Parker Hannifin
Corporation

A Winning Heritage

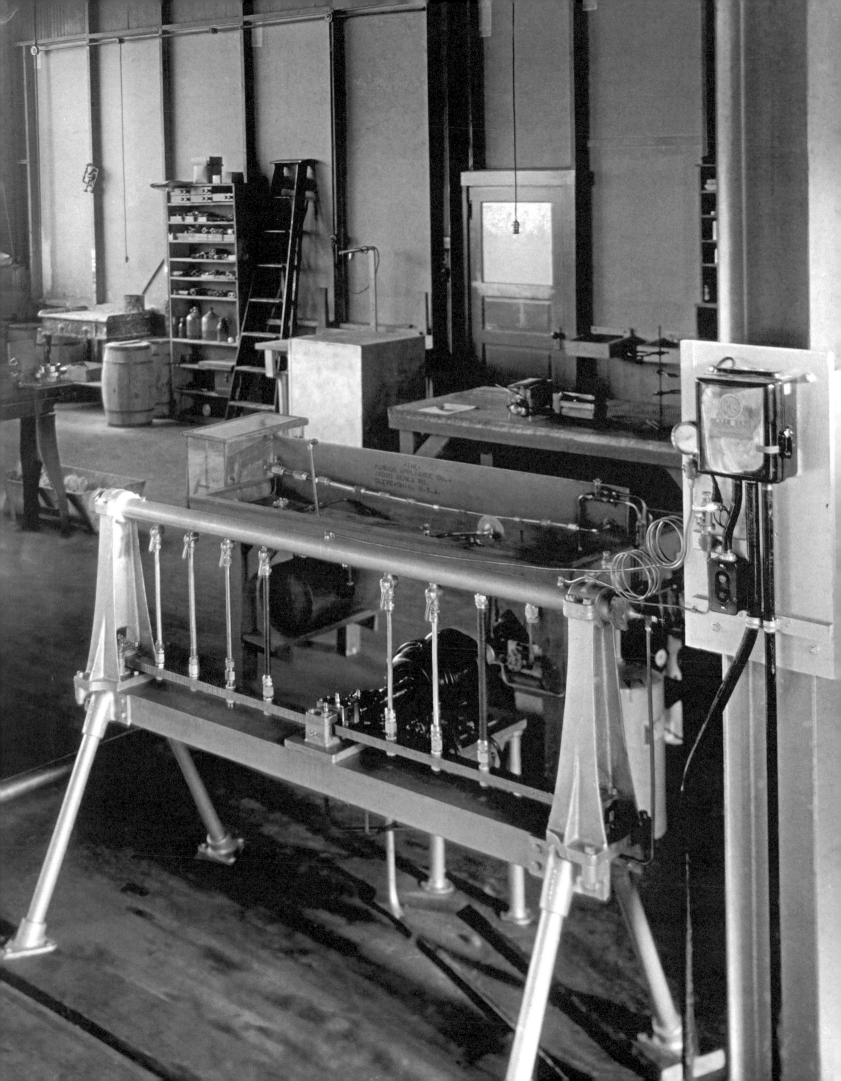

Parker Hannifin
Corporation

A Winning Heritage

Jeffrey L. Rodengen

Edited by Heather Lewin
Layout by Elijah Meyer

Write Stuff Enterprises, Inc.
1001 South Andrews Avenue
Fort Lauderdale, FL 33316
1-800-900-Book (1-800-900-2665)
(954) 462-6657
www.writestuffbooks.com

The publisher has made every effort to identify and locate the source of the photographs included in this edition of *Parker Hannifin Corporation: A Winning Heritage*. Grateful acknowledgment is made to those who have kindly granted permission for the use of their materials in this edition. If there are instances where proper credit was not given, the publisher will gladly make any necessary corrections in subsequent printings.

Publisher's Cataloging in Publication
(Prepared by The Donohue Group, Inc.)

Rodengen, Jeffrey L.
  A winning heritage : Parker Hannifin Corporation / Jeffrey L. Rodengen ; edited by Heather Lewin ; layout by Elijah Meyer.

  p. : ill. ; cm.

  Includes bibliographical references and index.
  ISBN: 978-1-932022-38-4

1. Parker Hannifin Corporation—History. 2. Automatic control equipment industry—United States—History. 3. Industrialists—United States—History. I. Lewin, Heather. II. Meyer, Elijah. III. Title. IV. Title: Parker Hannifin Corporation

HD9696.A964 P37 2009
381.45/6298/065

Completely produced in the
United States of America
10 9 8 7 6 5 4 3 2 1

Also by Jeffrey L. Rodengen

The Legend of Chris-Craft

IRON FIST:
The Lives of Carl Kiekhaefer

Evinrude-Johnson and
The Legend of OMC

Serving the Silent Service:
The Legend of Electric Boat

The Legend of Dr Pepper/Seven-Up

The Legend of Honeywell

The Legend of Briggs & Stratton

The Legend of Ingersoll-Rand

The Legend of Stanley:
150 Years of The Stanley Works

The MicroAge Way

The Legend of Halliburton

The Legend of York International

The Legend of Nucor Corporation

The Legend of Goodyear:
The First 100 Years

The Legend of AMP

The Legend of Cessna

The Legend of VF Corporation

The Spirit of AMD

The Legend of Rowan

New Horizons:
The Story of Ashland Inc.

The History of American Standard

The Legend of Mercury Marine

The Legend of Federal-Mogul

Against the Odds:
Inter-Tel—The First 30 Years

The Legend of Pfizer

State of the Heart: The Practical Guide
to Your Heart and Heart Surgery
with Larry W. Stephenson, M.D.

The Legend of Worthington Industries

The Legend of IBP

The Legend of Trinity Industries, Inc.

The Legend of
Cornelius Vanderbilt Whitney

The Legend of Amdahl

The Legend of Litton Industries

The Legend of Gulfstream

The Legend of Bertram
with David A. Patten

The Legend of Ritchie Bros. Auctioneers

The Legend of ALLTEL
with David A. Patten

The Yes, you can of Invacare
Corporation
with Anthony L. Wall

The Ship in the Balloon:
The Story of Boston Scientific and the
Development of Less-Invasive Medicine

The Legend of Day & Zimmermann

The Legend of Noble Drilling

Fifty Years of Innovation:
Kulicke & Soffa

Biomet—From Warsaw to the World
with Richard F. Hubbard

NRA: An American Legend

The Heritage and Values of RPM, Inc.

The Marmon Group:
The First Fifty Years

The Legend of Grainger

The Legend of The Titan Corporation
with Richard F. Hubbard

The Legend of Discount Tire Co.
with Richard F. Hubbard

The Legend of Polaris
with Richard F. Hubbard

The Legend of La-Z-Boy
with Richard F. Hubbard

The Legend of McCarthy
with Richard F. Hubbard

Intervoice: Twenty Years of Innovation
with Richard F. Hubbard

Jefferson-Pilot Financial:
A Century of Excellence
with Richard F. Hubbard

The Legend of HCA

The Legend of Werner Enterprises
with Richard F. Hubbard

The History of J. F. Shea Co.
with Richard F. Hubbard

True to Our Vision: HNI Corporation
with Richard F. Hubbard

The Legend of Albert Trostel & Sons
with Richard F. Hubbard

The Legend of Sovereign Bancorp
with Richard F. Hubbard

Innovation is the Best Medicine:
The extraordinary story of Datascope
with Richard F. Hubbard

The Legend of Guardian Industries

The Legend of
Universal Forest Products

Changing the World: Polytechnic
University—The First 150 Years

Nothing is Impossible: The Legend
of Joe Hardy and 84 Lumber

In it for the Long Haul:
The Story of CRST

The Story of Parsons Corporation

Cerner: From Vision to Value

New Horizons:
The Story of Federated Investors

Office Depot: Taking Care of Business—
The First 20 Years

The Legend of General Parts:
Proudly Serving a World in Motion

Bard: Power of the Past,
Force of the Future

Innovation & Integrity:
The Story of Hub Group

Amica: A Century of Service
1907–2007

A Passion for Service:
The Story of ARAMARK

The Legend of Con-way:
A History of Service, Reliability,
Innovation, and Growth

Commanding the Waterways:
The Story of Sea Ray

Past, Present & Futures:
Chicago Mercantile Exchange

The Legend of Leggett & Platt

Winning the Arch Way:
The Story of Arch Aluminum & Glass

The Road Well Traveled:
The Story of Guy Bostick and
Comcar Industries

The Legend of Brink's

Kiewit: An Uncommon Company

TABLE OF CONTENTS

INTRODUCTION

PARKER HANNIFIN, TODAY A MULTIBILlion dollar corporation with a global reach, finds its beginnings in the vision of one man—inventor and businessman Art Parker.

In 1918, Art, a 33-year-old engineer, began Parker Appliance Company in Cleveland, Ohio, investing the $6,000 he had saved while serving the United States during World War I. The first product Art had for sale targeted the burgeoning automobile industry—a pneumatic braking system to harness compressed air to stop heavy vehicles effectively and safely. Ironically, on an ill-fated sales trip to Boston in 1919, the truck carrying the company's inventory careened off a hilly Pennsylvania road, destroying every product the company had for sale.

Needing time to rebuild, Art began working and saving money. By 1924, Art had saved enough to reopen his company's doors and continue his passion for engineering and invention, and Parker Appliance Company was in business again. By the early 1930s, after a number of successful trade show exhibitions, Parker Appliance broadened its customer base within the aviation and automobile markets, boosting sales to $2 million by the end of 1934.

During World War II, Parker Appliance responded to America's needs by serving the U.S. government exclusively—it had no other customers. Just before the war's end, the company suffered an unexpected, major loss when Art died shortly after shoveling snow with his sons on January 1, 1945. When the war came to a close, the company was almost forced to close its doors, as the government was no longer in need of its services.

Art's widow, Helen, was advised to liquidate the company, but instead she cashed in his life insurance policy and poured the money back into the business. She also sought new management, and Parker Appliance slowly began to recover and prosper. In 1957, it merged with Hannifin Manufacturing Corporation to become known as Parker Hannifin.

During this time, Patrick S. Parker, Art's youngest son, was learning the business, earning his college degree, and sustaining his father's legacy of inventing new products and testing new engineering ideas. After many years as an employee in various capacities, Pat became president in 1969, a title he retained until 1977.

A succession of strong and insightful leaders from Allen "Bud" Aiman (1977-1981), to Paul Schloemer

(1981-1993), to Duane Collins (1993-2000), to Don Washkewicz (2000-present), drove the company forward through turbulent economic times, a shifting industrial market, and growing pains on the international level as Parker Hannifin grew its wholesale operations and branched out into distributorships. By this time, the competitive environment was very different from when Art began his company in the tiny loft in Ohio. A change was necessary to rejuvenate the company's successful, albeit steady, position.

In 2000, Don Washkewicz, whose Parker Hannifin career had spanned 28 years at the time, became president and COO. Although Parker Hannifin continued to prosper, Washkewicz felt that the company had yet to tap its full potential. The new president began a whirlwind tour of more than 200 Parker Hannifin facilities to understand intimately what was happening at the ground level, and to seek any new ideas individual facilities might have to improve performance for all of Parker Hannifin's facilities. This yearlong study culminated in what would become the Win Strategy—a three-pronged program to provide exemplary customer service, improve financial performance, and sustain profitable growth.

Washkewicz was then challenged with implementing the Win Strategy across all divisions and groups in the United States, Canada, Europe, Asia Pacific, Australia, the United Kingdom, and Latin America. For a company deeply rooted in its entrepreneurial and decentralized culture, it was a difficult but necessary transition. After all employees were trained and on board, the new strategy's result was undeniable: by 2005, company-wide sales had climbed to $8.2 billion, an increase of 17 percent over fiscal year 2004.

By 2009, Parker Hannifin had become a global innovator, its products touching many aspects of daily life, from helping to keep refrigerators cool, to advances in renewable energy and life sciences, to creating energy recovery braking systems on heavy-duty vehicles, to contributing to every major aerospace program in existence today. It continues the heritage founder Art Parker and his son Pat created by focusing on the future of engineering and positioning itself as the worldwide leader in motion and control technologies.

ACKNOWLEDGMENTS

MANY DEDICATED PEOPLE ASSISTED IN THE RE-search, preparation, and publication of *Parker Hannifin: A Winning Heritage.*

Several key individuals associated with Parker Hannifin provided their assistance in development of the book from its outline to its finished product, led by Senior Communciations Specialist Erica Isabella. The team included: Duane Collins, Christopher Farage, Allen Ford, Aidan Gormley, Dave Grager, Jim Jaye, Tom Meyer, Tim Pistell, Dan Serbin, Don Washkewicz, Jim Wood, and Elaine Zettelmeyer.

All of the people interviewed—Parker Hannifin employees, retirees, customers, distributors, analysts, and friends—were generous with their time and insights. Those who shared their memories and thoughts include: Bill Armbruster, Ron Arthur, Jim Baker, Lee Banks, Bob Barker, Barney Barnd, Dick Bertea, Bob Bond, Mike Boyles, Pete Buca, Maurice Castoriano, Gustavo Cudell, Dana Dennis, Raymond Doyle, Heinz Droxer, Bill Eaton, Bill Eline, Luis Antonio Frade, Lonnie Gallup, Bryan Goodman, Randy Gross, Steve Hayes, Tom Healy, Pam Huggins, Kjell Jansson, Rick Kanzleiter, Marwan Kashkoush, Franz Kaspar, Syd Kershaw, Klaus Kohler, Joe Kovach, Mark Kugelman, Robert Lawler, Dolores Lyon, Ricardo Machado, Al Maurer, Craig Maxwell, John McGinty, Pat McMonagle, Jim Mockler, Jack Myslenski, Frank Nichols, Mike Noelke, John Oelslager, Ken Ohlemeyer, Streeter Parker, David Parks, Harry Payling, James Perkins, Tom Piraino, Tony Piscitello, Don Raker, Cliff Ransom, Carey Rhoten, Edward A. Roberts, David Rudyk, Charly Saulnier, Ursula Sawyer, Paul Schloemer, Tom Sear, Patti Sfero, Roger Sherrard, Donald Smrekar, Denny Sullivan, Lex Taylor, John Treharn, John Van Buskirk, Nick Vande Steeg, Joe Vicic, Jeff Weber, Bill Webster, John Wenzel, Tom Williams, Richard Wright, John Zakaria, Larry Zeno, and Don Zito.

Research Assistant Beth Kapes conducted the principal archival research for the book, while Senior Editor Heather Lewin managed the editorial content. Graphic Designer Elijah Meyer brought the story to life.

Finally, special thanks are extended to the staff at Write Stuff Enterprises, Inc.: Elizabeth Fernandez, senior editor; Sandy Cruz, vice president/creative director; Roy Adelman, on-press supervisor; Abigail Hollister and Martin Schultz, proofreaders; Mary Aaron, transcriptionist; Elliot Linzer, indexer; Amy Major, executive assistant to Jeffrey L. Rodengen; Marianne Roberts, executive vice president, publisher, and chief financial officer; and Stanislava Alexandrova, marketing manager.

Art Parker (leaning against table) in Parker Appliance Company's first facility—a rented loft on Cleveland's West Side, circa 1918.

CHAPTER ONE

CREATING AN
INDISPUTABLE FORCE
1918–1928

Art Parker started his business with $6,000 in savings.

*Cheer up, we're both in one piece, still in our 30s, smart, single, and good
engineers. The world really needs guys like us. Look on the bright side. We came
to Pittsburgh in a $1,500 truck, and we're riding home on a million-dollar train!*

—Art Parker, founder of Parker Appliance Company, after
an automobile accident destroyed the company's entire inventory

IT WAS AN IDEA FROM ONE INDIVID-
ual that, in time, would affect the
lives of millions.

In 1918, Arthur (Art) LaRue
Parker, a 33-year-old engineer, began
a quest to develop a pneumatic braking system to harness compressed air
to stop heavy trucks and buses effectively and safely. With this in mind,
and his intellectual ability and heart-
felt enthusiasm as his guides, Art
founded Parker Appliance Company
in Cleveland, Ohio, in a tiny loft he
rented on the city's West Side. His concept of compressed
air as a means for power was the start of a legacy of
motion and control technology that now touches the
lives of nearly everyone on earth—and beyond.

The evolution of Parker Appliance Company into
Parker Hannifin Corporation is not just a historic
account of the transformation of technology, but also of
the humanity that guided the company's founder and
his family. Although Parker Hannifin is now a worldwide
motion and control enterprise, the company has never
lost sight of its culture, which has always placed great
importance on the interests and innovation of others.

Applying Ingenuity

Born November 16, 1885, Arthur
LaRue Parker was the youngest son
of William and Margaret Parker, both
originally from New York.[1] The
Parkers established their home in
Cleveland, which led Art to attend
the Case Institute of Technology.[2] As
a student of the fourth college in
the United States to focus on technical education, Art completed a bach-
elor of science degree in electrical
engineering. During his senior year, Art's thesis, a hypoth-
esis on the "Experimental Study of the Performance
of Automobile Storage Batteries," became a precur-
sor to the interests and ideas he developed later in
his career.[3, 4] With his degree in hand, he began his career
in engineering.

A painting depicting Art Parker, deep in thought at his desk,
hangs in the lobby of Parker Hannifin's corporate headquarters
in Cleveland, Ohio.

In 1907, Art began working as an experimental engineer for Willard Storage Battery in Cleveland—his job focused on the emerging automobile industry.[5] Art began studying the new concept of mass production, and quickly noticed its significance to the expanding field of technology. It would allow for the production of large quantities of items at a lower cost. While at Willard Storage Battery, Art began looking beyond electrical toward mechanical engineering. This offered the challenge of hydraulic control, which uses fluids under pressure to control parts in machinery.[6]

The first evidence of Art's vision of the potential that hydraulic machinery held was described in his first U.S. patent. Issued on September 28, 1909, patent number 935,051 was titled "Device for Regulating the Speed of Generators to Secure Constant Potential."[7] This demonstrated Art's intrigue with motion and the ability to control it, as his declaration in the patent's document stated:

It frequently happens that a generator is driven by a prime mover, the speed in which will vary, sometimes within narrow limits and again between wide limits … I have shown and described a particular form of differential mechanism, as well as a particular form of brake. It will be apparent that the construction herein set forth provides an efficient means for operating a generator at a constant potential, and accomplishes this result whatever may be the range of speed of the prime mover.[8]

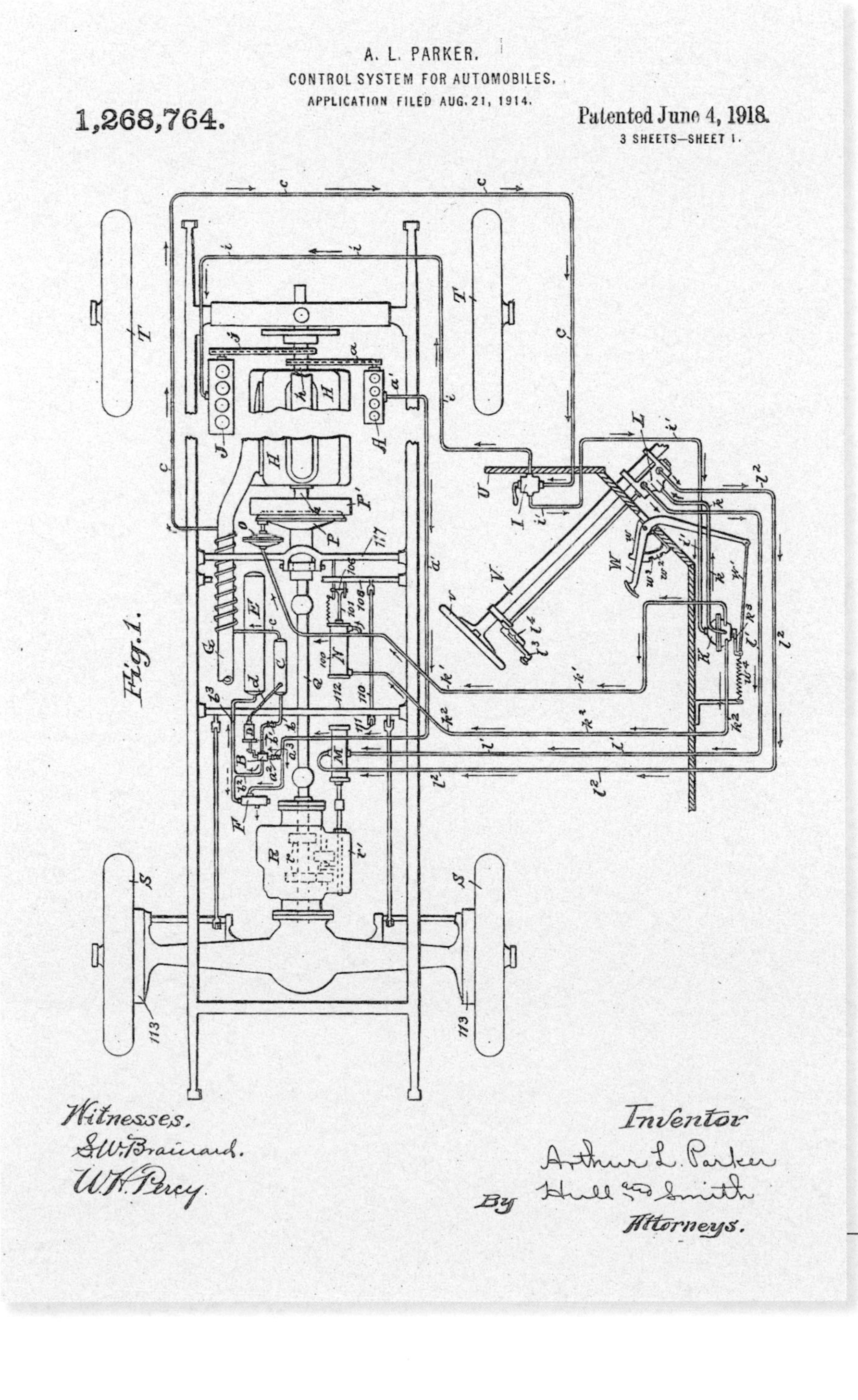

Aspirations Interrupted

Art began focusing on the development of his idea for a pneumatic brake booster system for use in trucks and buses.

In 1918, Art rented a tiny loft on the West Side of Cleveland to set up his company, the Parker Appliance Company. The word "appliance" was not used to describe household devices but to stress the ingenuity of converting one form of energy into another type of energy. To assist in the development and marketing of his first invention, Art hired his friend Carl E. Klamm, a talented engineer from Case Institute of Technology.

Klamm aided Art with the creation and implementation of a pneumatic brake system design. Patented on June 4, 1918, the "Control System for Automobiles" (patent

A. L. PARKER.
CONTROL SYSTEM FOR AUTOMOBILES.
APPLICATION FILED AUG. 21, 1914.

1,268,764.

Patented June 4, 1918.
3 SHEETS—SHEET 1.

Fig.1.

Witnesses.
S.W. Brainard.
W.H. Percy.

Inventor
Arthur L. Parker
By Hull & Smith
Attorneys.

A schematic drawing of an early truck that incorporates Parker pneumatic controls.

AN INDUSTRY TAKES FLIGHT

IT'S A LITTLE KNOWN FACT THAT CLEVELAND WAS an important hub for the earliest achievements of aviation in the United States. It was home to ingenious aviation pioneers and several aircraft companies in the early 1900s and had one of the largest and busiest airports in the world in the 1920s and 1930s.[1,2] Cleveland Municipal Airport deployed the first airfield lighting system and air traffic control tower in the country.[3,4] As Detroit was becoming known as the "Motor City" because of Henry Ford's automobile, Cleveland was becoming the "Cradle of Aviation."

In the early 1900s, flight was an amazing feat to most Americans. Resort owners hired aviators to perform aerial stunt shows. One of the earliest shows was held August 31, 1910, when Glenn Curtiss, the first to receive a U.S. pilot's license and inventor of airplane engine innovations, flew over Lake Erie completing what was, at the time, the longest over-water flight.[5]

In the fall of 1911, Al Engel crashed his airplane in an exhibition flight in one of Cleveland's eastern suburbs. Although the crash destroyed the aircraft, Engel walked away. He returned in 1912 with a new aircraft equipped with floats, allowing him to take off from and land on water. Engel's plane, the *Bumble Bee,* was equipped with a Curtiss engine. He flew extensively throughout northeastern Ohio for exhibition and passenger flights between 1912 and 1914.

Among the most notable aircraft companies in Cleveland was the Glenn L. Martin Company, which began manufacturing airplanes on September 10, 1917.[6] Martin was known for building the MB-1 bomber, a biplane used by the U.S. Army in World War I, and ultimately became a critical customer of the Parker Appliance Company.

With a growing aviation manufacturing industry, Cleveland hosted the legendary National Air Races from 1929 through 1949.[7] The nation's premier aviation event drew more than 100,000 to fill

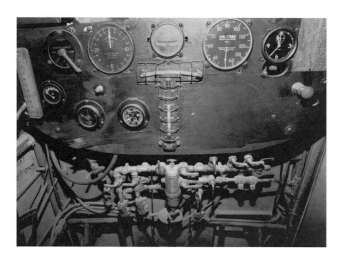

The *Spirit of St. Louis* instrument panel reveals Parker Appliance fittings just below the dashboard—fittings that enabled Charles Lindbergh's famous 33½-hour solo flight.

Cleveland Municipal Airport grandstands to watch the finest unlimited (referring to speed) air racers in the world.[8] With interest in aviation soaring from Charles Lindbergh's first transatlantic solo flight in 1927, planes from around the world raced a 10-mile rectangular course that combined high speeds with tight turns.

Cleveland also became home to the National Advisory Committee for Aeronautics (NACA) Glenn Research Center in the 1940s (NACA was the predecessor to NASA, the National Aeronautics and Space Administration). The center housed such inventions as the Altitude Wind Tunnel to perform the first wind tunnel tests on American jet engine prototypes and solve engine-cooling problems for the B-29 bomber of World War II.[9]

Today, many historic relics of Cleveland's aviation past, including the *Bumble Bee,* can be seen at the Crawford Auto-Aviation Museum at the Western Reserve Historical Society in downtown Cleveland.

number 1,268,764), was the beginning of Art's discovery that compressed air was an indisputable force:

Parker Appliance Company's early location in a loft on the West Side of Cleveland, circa 1918.

It is the general object of the invention to provide a system of control which is particularly adapted for use with and by fluid under pressure ... thereby to simplify the control of an automobile and to obtain a maximum speed, accuracy and efficiency in performing the various operations ... such as reversing.[9]

I wish to state, also, that I have found compressed air to be the most suitable medium for the shifting of gears of any that have been used for that purpose, or experimented within that connection. Its elasticity

makes it peculiarly adaptable to this purpose and much to be preferred to electricity for the shifting of gears, or even the manually operated devices, which are used almost entirely at the present time.[10]

After the excitement of receiving this landmark patent, Art was forced to refocus his energies toward a new challenge: World War I. While Austria–Hungary, Bulgaria, Germany, and the Ottoman Empire were

battling the Allied Powers of the United Kingdom, France, Russia, Italy, Belgium, Serbia, Montenegro, Portugal, Romania, Greece, and Japan, the United States remained neutral—until 1917, when a German submarine sank the British passenger liner, *Lusitania*, killing 128 Americans.[11]

As the United States entered World War I, Art enlisted in September 1918 and served as a transportation officer in France.[12] While he was stationed there, he noticed that the supply trucks used on the Western Front lacked the ability to brake effectively. He was sure he could correct this engineering shortfall.[13]

Germany surrendered November 11, 1918, after the first global conflict had claimed between 9 million and 13 million lives. The war formally ended after the Treaty of Versailles was signed by Germany and the Allied Nations on June 28, 1919.[14] Lucky to be alive, Art had saved $6,000 and had every intention of using the money for his business.

Art continued working with motion control technologies and gained a third patent. This patent provided an improved pressure-fluid system to correct a weakness in the automobiles developed during this era:

The primary object of my present invention is the provision, with a source of pressure fluid supply and pressure fluid system in communicative connection therewith, of means adapted to be operated at will for delivering fluid from the source to the system at any desirable pressure, and operative automatically to terminate such delivery when said desired pressure has been attained. This is obviously an advantage for it arrests the movement of all driving parts between the clutch and driving wheels, just as soon as the driving wheels are stopped thus relieving the transmission and differential gearing and shafts of undue strains.[15]

In 1919, Parker Appliance's sole customer was the Glenn L. Martin Company, the world's foremost aircraft assembly plant, based in Cleveland. Started in 1917, Martin's first big success was the

Art Parker's truck, filled with the company's entire inventory, is ready for a 1919 promotional tour from Akron to Boston.

THE U.S. PATENT PROCESS

TECHNOLOGY AND INDUSTRIALIZATION HAVE historically been driving forces in the United States. To acknowledge the need for granting ownership of innovation, the country's founding fathers drafted into the U. S. Constitution the first national patent system.[1] The Patent Act of 1790 was written in part by Thomas Jefferson.[2]

Created to promote "the Progress of Science and useful Arts, by securing for limited Times to Authors and Inventors the exclusive Right to their respective Writings and Discoveries," patent applications took several months to be examined. Fifty-seven patents were issued between 1790 and 1793.[3] With a change to the Patent Act in 1793, a Patent Board was created to speed the process of issuing patents, and while some unproductive processes were eliminated by the Board, others remained until the creation of the United States Patent Office (now known as the U. S. Patent and Trademark Office) in 1836.[4,5]

While initial patents were restricted and carefully issued for inventions that solved practical problems, the mid-20th century allowed for granting patents to "everything made by man under the sun."[6] It was during this time that a method of grouping similar patents together was created. This patent classification system, along with hundreds of patent offices established in libraries, helped categorize the explosion of patents.

By the 1870s, the number of patent assignments averaged more than 9,000 per year, and this increased in the next decade to more than 12,000 transactions recorded annually.[7] Although these patents could

MB-1 bomber, a large biplane design ordered by the U.S. Army January 17, 1918.[16] This one customer helped the Parker Appliance Company experience moderate success.[17]

To showcase the company's achievements and further market its pneumatic control design to prospective clients interested in the automobile industry, Art planned a promotional tour from Akron to Boston in 1919. Art and Klamm equipped a truck with Parker's unique pneumatic booster brakes and loaded the truck and trailer with the company's complete inventory.[18] Little did Art know that this promotional tour would be the beginning of the end of his newly created company.

Traveling by automobile was an adventuresome undertaking in the early 1900s because of the poor road conditions of the time. While Parker Appliance's booster brakes were installed to aid their travel, the hills of Pennsylvania proved to be too much. After losing a wheel, the truck crashed down a mountainside, taking Parker Appliance Company's entire inventory with it. Thankfully, Art and Klamm walked away from the wreckage, yet the mood turned grim when the two realized that all of their company's capital had been eliminated.[19]

The ill-fated trip forced Art to claim bankruptcy and shut down Parker Appliance Company. Taking the Pennsylvania railroad back to Cleveland, Art refused to lose hope that his company would make a comeback. This positive attitude was apparent in a conversation Art had years later with his son, Patrick. He recalled his father's words to Klamm:

Cheer up, we're both in one piece, still in our 30s, smart, single, and good engineers. The world really needs guys like us. Look on the bright side. We came to Pittsburgh in a $1,500 truck, and we're riding home on a million-dollar train![20]

Stepping Back

Art took his optimistic outlook and applied for a job as an engineer at Cleveland's New York, Chicago, and St. Louis Railroad, also known as Nickel Plate Road.[21] By 1924, Art had saved enough money to restart his Parker Appliance Company. Art transitioned from

be viewed as small monopolies on certain products, they facilitated the rise of corporations throughout the late 19th century and the resulting tremendous economic growth of the United States.[8]

Master of the Patent

Throughout his engineering career, Art Parker was a master of patents. All told, he is credited with almost 160 successful patents—23 of which were awarded after his death in 1945. His first patent was awarded on September 28, 1909, for a "Device for Regulating the Speed of Generators to Secure Constant Potential." In the years that followed, he earned patents for coupling devices, valve mechanisms, and fuel distributing devices, among other technology.

After his death on January 1, 1945, he still received patents for research that he began. His work was supported by his wife Helen, who continued her husband's love of technology by submitting his patent applications to the U.S. Patent Office. His last patent was awarded on February 10, 1953—it was filed May 15, 1945—for a rotary plug valve seat.

Modern Patent Procedures

Today's patent applications must comply with a number of requirements and limitations established in Title 35 of the U.S. Patent Code.[9] These include that an invention must be "novel," meaning that its subject matter cannot be considered public knowledge. Additional lengthy technical requirements, including a specification (description of the invention), must be submitted and then examined for validity.[10]

The length of time between filing a patent application and receiving a patent from the U.S. Patent Office may range from 18 months to three years.[11] The existence and development of the U.S. patent system provides the essential stimulus to promote technologic and economic advancement.

exploring applications for vehicle brakes to industrial prime movers, or main power sources.[22]

In October of that year, Art reopened Parker Appliance Company in a building on Berea Road in Cleveland.[23] Focusing on pneumatic and hydraulic components for its automobile and industrial customers, the revived company began to reap success. Whether manipulating the use of oil or water for hydraulic technology, air or gas within pneumatic technology, or producing a variety of automotive and industrial fittings, Parker Appliance was quickly gaining a solid reputation.

As Parker Appliance grew, Art saw a need for an improved method of transferring power. This led to the creation of a revolutionary two-piece flared tube coupling, which would become the foundation of Parker Appliance's business. When filing the patent application for his invention in February 1925, Art wrote the following:

The objects of the invention are to provide an improved coupling of simple form and capable of quantity production at low cost; to provide a very tight joint between the tube and coupling members, *which will withstand practically any pressure without leaking and which eliminates or greatly reduces the undesirable effects of vibrational strains transmitted from tube to coupling. ...* [24]

This flared tube fitting, patented on March 1, 1927, became known as the "standard Parker fitting."[25] Made of brass, the product was revolutionary in its ability to fit couplings seamlessly with tubing. Among the first users of the standard Parker fitting were such industry leaders as the U.S. Air Compressor Company, Bailey Meter Company, Detroit Edison, and Goodyear Tire and Rubber.[26]

The Rise of the Aviation Industry

Art began studying the industry with aircraft pioneer Glenn L. Martin. Martin employed some of the innovators of aircraft, including Robert Gross, who would later take over the Lockheed Corporation in the 1930s, and Donald W. Douglas, Sr., founder of Douglas Aircraft in 1921 in Santa Monica, California.[27,28] From his contemporaries and customers of Parker Appliance

Company, Art realized the vast potential of the aviation industry.[29]

Soon after the creation of the flared tube fitting in 1927, the U.S. Navy also adopted its use.[30] Because the Navy had contracted with the Glenn L. Martin Company to build some of its planes and Parker Appliance was a supplier for Martin, Art was drawn into issues with aircraft fuel and hydraulic systems. He formulated solutions for fuel, oil, and control lines that led to the development of valves specially designed for use with one of his first inventions, the flared tube fitting. The first valves to be manufactured by Parker for the aircraft industry were plug valves, which became indispensable for the prevention of fuel or oil leaks. Shortly after creation of these valves Art designed disc and cylindrical valves for use in airplanes.[31] As aircraft grew in size, the industry needed more compact, lightweight controls and valves.[32]

Making History

Art and Parker Appliance's reputation for producing reliable, hydraulic connectors for the aviation industry became so well known in the late 1920s that Charles Lindbergh called on Art to develop his historic aircraft's fuel transfer system.[33] While Lindbergh had already earned a reputable name among pilots, he was eager to be the first to fly solo nonstop from New York to Paris. This challenge had been made in 1919 by New York City hotelier Raymond Orteig, who offered $25,000 to the first person who accomplished the feat. Several who had tried were either killed or injured while competing for the "Orteig prize."[34]

Lindbergh was certain of his possible success if he had the right airplane and systems. After persuading nine St. Louis businessmen to help finance the cost of the attempt, Lindbergh chose Ryan Aeronautical Company of San Diego to manufacture a special plane he helped to design.[35] Lindbergh tested his plane, the *Spirit of St. Louis*, by flying from San Diego to New York City on May 10–11, 1927, with an overnight stay in St. Louis. By accomplishing the flight in 20 hours and 21 minutes, Lindbergh set a new transcontinental record.

His aircraft, however, was plagued by persistent fuel system leaks. After Lindbergh called on the expertise of Parker Appliance, Art developed a leak-free fuel system for Lindbergh's aircraft, which enabled him to take off

May 20, 1927, from Roosevelt Field, near New York City.[36] After arriving at Le Bourget Field, near Paris, on May 21, Lindbergh had completed the first transatlantic solo flight and was transformed overnight from an unremarkable mail plane pilot into an American hero. He had flown more than 3,600 miles in 33.5 hours —an achievement that could not have been accomplished without Parker's reliable, high-pressure connections and Art's ingenuity.[37]

Creating a Family

As Parker Appliance gained recognition as the premier designer and manufacturer of precision hydraulic devices in the aviation and automotive markets in the late 1920s, Art married.

As the third employee and first female hired by Parker Appliance, Helen M. Fitzgerald joined the company as Art's secretary after she graduated from secretarial school. Women had just won the right to vote in the United States, and this newfound liberation prompted many young women, like Fitzgerald, to seek independence through employment.[38] A daughter of a large Irish family from Cleveland's West Side, Fitzgerald began a romance with Art, although this relationship seemed unlikely because of the 20-year age difference.[39] Art would surprise Fitzgerald by proposing after asking her into his office for dictation.[40]

In December 1927, 41-year-old Art and Fitzgerald eloped—the two were married in Pittsburgh while on a business trip. Not only was the young bride surprised by the turn of events, but Art's chief engineer, Klamm, may have been surprised as well. The excerpts from Art's letter to Klamm conveyed not only Parker Appliance's financial state, but also the fun Art and his new wife were having at delivering the message of marriage to their colleague:

If Glenn Martin's check comes in and other funds—wire me fifty dollars at Wm. Penn Hotel— Pittsburgh—otherwise do not bother. You will probably be a little surprised, but I have taken possession of Miss Fitzgerald for good—you can arrange for another girl in the office—we will be home after the first of the year. You may tell Bigelow and, if advisable Brown, but for the time being it will be better not to spread it any further.

Art Parker and Helen Fitzgerald's wedding photo in 1927.

Mrs. Parker is frightened and worried for fear this shock may be fatal to you. I told her that you are quite familiar with the unexpected and that it would take more than this news to shake you up.[41]

A short postscript from the new Mrs. Parker was attached to Art's note: "Mr. Klamm: I'll let you kiss the bride when we return."[42]

Within two years of marriage, Art and Helen had a son. Patrick S. Parker was born October 16, 1929, and while three additional children would complete the Parker family, Patrick would play a pivotal role in the future of Parker Appliance.

Looking Toward the Future

The early years of Parker Appliance involved a constant struggle to keep the business viable while Art introduced revolutionary product designs to the American automobile and aviation industries. One example was the patent he applied for on September 12, 1929. To create useful improvements in couplings, Art invented the combined tube and pipe coupling.[43] Art wrote in patent number 1,774,841:

An object of the invention is to provide a coupling which may be used for selective connection to either a pipe with standard pipe threads thereon, or to a tube having a flared end. A further object of the invention is to provide a coupling of the above type wherein a pipe thread on the coupling may be used in connection with a pipe thread on a coupling nut for joining the flared end of a tube to the coupling.[44]

This patent further demonstrated Art's ability to invent products that were flexible in their application. His understanding of how to create beneficial, profitable products for industrial use would aid Parker Appliance's growth and also help it survive what would become one of the darkest times in American economic history.

The lathe shop at Parker Appliance Company's building on Euclid Avenue, circa 1930s.

GRADUAL GROWTH, UNCERTAIN TIMES

1929–1939

Sales reached $3 million by 1939.

Our success is founded on fair dealing, hard work, coordination of effort, and quality of products.

—Art Parker, founder of Parker Appliance Company

THE "ROARING TWENTIES" HAD fueled an economic and industrial boom within the United States. Parker Appliance harnessed this momentum through Arthur L. Parker's inventiveness. Propelled by an increasing number of patents for innovative technology, the company took advantage of opportunities in both the automobile and aircraft industries.

Parker Appliance became increasingly important to the success of these fledgling industries through Art's inventions, which included the two-piece standard Parker flared tube coupling and its ability to "provide a very tight joint between the tube and coupling members, which will withstand practically any pressure without leakage."[1] Because of the growing demand for Parker fittings, Parker Appliance needed to employ the mass manufacturing method that Henry Ford established in the automobile industry.[2] Although Art embraced mass production methods, he would not allow any compromise in workmanship or quality. This attention to detail attracted important customers such as General Motors Aviation and the Ford Tri-Motor Aircraft Company.[3]

Parker Appliance was quickly becoming a preferred employer in Cleveland as Art's rapidly evolving designs continued to attract new customers.

"Our success is founded on fair dealing, hard work, coordination of effort, and quality of products," Art said. This philosophy would become core to the company's culture for decades to come.

Battling "Black Tuesday"

The profitable business climate that Parker Appliance and other U.S. companies had experienced was about to collapse.[4] On October 29, 1929, also known as "Black Tuesday," the stock market crashed, signifying the beginning of the Great Depression.[5] As banks failed and businesses closed, more than 15 million Ameri-

The Parker Appliance Tube Coupling Price List book from 1932.

number 2,102,214, the "Art of Preserving Seizure of Contacting Surfaces of Soft Alloy and Like Materials."[10]

To showcase Parker Appliance's accomplishments, such as the first production of copper tubing for hydraulic installations, Art began exhibiting the company's products at national industry shows.[11] After a successful showing of hydraulic fittings, tubing, and components for aviation use at the International Exposition of 1930, and another exhibition at the 1932 Power Show, Parker Appliance broadened its customer base in both the aviation and automobile industries. Sales reached $2 million at the end of 1934.

cans became unemployed nearly overnight.[6] Although other businesses faced decimating losses, Parker Appliance managed to survive by a thin margin—and Art credited the company's survival to the dedication of his employees.[7]

Although the financial situation was dire, Parker Appliance continued to gain attention from the aircraft industry. For an industry where weight was a crucial element, Parker Appliance's first aluminum alloy fittings, known as "Dural" fittings, were a welcome innovation. They weighed significantly less than the traditional brass fittings.[8] These led to the development of a line of lubricants for use with flared tube couplings, enabling threads to fit together smoothly.

Art's formulas for lubricants and hydraulic fluids were handwritten in a small leather "recipe book," which his wife Helen then typed.[9] Each recipe contained chef-like tips, including a formula for a lubricant called Sealube. The creation of these "recipes" led to another patent,

Fostering Goodwill

In addition to developing and producing his new inventions, Art understood the importance of maintaining a company culture that met his employees' needs as well as contributed to their well-being. He expressed these thoughts in the first issue of Parker Appliance's internal newsletter in 1934:

I have often contemplated ways and means for promoting a closer fellowship and better understanding of mutual events and problems among this group of men who spend nearly a third of their time here at the Plant. … This paper may mean much to the progress and prosperity of members of this organization—through its columns new talent and abilities may be discovered, new confidence may be inspired and your daily tasks may be less arduous through new inspirations and the promotion of new sports and social activities.

Conditions such as we have successfully encountered and waded through during the existence of this business, are an inspiration … let everyone look forward to greater responsibilities and actively enter into our group activities and contribute his share to the success thereof.[12]

Art also provided extracurricular activities for his employees, giving them a chance to socialize outside the constraints of the work environment. The company sponsored a

Above: Parker Appliance was the first to introduce copper tubing for hydraulic installations in the early 1930s, and the first to use tubing for instrumentation of power plants. This copper tube shipment, from the Euclid Avenue building, took place in the late 1930s.

Right: Art Parker was meticulous in documenting his "recipes" for everything from Sealube to Gaslube in a "recipe book."

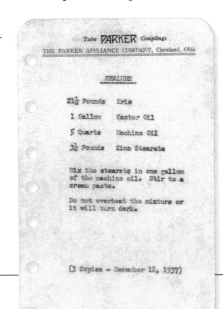

SURVIVING "BLACK TUESDAY"

How could a start-up company operating out of a rented loft survive the worst economic collapse of the modern industrial world? While the Parker Appliance Company's pneumatic brake booster system was making strides in the mid-1920s, it was the application of technology for industrial purposes, as well as other devices Parker Appliance manufactured, that allowed for the company's survival.

With skeptics criticizing the use of aviation for commercial use, Art always maintained his belief in the future of flight. Congress passed the Kelly Act in 1925, turning over operation of federal airmail routes to private parties through competitive bidding.[1] This led to the birth of civil aviation. The newly created Cleveland-Hopkins International Airport gained the greatest benefit through not only airmail routes, but also airlines that began carrying passengers. Four thousand aircraft cleared the field in 1925. In 1926 the total reached 11,000, and a year later, volume had grown to 14,000.

On the heels of Charles Lindbergh's historic flight from New York to Paris, Parker Appliance ran an advertisement in the June 20, 1927, issue of *Aviation* magazine that stated:

Captain Lindbergh's fuel flowed safely through "Parker" tube couplings. We express our sincere appreciation and gratitude to Captain Lindbergh for his masterful performance.

In the period of commercial aviation just ahead—when municipalities, corporations, and individuals fully realize the reliability, utility, and economic advantages of present day aircraft in competitive business activities;

When the demand for aircraft strains production facilities and automotive history is eclipsed;

Production and development of "Parker" tube couplings, fittings and fuel line equipment will keep pace with the demand.[2]

Parker Appliance's aviation innovations gained recognition after Charles Lindbergh's famous transatlantic flight. *(Photo courtesy of AP/WIDE WORLD PHOTOS.)*

Marketing its successful fuel line application for Lindbergh's plane, the *Spirit of St. Louis,* Parker Appliance's reputation as the manufacturer of choice for the aviation industry grew. By elevating its status with fast-growing Cleveland companies, such as the world's foremost aircraft assembly plant, the Glenn L. Martin Company, as well as aviation experts across the country, the late 1920s brought financial security for Parker Appliance.[3]

Parker Appliance supplied parts for the Ford Tri-Motor metal monoplane, which was used to shuttle passengers in a 100-minute flight to Detroit.[4] In 1929, it was $18 for a one-way ticket and $35 for a round-trip ticket.[5]

As the Depression made its mark on the country—a quarter of the U.S. workforce was without jobs, and many were homeless by 1933—Parker Appliance had enough orders from the aviation industry to survive 1929 by a thin margin. The company even maintained steady paychecks for its employees.[6] Using the same assembly-line manufacturing techniques as the automobile industry, Parker Appliance employees kept manufacturing fittings, couplings, and washers to help the company survive during this difficult time.[7]

bowling league that pit departments against one another in the spirit of healthy competition. He even held a dinner for employees in his own home, according to the February 1935 company newsletter. As the guests entered Art's home, women received corsages of gardenias, while men were given red carnations. The group played word games and billiards, and had fortunes told. Art also hired a magician for entertainment.[13]

Moving On

The workforce grew steadily despite the ongoing Depression—from 38 employees to 250—and space was dwindling in the rented loft on Cleveland's West Side. To continue to meet customer needs—which was eventually facilitated by the demise of the Hupp Motor Car Corporation—the move to larger facilities was inevitable.

While Cleveland was known for its aviation industry, it also had an automotive industry, primarily from the popularity of the Cleveland Automobile Company's

Art Parker purchased a 450,000-square-foot building at 17325 Euclid Avenue after the company outgrew its West Side loft.

"Cleveland" five-passenger touring car. Despite the impressive performance of the 1920 Cleveland Model 40 Touring Car, its success would not withstand the long-term recession. After the Hupp Motor Car Corporation purchased Cleveland Automobile Company in 1928, the car was transformed into the "Hupmobile." Although the company was based in Detroit, Hupp maintained a 450,000-square-foot automotive plant on Euclid Avenue in Cleveland.

Hupp went into bankruptcy in 1934. Art heard of Hupp's difficulties and thought the plant on Euclid Avenue would be ideal for his company's needs.[14] He needed to secure legal assistance immediately to help assess the situation and guide a possible transaction.

The engineering department (below) and the tool room (right), pictured in the late 1930s, were then housed at the new building, known as the Euclon building.

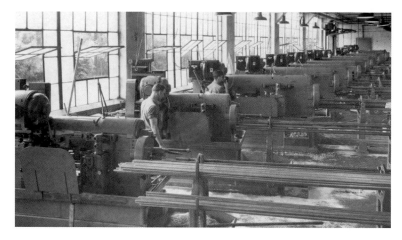

Although it was a Saturday, a young attorney named James A. Weeks was working in the office of Cleveland's Thompson, Hine & Flory. Art offered Weeks the challenge, and the two drove to Hupp's headquarters in Detroit that Monday. After waiting hours in the lobby, the two decided to get something to eat. While walking along the street, a newsboy related the headlines that Hupp had gone into receivership—Art and Weeks eagerly returned to Cleveland. Art and Weeks made a successful offer for the plant, and Parker Appliance had a new home.[15]

In December 1935, the company's internal newsletter recorded memories of those leaving Parker's "grand old building":

Sometimes we never realize how much we will miss a thing until it is taken away. However, a memory is something that cannot be taken away. ... Mr. Parker, remember when we had so much room [in the rented loft] that you used to park your Buick inside the building where the stockroom now is?[16]

Because the move to Euclid Avenue held uncertainties for the company, Art continued to boost employees' morale in the newsletter. His monthly correspondence was intended to give them hope for improved profitability, something not achieved easily in 1935 despite the steady volume of orders:

We can well hope that this is an AVERAGE year, and that we will have many better ones—some not so good, but that the average will be no worse than '35. One of the advantages of ignorance of the future is that we can go ahead with ambition and confidence—who wants an accurate prophet—who wants to really know what the future holds? Real knowledge of the future would take from us the fun of adventuring and experimenting, and trying out the ideas and plans that come to us each day.[17]

In spite of the company's growth prior to its move to Euclid Avenue, Art leased out much of the mammoth-sized building to help with costs.[18, 19] As the company settled into its new headquarters in January 1936, Art described the changes and how he felt they would affect the company:

Here we are in the new plant and all we have to do is make the new place go efficiently. In the past we have built a FAIR reputation for prompt deliveries and attention to customers' requirements. If we are to hold our performance even to past standards (we are, however, bound to improve our past performances) we must revise our methods to meet the new conditions encountered in this larger plant.
It is strange to step into our bigger quarters and the leg work wears you down. However, we now have our ding-dong call bells and our elaborate phone system all chiming in unison—so use the phone and save the legs. All we need is a lot of business—more folks to do jobs and the same old cheerful spirit. Don't get discouraged—everything is shaping up in grand style.[20]

Earning Respect

Art was happy to recognize the efforts of the iron benders and the employees in the foundry, tool room, and pattern shop, as well as those in the maintenance, automatics, and inspection departments. But he also

wondered what prompted people to seek employment at Parker Appliance. In a 1937 contest, employees were asked to pen letters explaining why Parker Appliance was a great company. One of the winning entries came from Mrs. Anna Mikula, an employee's wife, who wrote the following:

> … the everlasting personal interest of Mr. Parker in the welfare of the Parker employees and their families. The open door to the superintendent shop office for all employees, where any and all technical mechanical troubles, grievances and even personal feelings are given unbiased personal thoughts … the continued employment assuring a steady income … the continued research and experimentation on the different valves and fittings are the direct reasons for Parker materials being ahead of the field.

Initially, Parker Appliance used only a small portion of the Euclid Avenue facility, renting space to other companies.

ASSEMBLING AMERICAN INDUSTRY'S FUTURE

IN 1908, HENRY FORD REALIZED HIS LIFELONG DREAM of producing a reasonably priced, reliable, and efficient car by creating the Model T. Because the Model T was easy to operate, maintain, and handle on rough roads, it was an immediate success with the public. As other companies catered to the affluent, Ford offered an automobile within economic reach of most Americans. At its debut, the Model T could be purchased for $825, and four years later, the price dropped to $575.[1] By 1914, Ford claimed his company held a 48 percent market share, with the Model T representing half of all cars in America by 1918.[2]

In 1910, Ford opened a large factory in Highland Park, Michigan. It was at this plant that Ford would forever change the way in which industry approached manufacturing.[3] By combining precision manufacturing, standardized and interchangeable parts, and a division of labor, the continuous moving assembly line was created. A carefully timed conveyor belt delivered parts to workers who remained stationary and added one component to each automobile as it moved past them.[4]

As the Model T was produced in record time and numbers, the Ford Motor Company became the largest automobile manufacturer in the world. This moving assembly line revolutionized automobile production by decreasing time and costs, and other companies were intrigued. They studied the mech-

Last but not least, the formation of a Parker Welfare Committee that arranges the evening programs plus a family picnic breaks up and offsets any dull moments in the Parker routine.[21]

As Parker Appliance Company's involvement with the aviation industry became prominent, Art Parker added wings to his Parker Appliance logo, photo circa 1938.

Along with respect and recognition from employees and their families, Parker Appliance's customer base was growing outside the aviation and automotive fields. As the Mount Sinai Medical Center in Cleveland expanded during the 1930s, the hospital was completely piped with Parker fittings. At the same time, the city of Cleveland's pumping plants, filtration stations, and power plants modified plumbing to incorporate Parker fittings.[22]

Expansion was also seen in other ways. Art employed Railway Express to speed the delivery of Parker Appliance components from Euclid Avenue to meet any demand of the expanding aviation industry.

As airplanes increased in size, servomechanisms provided additional mechanical power for activating flight control surfaces (ailerons, rudders, and elevators),

flaps, air brakes, and landing gear.[23] Parker Appliance made certain that Art's patents could be applied in a variety of ways for fluid handling and motion control. Parker Appliance's involvement in aviation became so prominent that wings were incorporated into the company's triangular logo.

Examining Global Industry

Although national recognition for Parker Appliance products had increased, it was time to explore global opportunities.

Art began eyeing overseas developments in the aviation industry. In 1938, only Germany could match

---

Assembly-line workers contribute to the production of A-20 attack bombers in 1942. *(Photo from the Franklin D. Roosevelt Library collection [NLFDR], courtesy of the U.S. National Archives & Records Administration.)*

anized conveyor belts that moved among workers' stations to see if the method could be applied to their own products.

Art Parker also examined the assembly-line concept, and he thought that it would facilitate the manufacturing of his own products. At the time, there was high demand for the two-piece standard Parker flared tube coupling, which could be manufactured using the new technique.

But Parker Appliance also prided itself on maintaining product quality while meeting large orders. This attention to detail attracted important new customers such as General Motors Aviation and the Ford Tri-Motor Aircraft Company to solidify its reputation as a professional, dependable manufacturer.[5]

Parker Appliance received steady orders that required assembly line technology even through the Depression. Art's incorporation of this manufacturing method allowed the company to meet the largest orders it would ever receive throughout the late 1930s—orders from the U.S. government that would prepare the country's armed forces for World War II.

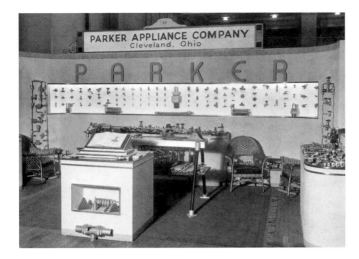

Displaying Parker Appliance's products nationally was important to Art Parker, and the company often attended the Power Show in New York City. The Parker Appliance Power Show display in 1936 (left) and in December 1939 (below). *(Photo below by Herbert Studios.)*

the United States in aircraft technology, and Art thought it might be the next market for Parker aircraft components.[24] That year, invited by German officials familiar with Art's expertise, he spent three months visiting the country's aircraft facilities.

Fully expecting to find German innovation comparable to that in the United States, Art was surprised by what he discovered. After touring the country's aircraft facilities, he became convinced that Germany possessed groundbreaking aviation technology that was slated for use in war—with the United States as a target.[25]

After Art's tour of Germany, he believed war was imminent. He refused Germany's invitation to supply its aircraft components, returned to the United States, and placed the largest single machine tool order that Cleveland manufacturer Warner & Swasey had ever received.[26] Art intended to develop components for critical fuel-handling systems for a variety of U.S. military aircraft.[27]

As the machinery order was delivered to Parker Appliance, Germany became increasingly belligerent under Adolf Hitler, the leader of the Nazi party. Germany invaded Poland in September 1939, signifying the beginning of World War II.[28]

Final Preparations

Before the war in Europe began, Art converted Parker Appliance into a corporation (on December 30,

1938). Shortly after, the company made a public offering of its stock and sold 100,000 shares to raise additional capital to prepare for the inevitable orders from the U.S. government.[29, 30]

Art also made arrangements in the United States to secure licenses under a number of patents, which, together with Parker patents, broadened his technical base. By mutually initiating license agreements with others in the aviation industry, Art gave these companies the authority to use Parker innovations without the threat of infringement. This strategy, combined with Art's decision to place less emphasis on the automotive marketplace, prepared Parker Appliance for the largest orders the company had ever received.[31]

With Parker Appliance's workforce growing, 40 patents in hand, and sales reaching $3 million in 1939, the company was ready to answer the nation's call to arms.[32]

This July 1943 cover of Parker Appliance's internal newsletter, *Fitting News*, showcased the company's support of war bond purchases during World War II.

SUPPLYING THE U.S. FOR FREEDOM

1940–1945

1940 Sales: $3 Million | 1945 Sales: $21.9 Million

With a skilled Research Department, fully integrated plant facilities, a nationwide sales and service organization and high reputation for production quality and dependability, your Company stands ready for what may come in the post-war era.

—Art Parker, founder of Parker Appliance Company

AS WORLD WAR II BEGAN, U.S. MANUFACTURERS were readying for increased production to support the nation's troops. Because of Arthur L. Parker's expertise within the aircraft industry, Parker Appliance was prepared to fill product orders from the government. The nation's aircraft builders needed a steady supply of specialized couplings, valves, and other hydraulic piping systems. This became the company's main focus. To fill the increased number of orders, Parker Appliance grew from 910 employees in 1940 to approximately 2,600 in August 1941.[1] Other changes were also inevitable as a result of this new business focus.

Parker Appliance suspended manufacturing industrial products for private companies to support the war effort completely, and most of the work was accomplished in Cleveland, Ohio. Art knew the West Coast was essential geographically to service the aircraft industry effectively, so he established the Pacific Coast Division of Parker Appliance in Los Angeles in 1940.[2] This 14-acre rented plant contained complete manufacturing facilities to expedite production and delivery services for West Coast customers.

Although Art's attention was focused on his company's expansion through additional staff and manufacturing facilities, his commitment to innovative engineering never wavered. He gained 12 additional patents in 1940. From improvements to a gas engine energizer to a fuel-distributing device to a variety of valve assemblies, Art was determined to help provide useful technology to the United States as it was drawn into the war.[3,4,5]

Growing with the Times

With production in Cleveland and Los Angeles progressing smoothly and Parker Appliance's workforce nearly tripling, Art continued the expansion of the company. Three new plant buildings were constructed adjacent to the building in Cleveland.[6] Designed

---

World War II war bond drives were so integral to Parker Appliance's support of the war effort that an official mascot salesman, "Parkie," was created in the company's foundry to market the bonds, circa 1943.

for production, these buildings cost $400,000. More than $1.5 million was spent on machinery and equipment, in addition to the approximately $1 million of machinery purchased in 1940.[7] Art described the impact these additions would have on the company:

Completion of the plan building program will add about 90,000 square feet of floor space to productive facilities. Present operations cover more than 180,000 square feet.[8]

Although costs were mounting, Art knew that his efforts to supply quality products to the government were important. According to the *Cleveland Plain Dealer*, a local newspaper, Parker Appliance was doing everything possible to meet the government's orders:

Keeping pace with increasing demands of the booming aircraft industry, the company has boosted its production and is operating two 11-hour shifts daily in most departments. Some departments are working three shifts a day, six days a week. About 50,000 types of piping appliances are made by the company, which also fabricates tubing for special needs. Company officials estimated that the average trainer plane carried around 300 couplings, valves, and other Parker parts of various shapes and sizes. Four-engine bombing planes, they added, required more than 3,000 specialized fittings to control the flow of liquids and air.[9]

Parker Appliance's link tube installations were used for "locomotives, chips, power plants, machine tools,

chemical operations, and scores of other uses." The U.S. Navy was also using Parker Appliance equipment for "servicing jobs on naval vessels."[10]

While its main plant was heavily dedicated to forgings that formed metals into parts in its foundry, Art was busy calculating what was needed to meet the military's expectations as well as planning for the future needs of the aviation industry.

"Sealing" Parker Appliance's Fate

While the expansion of Parker Appliance's Cleveland operations and the creation of the Pacific Coast Division were necessary, Art found that with growth came new problems.

The pressure to produce increased when the Japanese bombed Pearl Harbor on December 7, 1941. Although the United States had hoped to stop Japan's advance through oil embargoes, Japanese forces had gained momentum, killing more than 2,000 in Oahu, Hawaii, and effectively marking the United States' formal involvement in the war.[11]

The United States needed to respond forcefully, but the most difficult problem in the emerging field of fluid-power systems for aircraft and naval ships was

---

With production demands constantly increasing from the government, Art Parker began an expansion program that included construction of three new plant buildings to adjoin the Euclon building, costing the company $400,000, circa 1941.

how to seal petroleum-based oils. While natural rubber seemed the best conduit, it did not hold up well to prolonged exposure to petroleum-based fluids. Rubber was also difficult to obtain as the United States' supply from Sumatra, Borneo, and other rubber plantations was cut off because of the war.

To alleviate this shortfall, the U.S. government instituted a massive program to replace natural rubber with Government Rubber-Styrene (GRS). Although it was an effective application for tires and water hoses, GRS lost its elastometric, or rubberlike, properties with prolonged exposure to mineral-based fluids.[12] High pressure and high temperatures from the new hydraulic systems in aircraft and trucks also proved too much for other sealing devices, such as wax-impregnated sennit and leathers.

With a heavy subsidy from the government, natural and synthetic rubber suppliers—including Goodrich, Goodyear, Standard Oil, and Firestone—quickly developed "Buna-N." Buna-N could swell and retain military specification hydraulic fluids, in addition to withstanding long exposure to the fluid.[13] It was the best alternative to natural rubber. While the result was the ultimate tool in delivering performance, the

The Parker Appliance Employee Orchestra provided the Big Band sound, from behind proudly displayed company logos, for a Bond Employee Talent Show fundraiser. The bandleader, Frankie Laine, was a versatile lathe operator who would go on to become a nationally famous vocalist in the 1950s. One of his hit songs was "Ghost Riders in the Sky."

chemical process of producing Buna-N was beyond what rubber supply manufacturers had agreed on. Because Goodrich and its colleagues were only supplying the compound ingredient for Buna-N, rather than producing rubber themselves, Art saw an opportunity for future growth.

Art added a research and development (R & D) laboratory in one of the new buildings on Euclid Avenue. The laboratory was created specifically to develop rubberlike substances, as well as a series of lubricants.[14] It was led by a young mechanical engineer, Robert C. Fuhrman, and a graduate rubber chemist, E. J. (Manny) Carlotta. While the development of rubberlike substances was important, a much higher priority for the R&D team was to create lubricants needed for the

SURVIVING AGAINST ALL ODDS

As THE UNITED STATES WAS STRUGGLING FOR FINANcial survival amidst the ruins of the Great Depression in the early 1930s, Germany turned toward a new leader in hopes of economic recovery. Adolf Hitler appealed to the lower and middle classes through promises of restructuring the German economy and rearming its military.[1] While heading the National Socialist German Workers' Party (better known as the Nazi Party), Hitler rose to power and became chancellor of Germany on January 30, 1933.

One month after being appointed chancellor, Hitler legalized the incarceration of political opponents and those who opposed his leadership. According to the Presidential Order, " … those who endanger human life by their opposition will be sentenced to penal servitude, or in extenuating circumstances to a term of imprisonment of not less than six months. …"[2]

A short six weeks later, the first Nazi concentration camp, known as Dachau, officially opened in an abandoned gunpowder factory.[3] The local German newspaper, *Munchner Neueste Nachrichten*, published a statement regarding the camp:

The Munich Chief of Police, Himmler, has issued the following press announcement: On Wednesday, the first concentration camp is to be opened in Dachau with an accommodation for 5,000 persons. All Communists and—where necessary— Reichsbanner (a Social Democratic party militia) and Social Democratic functionaries who endanger state security are to be concentrated here, as in the long run it is not possible to keep individual functionaries in the state prisons without overburdening these prisons, and on the other hand these people cannot be released because attempts have shown that they persist in their efforts to agitate and organize as soon as they are released.[4]

By May 1, 1933, 1,200 inmates were held at Dachau; by the end of the year, there were 4,821 registered prisoners.[5]

---

fittings and valve departments.[15] E. W. "Ned" Hollis, former vice president and general manager of Parker Appliance's rubber division, explained:

Two of the main ingredients in most of these compounds were castor oil and sheep fat. The manufacturing process involved cooking the ingredients in huge steam kettles for many hours, which would permeate the atmosphere of the entire plant and neighborhood with a fragrance that did not compare favorably to Chanel No. 5![16, 17]

As production of lubricants increased, so did the creation of Parker Appliance devices designed to use O-rings (solid-rubber seals that "seal in" fuel). Bulkhead fittings, engine primers, selector valves, shut-off valves, and needle valves needed quality seals to function properly. Unfortunately, Parker Appliance's O-ring suppliers were not dependable. Art ordered his R&D team to develop a chemical-based rubber compound that would enable Parker Appliance to produce its own O-rings, as well as similar seals and gaskets. After he purchased laboratory presses, molds, mixers, and other equipment, Parker Appliance was immersed in the rubber business.

The technology surrounding hydraulic systems for landing gear, flaps, control surfaces, bomb bay doors, and control "servo-systems" required for aircrafts was also evolving. Hollis reminisced about the war production days in Parker Appliance's rubber division:

The efficiency and flexibility of tubing and tube fittings in plumbing together multiple engines and multiple tanks provided a baseline of products, but it was a natural evolution to provide many other component parts of the fuel system harness. Selector

Arthur Kerdemann was among the 12,000 Jews and 4,000 Aryans who were marched through Dachau's gates in 1938, but was one of the few who left alive. After being arrested for allegedly killing a German diplomat, Kerdemann spent five months at Dachau. His relatives had obtained a passport for him to Shanghai—the Nazis were releasing all who could get passage out of the occupied territory. At the last minute, Kerdemann was able to join his sister in England where he stayed for five months before sailing to the United States.[6]

Kerdemann began working at Parker Appliance Company in Cleveland. Through his work in the tool design department, he appreciated the freedom and advantages the country had to offer.[7] When he was interviewed for a story on his experiences for Parker Appliance's internal newsletter in 1943, Kerdemann stated that he almost felt grateful for his troubles— if he had not been arrested in Germany, he might not have traveled to the United States.[8]

Yet the struggles he encountered at Dachau could not truly be understood by Americans not fully aware of Hitler's wrath overseas. Kerdemann had been told he was being watched by the Gestapo in Germany and that he should not talk of his experience within that country as he would be returned

Arthur Kerdemann of Parker Appliance's tool design department spent five months in Dachau, Germany's first concentration camp, circa 1943.

to camp immediately. Elsewhere, however, he was at liberty to say all he pleased.

"Because they won't believe you anyway," Kerdemann said. "The peculiar part, is that most people don't."[9]

valves, shut-off valves, level control valves, boosters— even fuel filters. And almost every one of these devices required sealing against leakage. More O-rings, more special design seals.[18]

The importance of Parker Appliance's R & D division became paramount in an environment laden with war's erratic demands. The belief at Parker Appliance was that "future development comes only as a direct result of intelligent planning."[19] Yet, the company admitted that preparing for new products to be created and sold for the after-war market was very difficult. Anticipating what products would be needed and when they should be available would have been "pure speculation in that the date of the war's end is absolutely unpredictable."

The company continued to grow, although this was not immediately reflected in the bottom line. Net income for the fiscal year ending 1943 was just more than $1.2 million. While this figure was down slightly from the year before because of the substantial increase in facilities and personnel, Art remained confident. According to the 1943 Annual Report:

[The] expansion has been well controlled, and … our facilities will be fully occupied in the post-war period. … With a skilled Research Department, fully integrated plant facilities, a nation-wide sales and service organization and high reputation for production quality and dependability, your Company stands ready for what may come in the post-war era.[20]

Throughout 1941 and 1942, Parker Appliance expanded with 12 nationwide sales and service facilities based in New York; Washington, D.C.; Atlanta;

Dayton; Detroit; Chicago; Dallas; Kansas City; Los Angeles; San Diego; Seattle; and Montreal, Canada. A key player in spreading the attributes of Parker products was the "Parker Service Engineer" who served as a liaison between the company and the customer. This industrial concept, introduced in the early 1940s, was one that Art watched carefully to ensure his Engineering and R & D departments were aware of the evolution of customer needs.[21]

Women Join the Workforce

Parker Appliance's employees worked around the clock following the Japanese attack on Pearl Harbor. "Twenty-four hours out of every twenty-four-hour day and seven days out of every seven-day week, the machines are running and Parker folks are working hard … for VICTORY," stated the January 1943 issue of the company's internal newsletter, *Fitting News*. To ensure the plants could run at this pace, the company

needed to fill its ranks being depleted by the war. Parker Appliance began hiring women to meet the need for able-bodied workers.

Although millions of American women were already working in plants similar to Parker Appliance across the country, U. S. War Manpower Commission Chief Paul V. McNutt stated that "one out of every six women over 18 and not now employed will be needed in the nation's labor force by the end of 1943 and one out of every four—possibly three—housewives between 18 and 44 will be employed in the nation's war effort by that time."[22] At the beginning of 1943, female employees represented 30 percent of the U.S. factory workforce, and this number was growing

At a national trade show, Parker Appliance demonstrates the vital role women played in manufacturing its products to support the war.

Parker Appliance employees supported World War II efforts in many ways, as seen by this billboard on London Road in Cleveland that encouraged blood donations.

at the rate of 125 new female employees each month.[23] The January 1943 issue of *Fitting News* described the effect of women in Parker Appliance's workforce:

No task is too small and few too heavy for the women as they fill the gaps in the production lines. They did not come to usurp men's places beside the machines. They have come to help as they were needed in Parker's part in this gargantuan endeavor to keep the machines rolling. As evidence that women at Parker are sincere in their participation in industrial war work is the fact that in the early spring of last year over 200 of the female employees voluntarily contributed a day's pay to the Pearl Harbor Fund.[24]

Employees Help the War Effort

As production continued incessantly, Art knew that his employees' personal needs had to be met as well. He provided social outlets, such as bowling and softball leagues, which offered prize money, and numerous variety shows, which showcased the talents of Parker employees. While these variety shows were created for entertainment and enjoyment, the overall purpose remained serious as they were opportunities to urge employees to buy war bonds. The idea of raising funds for war bonds at Parker Appliance's Cleveland headquarters became so popular that Hollywood star John Garfield visited the plant December 5, 1942, and told employees that "buying war bonds is not only a good investment for your money, but the patriotic duty of every good American."[25]

By October 1943, employees had bought more than $900,000 in all types of bonds.[26] The war bond drives became ingrained in the Parker Appliance culture.

SAVING THE COUNTRY THROUGH BONDS

During one of its war bond drives to support World War II efforts, Parker Appliance hosted Hollywood actress Greer Garson, seen here amidst a crowd with Art Parker (left) and Cleveland's Mayor Frank J. Lausche (right).

As the United States entered World War II, there was a national call for defense that every American was willing to pay for—literally. Defense bonds were sold to finance the war effort. When the Japanese attacked Pearl Harbor on December 7, 1941, the U.S. government changed the name to war bonds. After President Franklin D. Roosevelt bought the first bond May 1, 1941, everyone from artists and movie stars to young women at makeshift stands pleaded with Americans to "buy war bonds."[1]

To promote these Series E bonds, the campaign stirred the conscience of Americans by appealing to both their financial and moral stake in the war. By buying bonds, which were offered in various denominations, they could show patriotism by sacrificing their hard-earned money. However, the average hourly pay rate at the time was 85.3 cents an hour, and investing was difficult for most.[2] In 1942, the value of the dollar was steep (equal to $12.59 at the end of 2007).[3]

Through advertisements created and endorsed by the government as well as those generated by private companies and organizations, the First War Loan Drive began November 30, 1942. Sales totaled almost $13 billion—$1.6 billion were sold to individuals, and the rest were purchased by corporations and commercial banks.[4]

Much of the sales' success was a result of Hollywood's involvement. After film star Carole Lombard was killed in a plane crash following a bond rally in

which she had raised some $2.5 million, Hollywood became involved with a "Stars Over America" bond blitz. With 337 stars working 18 hours a day throughout the country's bond drives, crowds of admiring fans followed with their wallets open.[5]

Parker Appliance employees were thrilled by film star John Garfield's visit to the plant December 5, 1942. In a surprise announcement, second-shift employees at the plant were shocked when Garfield stopped to talk about buying war bonds.[6] According to the Parker

Appliance January 1943 edition of the internal newsletter, *Fitting News:*

John Garfield made a deep impression on all Parker employees who met him, men and women alike. Straight-talking and unaffected by his national renown as a motion picture actor, he specializes in visiting war plants.[7]

Garfield made a lasting impression on Parker employees. During the war, Hollywood stars made seven tours through 300 cities and towns. As the war came to an end, the last proceeds from a "Victory Bond" campaign were deposited in the Treasury January 3, 1946, officially finalizing sales. Throughout the last five years of sales, the War Finance Committee sold a total of $185.7 billion of securities to more than 85 million Americans, including thousands at Parker Appliance who invested in the bonds.

Parker Appliance employees pledged more than 13 percent of their payroll to purchase war bonds through a payroll savings plan. Percy Brown (far left), co-chairman of the Greater Cleveland Bond Committee, congratulates Art Parker (far right) as Matt DeMore (center left) and Mayor Frank J. Lausche (center right) look on, circa 1943.

The Parker employees' variety show, "IMP Laments of 1943," was hosted by actress Nancy Kelly and Cleveland's Mayor Frank Lausche and showcased singing and comedy acts at Cleveland's Public Music Hall. The show raised $5,000 for the Red Cross. Additional support came from employee blood drives that helped "Cheat Death with Plasma Donations."[27] As the war divided nations, it also created a culture of family among Parker Appliance employees—a culture Art knew would ensure his company's survival through the war and during peace time. Art wrote the following in the company's 1944 Annual Report:

Parker Appliance winners of the war bond drive sales contest enjoyed a trip to the Willow Run bomber plant in Michigan, home of the B-24 Liberators, as a reward in September 1944.

Fluid Power in aircraft and other war products is firmly established as the modern method of efficient transmission of power. Our war-time products are our peace-time products and we will enter into peace time work as our customers again resume their civilian production. Your management is conscious of our obligation to continue all efforts to bring the war to a victorious conclusion and establish sound economic conditions for the post-war period.[28]

Parker Loses Its Leader

Art became concerned about the U.S. government's insistent requests for hydraulic equipment in comparison to its lesser demands for aircraft production. This lopsided distribution of work was worrisome, even as it kept Parker Appliance's profit well above the $1 million mark at the end of fiscal year 1944.[29] Although Art tried to

persuade war production authorities that other vital defense manufacturing was being neglected, the government maintained its steady stream of orders.[30]

Manufacturing at Parker Appliance continued to grow—as did Art's family. He and Helen had four children: Thomas, Joyce, Cynthia, and their oldest son, Patrick, who was now a teenager. While Art tried to be a part of his children's lives, almost all of his time was committed to Parker Appliance's military production.[31] Even as his success mounted—Parker Appliance's triple-type-U fitting became the only fitting used by the U.S. Air Corps—the years of continual pressure of meeting the government's demands took its toll.[32] On January 1, 1945, Art suffered a heart attack and passed away at his home just hours after shoveling snow with his sons.[33] The *Cleveland Plain Dealer* reported:

The industrial community of Cleveland suffered a severe loss on New Year's Day with the death of Arthur L. Parker, founder, president, and general manager of the Parker Appliance Co. "A master of many sciences … a creator of industry … and a citizen of vision." These were the words with which, in December 1943, Dr. William E. Wickenden, president of Case School of Applied Science, bestowed the honorary degree of doctor of engineering on this Case graduate.[34]

As Parker Appliance employees mourned the sudden death of their leader, Helen reeled from the loss. Her grief escalated when, just five months after her husband's death, Germany surrendered to Allied forces, and the war soon ended. While families welcomed home loved ones, Helen was left with the quieted machines at Parker Appliance. The company had virtually no business, either military or commercial.

Patrick described both the drastic drop in business and his mother's attitude toward Parker Appliance at the time:

The company's only customer—the U.S. [war effort]—abruptly went out of business. All that was left at Parker were termination claims, inventory, and work in process. Within weeks, employment [at Parker Appliance] dropped to less than 300. All facilities were idled, and the only work available was identifying the millions of partially completed pieces lying around the factory floor.[35]

Art Parker in the mid-1940s, just prior to his death. *(Photo by Euclid Studio, Inc.)*

[Helen] was made of tough fiber. She resisted any suggestion of sale or liquidation of the company … she insisted that strong professional management be recruited, and that the company be rebuilt—a difficult assignment by any measure, and certainly one that had no sure prospect of success.[36]

Art's widow was left to decide between what some thought were her only options—bankruptcy or liquidation of her husband's dream. Yet she refused to give up on a company that her husband had painstakingly built. The year ahead would give Helen the opportunity to prove that Parker Appliance could not only survive, but also regain its place as the premier technological supplier to industry.

THE TERRY STEAM TURBINE CO.
MAIN OFFICE AND WORKS
HARTFORD 1, CONN.
P. O. BOX 1200

June 11, 1946

The Parker Appliance Company
17325 Euclid Ave.
Cleveland 12, Ohio

Attention - Mr. Paul Kozak, Jr.
            Advertising Manager

Gentlemen:

      In accordance with your request of June 3rd,
1946, we are pleased to send you herewith photograph of
a Terry Steam Turbine which employs Parker fittings.
This turbine is rated 1700 H.P. at 4750 R.P.M. It is
equipped with an oil relay variable speed governor and
operates with steam conditions of 140#, 450°T.T., 26".
It drives a large blower in one of the country's leading oil refineries.

      We sincerely hope that you will find this
photograph of interest.

                Very truly yours,

                THE TERRY STEAM TURBINE CO.

                Advertising Manager.

Ack
7-23-46

After World War II contracts were cancelled and Parker Appliance's financial state was spiraling downward, the new management of S. B. "Ghost" Taylor, president, and Robert W. Cornell, vice president, looked to marketing the usefulness of Parker Appliance's products, as seen here in this Terry Steam Turbine in 1946. *(Inset photo by George E. Meyers, Inc.)*

STARTING OVER

1946–1950

1946 Sales: $21.9 Million | 1950 Sales: $7.1 Million

Mr. Parker is no longer with us. The best tribute to his memory that the Parker people can make is to carry on and build on the foundation he has created ...

—Herbert I. Markham, president, Parker Appliance Company

AS THE POSTWAR ERA BEGAN, Helen Parker knew the survival of her husband's company rested on her shoulders. With bankruptcy or liquidation an almost certain result of the war's end and Arthur L. Parker's death, Helen channeled her grief into saving the company. Under these dire circumstances, a special meeting of Parker Appliance Company's board of directors was held January 18, 1945. Herbert I. Markham, vice president at Parker Appliance since August 1942, was elected president and Art's first employee, Carl Klamm, was made special sales engineer.[1]

In a reassuring note to employees, Markham delivered a message of calm amidst turbulent change:

The Parker Appliance Company is an example of what America stands for. In it you see how men with the vision and courage of Arthur L. Parker can build a company for the employment of people for service to the community and the industrial enterprises of the entire country.

Mr. Parker is no longer with us. The best tribute to his memory that the Parker people can make is to carry on and build on the foundation he has created with the

end in view that The Parker Appliance Company may become a greater and stronger factor in its various fields of operation. I ask the cooperation of all the Parker organization that this may be accomplished.

With the presidency filled, Helen faced the evolving industrial landscape affected by the war's inevitable conclusion. She felt compelled to seek professional management outside the company to help reverse its downward spiral—at the time, it was nearly broke.[2] Parker Appliance's mainstay military orders had ended as the Allies commanded victory.[3]

Helen realized a new course was necessary to rebuild the industrial component business of Parker Appliance. The company's banker, Charles C. Sigmier of the Cleveland Trust Company, suggested she hire S. Blackwell "Ghost" Taylor of Cleveland's Reliance Electric Company

Parker Appliance Company struggled to stay solvent after the end of World War II and began manufacturing molds to create miniature plastic bottles to advertise Coca-Cola.

as president.[4] Trusting Sigmier's advice, Helen shifted Markham to chairman of the board, hired Taylor as president, and also hired Robert W. Cornell, a young business associate of Taylor's, as vice president to help guide the company. Helen also invested Art's $1 million life insurance policy into the business to assist the company through the rebuilding process.

Staying Solvent

The first course of business for the new management team was the necessary sacrifice of nearly three-quarters of Parker Appliance's workforce. With employees dreading the inevitable, the workforce was cut drastically by the middle of 1945.[5] Although a small workforce was maintained, the corporate books were in disarray. According to Markham and Taylor, there was an effort to concentrate all Cleveland manufacturing into the main plant.[6] Survival tactics included the sale of

two of the newly added Cleveland plants (built under Art's guidance), located at St. Clair Avenue and London Road. War contract terminations, which dissolved practically all of the company's war contracts and subcontracts, and the resulting curtailment of production caused internal friction among the remaining employees.

"There was so much capacity around … it was a dog-eat-dog period of time," Art's son Patrick Parker stated years later.[7]

Employment Difficulties

Both Markham and Taylor tried to reassure the remaining employees during the year following Art's death with hope for "new business conditions" following the war's end.[8] Yet issues of costs and price ceilings were a constant concern.[9]

Even during the rehiring process of those who were laid off, tensions continued to mount as disputes over

After Art's sudden death, at a special meeting of Parker Appliance Company's board of directors, Herbert I. Markham was elected interim president.

At that same special meeting, held January 18, 1945, Carl E. Klamm, Parker Appliance's first employee, was appointed to special sales engineer.

seniority arose. Workers went on strike August 22, 1945. With aid from the American Federation of Labor's International Association of Machinists Company, 2,000 picketers assembled at Parker Appliance's gates to bring concerns to management about the seniority provisions of the union's contract in the laying off and rehiring of workers.[10]

Although the machinists were on strike, the company's office workers continued to report to their jobs—even as the picket lines were making this increasingly difficult.[11] The strikers became forceful when Cleveland police officers began escorting office workers through the line to enter the plant. Two automobiles were damaged during the scrambling, reported the *Cleveland Plain Dealer*.[12] Two policemen and 14 strikers were injured as mounted officers attempted to resume order.[13]

The next day, Taylor announced the closing of Parker Appliance for an indefinite period.[14] Office workers were

told to remain at home to avoid any disturbances between police and picketers. In a statement to the *Cleveland Plain Dealer*, Taylor said that there could be no negotiation of grievances until workers dropped their strike and resumed their places in the plant because of a no-strike clause in the contract between the company and the machinists' union.

"That clause was in the contract even before the war, and we feel that it is binding. We cannot see our way to negotiate while the strike is on, and the contract is being violated by the union," Taylor said. "By keeping the office workers out of the plant, the union has prevented our efforts to get more work for our men."

Negotiations came to a standstill because agreement could not be reached about the recognition of foremen, organized in a separate local of the Machinists Union. However, on October 10, the issue of recognizing foremen was withdrawn, and parties agreed to negotiate the matter of seniority.[14] As negotiations were finalized,

On the advice of the company's banker, Helen Parker hired S. B. "Ghost" Taylor as president and moved Herbert Markham to chairman of the board.

Robert Cornell, a young business associate of S. B. Taylor, was hired as vice president to further usher in the new postwar era of Parker Appliance.

A WIDOW'S FAITH

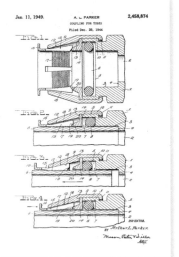

U.S. Patent number 2,458,874: *Coupling for Tubes*, filed just a week before Art Parker's death.

O N THE HEELS OF ARTHUR Parker's death on January 1, 1945, his widow was left with four children and a company on the verge of losing its only customer, the United States government. As World War II came to an end, so did military supply orders for Parker Appliance Company, leaving the company without work and in a tumultuous financial state. Although most women of her generation would have walked away, Helen Parker became committed to saving her husband's dream—his company.

Moving quickly, Helen invested every penny of Art's $1 million life insurance policy into Parker Appliance.[1] With the guidance of attorney James Weeks of Thompson, Hine & Flory—a law firm that continues to serve Parker today—and the company's

banker, Charles C. Sigmier, Helen brought in new management and held onto hope that these decisions and her finances could save the company.[2] As S. B. "Ghost" Taylor and his colleague Robert Cornell assumed roles as president and vice president, respectively, Helen relied on their guidance for key business decisions—yet her role and convictions remained strong.

Although Parker Appliance turned to unconventional job contracts to pay its bills, Helen was determined to continue her husband's legacy of innovative technology.[3] Even through World War II, Art

employees reported to Parker Appliance's Cleveland plant October 22. Although Taylor and Markham acknowledged that the issues resolved were "fundamental," the strike took its toll on the already fragile company.[15]

Being Resourceful in the New Year

With a small workforce back in place, Taylor and Cornell began closely examining the company's busi-

Employees work in Parker Appliance's Rubber Division as it nears the uncertainty of bankruptcy or liquidation, circa 1945.

remained extremely active in the creation and improvement of several manufacturing designs. Patent number 2,458,874, filed just a week before his death, described an invention for improvements in a coupling for tubes and also in a coupling for a flareless tube[4]:

An object of the invention is to provide a coupling which is so constructed that a tube may be inserted in the coupling when the parts are assembled and gripped and sealed to the coupling so that it cannot be removed therefrom by a pull on the tube.

A further object of the invention is to provide a coupling of the above type with means whereby the grip of the coupling on the tube may be released when it is desired to remove the tube from the coupling.[5]

Art elaborated on his design's intention to provide consistently secure connections:

When it is desired to remove the tube from its coupling it is not necessary to disassemble the parts of the coupling. The operator will drive the sleeve inwardly. The inclined end thereof will engage the cam of the camming ring and expand the end of the sleeve outwardly so as to disconnect the serrated portion of the sleeve outwardly … from the tube. This will permit the tube to be

withdrawn from the coupling. … Any fluid leaking into the chamber and bearing against the gasket will force the gasket against the camming ring … and the fluid pressure tending to contract the gasket … will expand it against the body member and the tube and increase the tightness of the seal.[6]

Knowing Art's enthusiasm for and dedication to the improvement of Parker Appliance products, Helen submitted his works in progress for patent assignment. Based on a pending application Art had filed November 27, 1944, which detailed an engine primer, Helen submitted a new patent application December 10, 1946[7]:

An object of the invention is to provide a primer of the reciprocating piston type with a rotary disk valve for selectively distributing the fluid transferred by the reciprocating piston. … A further object of the invention is to provide a primer of the above type with spring means for holding the disc valve continuously in contact with its seat.[8]

Granted the patent for the engine primer September 28, 1948, it was clear that Helen's goal to continue Art's dream of implementing innovative, precise, and reliable designs for the industrial world was being realized. From January 1946 through February 1953, Helen spearheaded the promotion of 26 new patents under Arthur L. Parker's name.[9]

A tube bender works at a manufacturing station in 1945.

ness strategy. They had no doubt that Parker Appliance was ready for an economic upturn, but additional concerns needed to be addressed.

Peacetime manufacturing required significant rearrangement of the plant's production. At the end of the war, Parker Appliance's operations in Cleveland and Los Angeles had a considerable amount of machinery and equipment on rental from the Defense Plant Corporation.[16] While the company purchased $250,088 worth of the equipment by the end of the 1946 fiscal

year, the government removed the remaining equipment, and there were no plans for major expenditures for manufacturing facilities during the coming fiscal year, according to Taylor and Markham.[17]

Parker Appliance's principal products were diversified prior to the war. The company manufactured tube couplings, fittings, and valves for oil, fuel, and control lines in aircraft and hydraulic control systems and machine tools for air, water, oil, chemical, and fuel lines in manufacturing and power plants. But war production had shifted all the company's efforts into the aircraft industry, preventing it from serving industrial customers. Taylor and Cornell knew they could regain this customer base; however, to generate income, the company needed to re-diversify outside of its traditional markets.[18]

Taylor and Cornell converted the now-defunct war production facility into a plant that facilitated the company's ability to meet current market needs. Taylor and Markham released a statement regarding the matter:

The facilities of our Engineering Division and laboratory have been reorganized to meet the present demands of, and to insure adequate service to, our customers. Various new types of fittings, globe and needle valves, plug valves, and other items have been developed for the aircraft and industrial markets.

The tube fabrications facilities developed during the war for servicing aircraft requirements have now been adapted to produce bent tube assemblies for a wide range of industrial uses.

Our extensive wartime laboratory facilities have been converted to a new Special Products Division, which is producing molded rubber and plastic products and is enjoying a rapid growth.[19]

The company also sought work wherever it was available. Parker Appliance won a contract to produce bronze burial urns for the battlefields of Normandy.[20] It was the only work the company could find in 1946,

WAR AND CIGARETTES

BEFORE WORLD WAR I BEGAN, MUCH OF THE U.S. public consumed tobacco by smoking pipes and cigars or by chewing tobacco or "snuff." Yet, by the early 20th century, Americans preferred cigarettes, consuming more than 1,000 annually per smoker.[1] With convenient mass-produced cigarettes and "safety matches" in the form of matchbooks that allowed a portable means of lighting cigarettes, smoking became an easy and acceptable activity.

Men in the military and women working in industries that supported World War II were exposed to increased distribution of cigarettes. Physicians endorsed the placement of cigarettes in soldiers' ration kits during World War II, facilitating the belief that smoking relieved tension and produced no ill effects.[2] The marketing and free distribution of cigarettes to military personnel are believed to have played a prominent role in generating the high prevalence of smoking, with approximately 80 percent of World War II

soldiers smoking at least 100 cigarettes in a lifetime.[3] Marketing campaigns also linked the smoking of cigarettes to weight control, targeting female consumers.[4]

This smoking trend was further ignited through match manufacturers that capitalized on patriotic and military advertising on matchbook covers. In 1945, the price of a matchbook was about one-fifth of a cent to a vendor, and the U.S. Office of Price Administration (which controlled inflation during the war by ensuring price stabilization of some goods) insisted that a free book accompany every pack of cigarettes.[5] Soldiers as well as Americans at home were officially hooked.

Parker Appliance saw an opportunity to join other manufacturers in serving a need that was very popular at the time. In its March 1945 internal newsletter, *Fitting News*, Parker Appliance's Pacific Division touted its "postwar product ready for eager customers."[6] The first pipe, Smoker's Delight, No. 1, (S.D. [1]), was readied for inspection November 20, 1944:

according to Art's son Patrick Parker.[21] At 17, Patrick began his first summer job at the company's foundry by pouring metal into the urn molds.

Anticipating Customer Needs

Taylor and Cornell emphasized that customer service was the company's No. 1 priority. One example of this was through the creation and distribution of both the Parker O-Ring Handbook and the Parker Compound Manual.[22] The O-ring solid rubber seals, perfected by the R & D department, were marketed to a variety of customers for "sealing" needs to prevent the loss of fluid or gas. Depending on the size, O-rings could be used any number of ways from conveyor belts to water faucets.

With little information available publicly about the O-ring or its technology, Parker Appliance's customers contacted the R & D department to resolve any difficulties with the O-ring. One such issue occurred with Pesco, a pump company that used an O-ring as a rotary shaft seal on one of its pumps.[23] According to Tommy McCuistion of Parker's Rubber Products division:

A special compound had been developed for this application and worked well until the mold became worn and there was difficulty in meeting Pesco's tolerance specifications. Some of the O-rings were oversized on the inner diameter, and Pesco would reject them. A new mold was built, and the O-rings were now on the side of the tolerance and had to be restricted over the shaft when installed.[24]

After a sudden rash of O-ring seal failures and the resultant use of a more expensive O-ring, Parker Appliance's R & D department investigated the initial problem. By building a small test fixture in its machine shop, two or three different cross sections of the rubber O-rings

---

It will be no surprise to Parkerites to learn that the Pacific Division has already completed the design of an item certain to cause a sensation when offered to eager postwar buyers … a new kind of pipe. A close examination reveals super-sales features such as: gnarled stem for easy grip by even novices, rich mahogany finish to appeal to both men and women smokers, small bowl for economy, plastic nonslip mouthpiece built for tooth comfort, bowl of solid long-wearing brass, built-in refrigeration unit for cooler smoking, and many others.[7]

Parker Appliance's Pacific Division created a "super-special postwar product" known as Smoker's Delight, No. 1 or S.D. (1). This invention was a sign of the times, providing the nation with another way to satiate its craving for tobacco.

Although it was not a cigarette, the S.D. (1) was touted as a better means to smoking tobacco and had the ability to burn a patented pseudo-tobacco, also created by Parker Appliance's R & D laboratory. This product had the "looks, tastes, and … the same effect as real tobacco, but costs much less and can be easily manufactured by the bale."[8]

As World War II was coming to an end, support of the cigarette-smoking phenomenon was commonplace—even the *Journal of the American Medical Association* published cigarette ads throughout the 1940s.[9] The loyal patronage of smoking could be seen throughout America's industry, and Parker Appliance would show its desire to contribute its research efforts to the postwar market of a tobacco-craving nation.

While partially a gimmick that made light of the smoking trend, Parker Appliance's interest in inventions that served the growing cigarette industry was a sign of smoking's popularity and its growing presence in Americans' lives.

Today, Parker promotes a healthy lifestyle with many smoke-free facilities.

were tested to simulate the conditions created by Pesco's pumps. According to McCuistion:

These tests indicated that when the O-rings were stretched on installation, heat would build up rapidly and failure would occur within a few minutes. However, when an oversized O-ring was used in the identical groove, the problem did not occur and hundreds of hours could be put on the O-ring at 1800 rpms.[25]

By publishing its findings, engineers in the R & D department were further intrigued by possible additional applications of O-rings. This information was also made available to its customers. The Parker O-Ring Handbook and the Parker Compound Manual were widely distributed to reach a broader market in a fast and inexpensive manner and also enabled the company to provide engineering solutions to customers' sealing problems.[26]

Even with new technology creating opportunities, many obstacles remained as 1948 drew to a close. Taylor reached out to Parker Appliance employees in its annual report for the year:

… You will probably be surprised to see that 55 cents of every dollar taken in went to employees' wages and salaries, and that less than 2 cents was left for net earnings after paying for materials, taxes, and

Parker Appliance's Research and Development laboratory continued to create innovative products in 1945.

other expenses. Material alone took 25 cents [per dollar]. Common stockholders—there are about 850 of them—the owners of the Company, have received nothing for the past three years.

These low earnings and our inability to pay dividends to those whose investment makes our jobs possible are a serious concern to your management and to every thinking employee. During the current year, with increased business, and more jobs, we must solve the problem of high costs and find ways to improve our performance as a Company. I hope you, as an employee, will help in every way you can, because we will need your help.[27]

Strength in Fluid Power

Taylor and Cornell recognized the growing opportunity in fluid controls and fluid power. Realizing that precision devices were needed to power machines doing heavy work, the field of fluid power became the foundation for Parker's future.[28] Taylor and Cornell believed that just as General Electric could provide a complete range of electrical components and products,

Parker Appliance could achieve the same prominence within the fluid power industry.[29]

Looking to the customers Parker Appliance had during the 1940s—Boeing Aircraft Company, Ford Motor Company, The Manitowoc Shipbuilding Corporation, and Westinghouse Electric & Manufacturing Company—the company hoped to prove the worth of its industrial applications.[30] By focusing on the company's proven products, including tube couplings for seamless tubing systems to transmit fluids or gas, precision valves, and fabricating equipment for mass production of tubular assemblies bent uniformly, Taylor and Cornell targeted their applications to many industrial markets.[31] From cooling mechanisms in refrigeration units to powering steam, air, and lubrication systems in steam, diesel-electric, and all-electric locomotives, Parker Appliance continued to extend its reach.

Learning from the Past

While the focus on national markets was paying off for Parker Appliance as 1949 ended, a new, yet familiar, threat was evident—one that could directly affect the company's survival.

It was June 25, 1950, when the North Korean army launched across the 38th parallel into South Korea, powered by a firestorm of artillery. With the help of Soviet 150 T-35 tanks and 180 aircraft, the North Koreans began the war.[32] An onslaught of 135,000 troops sent South Korean forces into retreat, and Seoul was captured on June 28.

Although the invasion came as a surprise to the United States—Congress was told the week prior that war was unlikely—the actions of North Korea convinced President Truman that World War III had arrived. With a substantial number of United States forces in Japan under the command of General Douglas MacArthur, President Truman ordered military force against North Korea.[33]

The United States was at war again, and the government quickly turned to Parker Appliance to supply its industrial equipment orders. But, having learned from experience, Taylor and Cornell refused to let the company depend blindly on the government as its sole customer.[34] With the help of Sigmier's financial advice, Taylor crafted contracts to aid the government as it began a build up of materials for the Korean War, but they were fashioned to assist Parker Appliance's survival. The terms provided for government sponsorship of production as well as project financing, which would protect the company once the war ended.[35] This new business helped Parker Appliance achieve more than $7 million in sales, its best effort since World War II.[36] Success was also attributed to standardization of its products, introduction of new items, opening of new markets, and greater manufacturing efficiency.[37] Taylor detailed the results in that year's report to shareholders and employees:

… The simplification of our product lines has also made it possible to realize over $500,000 in reduction of inventories. This has added to cash and makes it possible to finance a substantial increase in business.

The Korean War has caused a sharp increase in demand for many of our products. It is difficult to estimate at this time the full effect of the current emergency upon the immediate future of our business. However, we are preparing for increased volume, both in aircraft and industrial products. Many of the new products, which have been perfected since World War II—notably molded synthetic rubber products, new valves for aircraft fuel and hydraulic systems, components for jet engines, and devices for fast refueling of airplanes—are sure to be required in much greater volume … [38]

As the United States prepared for war throughout 1950, Taylor and Cornell were setting a steady course for Parker Appliance, ensuring that the company would be known as the world standard for hydraulic and fluid-handling systems.

For more revenue miles..

● The way to increase airline profits is to keep fixed charges airborne. A plane earns no money when it's on the ground.

Even more important than completing scheduled flights is the decreasing of ground time in the schedule. If your average cruising speed is 275 miles per hour, you lose 23 miles every five minutes you are delayed in an airport.

To refuel 7500 gallons of gasoline at a mere 50 or 75 gallons a minute costs as much time as a 200-mile flight. Measured in terms of passenger annoyance, of overloaded airport facilities, the loss may be even greater.

The obvious remedy is a more efficient, yet safe, method of refueling. Parker offers you that remedy in the new Underwing Fueling Equipment.

2

Parker Appliance Company used marketing materials, such as this page from its "To Turn Ground Time into Flight Time" bulletin, to promote its underwing fueling equipment, circa 1950s. This innovation allowed aircraft to accept up to 200 gallons of fuel per minute.

DEFYING THE ODDS

1951–1959

1951 Sales: $12.2 Million | 1959 Sales: $43.2 Million

Parker Appliance looked at itself and said that if one company [General Electric] can provide a total range of electrical components and electrical products, why should this not make sense for a total range of fluid components and fluid products? This was probably the single most important management decision made in the history of this corporation.

—Patrick S. Parker

As Parker Appliance company entered the 1950s, the company's new management team recognized the growing demand for industrial hydraulic and pneumatic products. By catering to America's industry, which was converting to the use of fluid controls and fluid power components, S. B. "Ghost" Taylor, president, and Robert W. Cornell, vice president, knew that Parker Appliance's precision devices would be successful.[1]

Charles C. Sigmier, the newly hired chairman of the board, was one of the authors of a corporate creed that evolved after World War II to help guide management efforts. The Parker Appliance creed included four basic points:

1. *Parker Appliance Company was not for sale.*
2. *Management would strive to reduce the percentage of government business overall, while still increasing actual sales to government customers.*
3. *Corporate growth would be through a combination of internal research and development as well as acquisitions; however, Parker had to be the dominant factor in any proposed merger.*
4. *Acquisitions would be sought principally to expand and fill out fluid power component product lines.*[2]

Although the volume of business had almost recovered to its pre-war level, employment was stable, and the company posted a small profit, Parker Appliance could be vulnerable if it relied solely on fulfilling the government's war production needs. As the Korean War progressed, Taylor and Cornell, with Sigmier's help, held strong to the company's goal of surviving past another war. Parker Appliance's contracts and government financing allowed it to thrive as it regained its former industrial business.[3]

Parker Appliance Expands

At the end of 1951, Parker Appliance's sales for the fiscal year totaled $12.2 million—a significant increase over the $7.1 million reached the preceding

---

In the 1950s, "Parky" was the official mascot for Parker Appliance O-rings.

year.[4] In addition to the increase of its defense production program, there was also a substantial rise in demand for aircraft and industrial products. Taylor and Sigmier also took a first step toward expanding Parker Appliance by organizing several wholly owned subsidiary companies.[5]

In 1950, Parker Appliance became the parent company of Eaton Screw Products Company, a small manufacturing business based in Eaton, Ohio.[6] The company was recognized as an outstanding small business in 1948 by *American Machinist* magazine.[7] Eaton Screw had suffered a fate similar to Parker Appliance as its founder, Horace Justice, died from a heart attack in December 1948. Robert C. "Barney" Barnd and two other investors bought the company from Justice's estate. While Barnd, a used car salesman, admitted he knew nothing about manufacturing, he was sure the company could continue to prosper with the employees it had in place.[8]

A year later, Cornell called Barnd and asked to see the Eaton Screw Company facility.

"After a tour of the facility, he shared with me the problems Parker Appliance was having in Cleveland in modernizing and cost reducing their manufacturing to improve profitability," Barnd recalled, adding that Cornell then asked if it were possible to buy Eaton Screw. "Being a car salesman," Barnd said, "I was always ready for a deal."[9]

After negotiating with Taylor and James Weeks, Parker Appliance's board member and legal counsel, Parker Appliance took ownership of Eaton Screw Products in October 1950. As a wholly owned subsidiary of Parker Appliance, Barnd became CEO, president, and general manager of Eaton Screw.[10]

"That little company was a marvel of what an automatic screw machine company should be. It was an outstanding operation," said Barnd.[11]

An aerial view of Parker Appliance Company's Cleveland plant, circa 1950s. *(Photo by Lloyd De Mers.)*

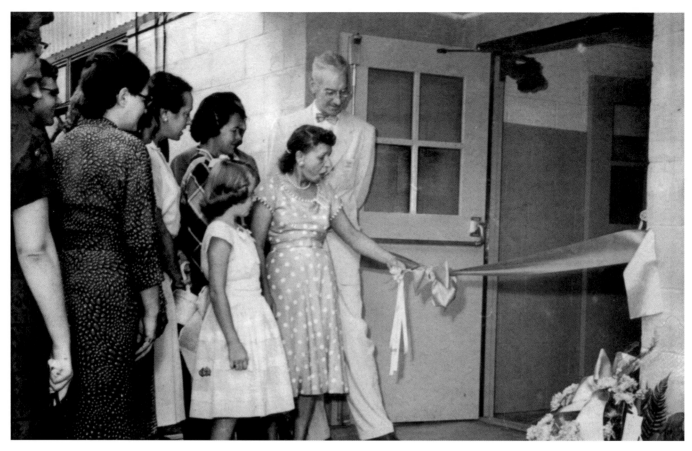

While this consolidation could have been intimidating for Barnd and Eaton Screw's employees, Taylor and Cornell made certain the company felt at ease with the merger. Barnd explained:

I was very impressed with Ghost Taylor and Bob Cornell. Taylor was quiet, but when he had something to say, it was very provocative. Bob had a great personality, and both were great listeners. If [Taylor and Cornell] were visiting, or if you were in one of the monthly managers' meetings, they both listened to you. Even as the company grew, Bob knew what was going on day-to-day, week-to-week, month-to-month. But he and Ghost delegated responsibility and expected you to keep them informed. Another thing I learned from Bob was that it was very important to build a team.[12]

After the consolidation of Eaton Screw, Parker Appliance acquired the Synthetic Rubber Products Company in Los Angeles.[13] During 1951, Parker Appliance finished construction on a new plant for its

In June 1950, Helen Parker officially opened the Berea Rubber Company, Berea, Kentucky, with S. B. "Ghost" Taylor.

third wholly owned subsidiary, the Berea Rubber Company in Berea, Kentucky. Berea began substantial production of synthetic rubber O-rings for military aircraft. Although the total cost of the plant and its equipment was estimated at $700,000, a mortgage loan under the Defense Production Act of 1950 covered almost three-quarters of the cost.[14]

While Taylor and Cornell were expanding the company's manufacturing operations, they turned their attention to a manufacturing facility located at 6506 Stanford Avenue, Los Angeles. Purchased by Parker Appliance and initially dubbed the company's Pacific Division, the plant was incorporated, and on August 1, 1951, Parker Aircraft Co. was born as a wholly owned subsidiary.[15] A lease agreement was created with the newly formed subsidiary and developed under a U.S. Air Force Facilities contract that supported the

PARKER PRESIDENT PLAYS AT THE HERMIT CLUB

AMERICA'S FIRST PROFESSIONAL THEATRICAL CLUB, The Lambs, was established in New York in 1874—shortly after that a similar society named The Hermit Club was formed in Cleveland.[1] As the social gathering place for amateur actors, singers, and musicians, what made The Hermit Club unique is that its performers were top executives at Cleveland's largest companies.[2]

Members of Cleveland's Gatling Gun Company (GGC), a military group created by ex-servicemen from the Spanish-American War who prided themselves on producing and performing musical comedies, were visited by some of The Lambs' performers in the early 1900s.[3] It was after this meeting that GGC member and Cleveland architect Frank B. Meade was encouraged to organize a club similar to The Lambs. The result was a private society called The Hermit Club, housed in a building erected in 1904 in Cleveland's theater district.[4]

The first Hermit Club building was modeled after the famous Lambs structure in New York, including an ambiguous entrance to pedestrians walking through its alley. Hidden between two large warehouses, The Hermit Club's location was chosen primarily because of its proximity to the Opera House.

Although The Lambs heralded great performing artists as members, including Fred Astaire, Irving Berlin, and John Philip Sousa, The Hermit Club was known for prominent business professionals whose hidden talents were on display for members only.[5] In 1928, The Hermit Club moved to Euclid Avenue in the new theater district and thrived. One member was Parker Appliance Company's president, S. B. "Ghost" Taylor.

Standing 6 feet, 5 inches tall, Taylor took on the nickname of "Ghost" in college because of the tremendous shock of light-colored hair he sported.[6] Many revered Taylor for his managerial skills but were not aware of his other talents.

"Ghost was a musician," said Robert "Barney" Barnd, whose company, Eaton Screw Products, was merged into Parker Appliance as a wholly owned subsidiary in 1950. "He was a no-nonsense manager, but he could be a fun guy."

Another Parker Appliance colleague remembered seeing Taylor perform.

"I got to know Ghost because he was a musician and belonged to The Hermit Club. He introduced me to the club and got me in," said Bill Webster, who was hired as an engineer by Taylor in 1950. "Ghost played the trombone, nobody knew that."[7]

While Taylor is gone, The Hermit Club and its performers reign as the country's only private club dedicated to the performing arts. Current members comprise a 25-piece orchestra, men's and mixed chorus, 19-piece jazz band, a drama troupe, and a chamber music group. A unique venue for the finest in business and the arts, Taylor was a privileged member who experienced what the plaque at The Hermit Club's entrance states: "Ye've shared the best."

production of fittings, valves, and other aircraft components.[16] Soon after, an additional 40,000-square-foot fittings plant was constructed at 5827 West Century Boulevard, Los Angeles.[17]

While the surge of mergers and new construction was unchartered territory for the company, Taylor, Cornell, and Sigmier stood behind these decisions. According to Parker Appliance's 1951 Annual Report, they felt that "this financial plan, while complex, provides the method whereby we may do our part in the defense effort without excessive risk to our shareholders."

Focused Creativity

The 1950s were a time of growth for Parker Appliance and also a period where decentralized management became the core principle that would drive the company. Taylor and Cornell, like Arthur Parker, relied on the creativity and dedication of the workforce for the company's success. The management emphasized an autonomous spirit for all staff—by believing in the abilities of each employee, Parker Appliance's workers in turn would create innovative and marketable products for the company. Yet, as Bill Webster, who was hired as an engineer in the Jet Division in Cleveland by Cornell in 1950, explains, the company was well-grounded and kept the creativity focused, realistic, and progressing:

What was really great and smart about Parker is that those of us that started in engineering worked in the laboratory. You didn't sit at a desk and start "engineering." You learned how to become a plumber. You put pipes together.[18]

Parker Appliance underwing fueling equipment included a nozzle with a 2½-inch hose to allow fueling up to 200 gallons a minute, circa 1951.

This autonomous, almost entrepreneurial, spirit, however, wasn't solely a quality of engineering-related sectors of the company. The Eaton Screw Product Division, for example, which was by this time thriving, was showing impressive numbers. Barnd's efforts as general manager were apparent when Eaton Screw—perhaps the first decentralized effort of Parker Appliance—became the lowest-cost producer of industrial hydraulic tube fittings, performing all operations up to packaging and warehousing.[19]

Even as Parker Appliance was spreading its industrial wings, the growing number of employees were shown continued respect. Company events, such as Parker Family Day, where more than 3,000 employees, families, and friends enjoyed a Sunday gathering, and the "Payroll Quiz," with employees competing to guess the company's annual wage total at the Cleveland plant, were held to honor the work done throughout the year.[20]

Employees were expected to adapt to different tasks and situations. Because hazardous materials and extreme heat were used daily, for example, a volunteer employee fire brigade became central to the Cleveland plant in the 1950s. Three brigade officers directed the overall emergency procedures; a number of employees—essentially "lieutenants" to the brigade officers—assisted in implementation; and a third tier was assigned the task of counting employees by floor and shift to assure full evacuation should a fire occur at the Jet Division, Rubber Products Division, or Fittings Division, etc.[21]

Diversification after the Korean War

After the United States, North Korea, and China signed an armistice on July 27, 1953, ending the Korean War, Parker Appliance remained strong because of planning by Taylor, Cornell, and Sigmier.[22] The trio took a lesson from industry giant General Electric (GE) and looked to offer an increasingly broad product line to serve a growing worldwide demand from an expanding customer base. In the case of Parker Appliance, however, it would be fluid power systems. In fact, according to Patrick "Pat" Parker, Art's son, the new strategy—that Parker Appliance would be "the GE of fluid power"—would become a motto throughout the organization. According to Pat Parker:

... If one company can provide a total range of electrical components and electrical products, why should this not make sense for a total range of fluid components and fluid products? This was probably the single most important management decision made in the history of this corporation. Perhaps the second most important decision was to stick to this philosophy and not to be guided away from it.[23]

Parker Appliance's drive to become a supplier of diversified inventory was evident with its purchase of a line of hydraulic pumps and valves for machine tool application from Sundstrand Machine Tool Company of Rockford, Illinois, in 1953.[24] Another directional hydraulic control valve line for aircraft was acquired that same year from Proof Industries Corporation of Cleveland.[25] Additional changes included transferring the manufacturing of all aircraft products from Parker Appliance's Cleveland plant to Parker Aircraft Company in Los Angeles to make room for increased production of its industrial products. These included metalworking equipment, such as turret lathes or welding machines; parts used in transportation vehicles, such as locomotives, airlines, or passenger cars; and power units, such as marine engines and steam engines.[26]

With Synthetic Rubber Products Company of Los Angeles liquidated into Parker Appliance and its formal operation changed to a branch of the Rubber Products Division in 1953, it was clear that more changes were ahead for the fast-growing company. By 1954, Parker Appliance had invested approximately $3.4 million into the Rubber Products Division.[27] Further action materialized in this sector of the company when Berea Rubber Products in Berea, Kentucky, became fully integrated into Parker Appliance on March 31, 1955.[28]

Now that Parker Appliance had the proper tools, its objective was to develop new products for aircraft and industrial customers. In 1956, the company focused on improved components for hydraulic, fluid, and fuel systems. Examples included the precision grinding required for high-performance aeronautical fluid system devices, such as the hydraulically actuated butterfly valve. Parker Appliance's Industrial Hydraulics Division in Cleveland also perfected a semi-automatic drilling machine to speed production of precision components, like the directional hydraulic control valves used on farm, earthmoving, and materials-handling equipment.[29]

Patrick Parker Begins His Career

During this time, Patrick Parker began forming his role within his father's company. While attending college, Pat returned to Parker Appliance each summer and worked many jobs within the Cleveland plant, including foundry laborer, machinist, and lift truck driver. After graduating from University School in Shaker Heights, Ohio, Pat continued his education at Williams College in Williamstown, Massachusetts, and Harvard Graduate School of Business Administration, Cambridge, Massachusetts.[30]

During his tenure with different part-time positions, Pat also served as an accountant—a role that Barnd at Eaton Screw saw firsthand. While Parker Appliance was formally taking over Eaton Screw Products, Pat accompanied several auditors to the company. The employees knew Pat's last name, but many were not aware that he was related to Art Parker.

Los Angeles–based Parker Aircraft Co. in 1959. The division of Parker Hannifin Corporation manufactured components for commercial, personal, and military aircraft.

"I worked with him during a visit to Eaton Screw for a few days and got to know him," said Barnd. "Somebody asked me who this Parker guy was, and I said, 'Well, I'm not going to say much about him, but I think you ought to treat him very nicely because I think one day he's going to be your boss.'"[31]

Although some may have formed instant opinions about Pat with this knowledge, his demeanor was not one of entitlement.

"When Pat first came down with the auditors, my wife and I lived in a three-bedroom apartment in Eaton, Ohio … and we had Pat up for a light supper, during the days when television first became popular," recalled Barnd. "When we went in the front room to watch the television, Pat sat on the floor with his legs crossed watching the screen with my three-year-old daughter sitting on his lap. He was just a very ordinary individual, a good businessman, and a good friend who loved people."[32]

After graduating from Harvard, Pat assumed a full-time job with Parker Appliance as a sales correspondent until he served in the Navy as a stock program officer from 1954 until 1957.[33] Just as it seemed fitting for Pat to be involved with Eaton Screw Products as Parker Appliance's first wholly owned subsidiary, his homecoming would once again be during a time of substantial change.

Parker Appliance Company acquires all of the stock of Hannifin Corporation in Des Plaines, Illinois, a leading manufacturer of hydraulic and pneumatic power cylinders, valves, and hydraulic presses. E. G. Peterson (left), president of Hannifin, examined several products with Parker Appliance President S. B. "Ghost" Taylor in October 1957.

Acquisitions Lead to a Name Change

As 1957 began, Parker Appliance purchased The Franklin C. Wolfe Company and its principal subcontractor, Mathewson Corporation, of Culver City, California, and Inglewood, California. Through this acquisition, the company picked up an important new line of complementary products for the aircraft and missile fields. The devices from Franklin C. Wolfe were efficient static-sealing products marketed as Gask-O-Seal, Lock-O-Seal, and Banj-O-Seal. This product line would sufficiently add precise sealing capabilities to Parker Appliance's already established O-ring line, but with applications specifically for aircraft "wet wing" fuel storage. The Inglewood branch specialized in precision fluid check valves and military standard tube fittings for aircraft fuel, hydraulic, and pneumatic pressure lines.[34]

On the West Coast, Parker Aircraft Company added a new facility for research and engineering.[35] Built at Century and Airport boulevards in Los Angeles, the

PARKER HANNIFIN EXPLORES THE FINAL FRONTIER

As World War II was coming to an end, it was not only defeat that had Germany's Chancellor Adolf Hitler worried, but also the capture of his country's rocket researchers.[1] German scientist Wernher von Braun led the world's first successful launch of a V-2 rocket as a weapon in 1942. At the end of the war, the scientists were in danger when Hitler ordered their execution. Von Braun led almost 125 rocket scientists and engineers to surrender to the Americans. After entering Allied territory, some of the group were eventually moved to Fort Bliss,

Texas, which was adjacent to White Sands Missile Range, in White Sands, New Mexico. In 1945, after the scientists refurbished and assembled the German V-2 rockets, the first was launched in the United States.

This enthusiasm for the space age was boosted by the research team in White Sands and by U.S. Air Force and Department of Defense jet testing. It led to the breaking of the sound barrier in 1947, and it appeared that Americans were the technological leaders of the world. Yet just a scant 10 years later, the Soviet Union shocked the United

building was part of the company's expansion program and cost about $600,000.

Decentralized management of the different divisions allowed for the diversification of products and elevated the company's profile in a variety of markets. This also opened the door to the distributor concept. Because the divisions were spread across the United States and linked to acquired companies, distributors became key business partners, offering products directly to customers.

While these acquisitions, new product lines, and building expansions were of great benefit to Parker Appliance, its history was forever changed with the next acquisition. On September 30, 1957, Parker Appliance acquired all of the stock of Hannifin Corporation, a leading manufacturer of hydraulic and pneumatic power cylinders, valves, and hydraulic presses, whose products had a wide industrial application.[36] By entering an agreement to purchase the Hannifin Corporation of Des Plaines, Illinois, for approximately

$7.5 million, Parker Appliance Company's name was changed to Parker Hannifin Corporation on October 1, 1957.[37, 38] The new company boasted nine divisions, 10 plants, and 129 distributors. The highly successful merger contributed to sweeping gains, as sales of $28.3 million in 1957 increased to $34.9 million in 1958, spiking pretax earnings nearly 25 percent to just less than $900,000 for the same period.

Approaching the "Final Frontier"

Even though the United States economy went into a recession in 1957—unemployment

A new logo was created after the 1957 merger of Parker Appliance Company and Hannifin Corporation. The dual-purpose "PH" not only stands for Parker Hannifin but also pneumatics and hydraulics.

States by launching Sputnik I, the first man-made Earth-orbiting satellite.

In response to scientific and political pressure, the United States created the National Aeronautics and Space Administration (NASA) effective October 1, 1958, to bolster national defense during the Cold War.[2] As the Soviet Union launched Sputnik II on November 3, 1958, carrying a dog named Laika, the United States was planning the launch of its first satellite.

With precision and success mandatory for its first satellite, NASA turned to Parker Hannifin Corporation. As a key supplier of parts for aircraft and submarines during World War II, the company was well-versed in the needs of national defense. Supplying fluid system devices became a priority for Parker Hannifin in 1958, enabling the launch of rockets like NASA's Vanguard missiles.

Parker Hannifin's reputation became so well known that von Braun visited its plant in Huntsville, Alabama, where he and his research team were also stationed at the U.S. Army's Redstone Arsenal facility.

"He [von Braun] was a very impressive individual," stated Paul Schloemer, former CEO and president of Parker Hannifin, who met with von Braun on several occasions. "He was the sort of fellow that when he walked in a room, you immediately felt his presence."[3]

Von Braun and his team developed the Redstone Rocket and later the Jupiter-C Rocket, which launched Explorer 1, America's first orbiting satellite, on January 31, 1958.

Dr. Wernher von Braun, director of the Marshall Space Flight Center in Huntsville, Alabama, is shown here with a model of the V-2 Rocket. *(Photo by NASA/courtesy of nasaimages.org.)*

hovered around 5 percent, and the economic growth rate was slower than that of the USSR (Union of Soviet Socialist Republics) and Western Europe—Parker Hannifin Corporation reported all-time highs for sales and earnings in 1958.[39] With sales of just under $35 million, this figure trumped sales in 1957 by more than $6.5 million.[40]

In addition to its variety of fittings and valves, accumulators, sealing devices, fuel-injection nozzles, and power cylinders and presses, Parker Hannifin began targeting the space industry with its products. After President Eisenhower signed the National Aeronautics and Space Act, establishing the National Aeronautics and Space Administration (NASA) on July 29, 1958, the

space race between the United States and the Soviet Union had officially begun—and Parker Hannifin was already helping its country.[41] As a leading supplier of precision fluid system devices to missile and rocket engine builders, military services, and astronautics research and testing facilities, Parker Hannifin was again creating groundbreaking technology.[42]

The following year, at the Langley Field facility in Hampton, Virginia, NASA was testing a space capsule that would carry America's first astronaut into orbit around the Earth. As the capsule, built by McDonnell Aircraft Corporation, underwent wind-tunnel tests, Parker Hannifin supplied many types of seals to ensure proper pressure. These seals included silicon rubber O-seals and O-rings, which were used to form the fastener and window mountings and the vital entrance hatch seal, periscope seal, emergency escape hatch seal, and the valve and instrument seal. Additionally, all the space capsule rivets were sealed with Parker Riv-O-Seals.[43]

The Parker Hannifin Corporation facilities spread across the United States after the 1957 merger of Parker Appliance Company and Hannifin Corporation.

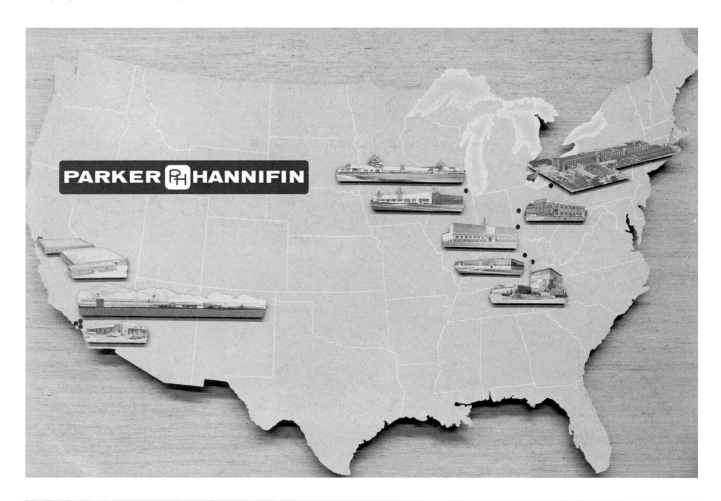

The company's annual Family Day event continued after the 1957 Parker Appliance Company and Hannifin Corporation merger. Here, in November 1959, Parker Hannifin Family Day draws more than 3,000 participants.

"Our experienced engineering staff is making it possible for us to increase our volume of highly engineered products for missiles as well as for aircraft, both commercial and military," wrote S. B. "Ghost" Taylor, Parker Hannifin's president, in the company's 1959 Annual Report.[44] With its industrial and defense footing firmly in place, Taylor confidently announced in September 1959 that Parker Hannifin predicted profits of $2.50 a share on sales of $50 million for the fiscal year ending in 1960.[45]

In 1960, the Lockheed Missile and Space Division in Sunnyvale, California, turned to Parker Hannifin for its expertise. Polaris, the U.S. Navy's long-range fleet ballistic missile, was scheduled for its first launch off the Florida coast from the USS *George Washington*, a nuclear submarine. Lockheed's researchers needed a reliable launching system for both the missile and submarine. This was accomplished through a variety of Parker Hannifin fluid handling and control devices—many of which were custom-engineered.

As the space race continued throughout the early 1960s with NASA marking achievements in aeronau-tics and space research, so did Parker Hannifin's commitment to the cause. By the end of 1961, a small plant was leased in Huntsville, Alabama, close to the George C. Marshall Space Flight Center, as a branch of Parker Aircraft Co. Division.

"This facility will permit us to improve our service on the increasing volume of business that we are receiving for 'Space' projects," Taylor stated.[46]

The future of space was limitless, and Parker Hannifin was determined to be part of its infinite possibilities.

the PARKER COUNTDOWN with
Apollo

Parker Hannifin parts used in the *Apollo 11* spacecraft were integral to the success of the moon-landing mission.

A DECADE OF CHANGE

1960–1969

1960 Sales: $50.7 Million | 1969 Sales: $197.3 Million

We don't have any 'misters' in this company.

—President Robert Cornell to Duane Collins,
a sales trainee who would later become CEO and Chairman,
after Collins addressed him as "Mr. Cornell."

As THE 1950S WERE COMING TO A close, Parker Hannifin Corporation was looking toward a great future. Reporting high records for sales and earnings between 1957 and 1960, President S. B. "Ghost" Taylor and Vice President Robert Cornell knew their management approach was effective in positioning the company for a substantial increase in sales.[1]

As space travel and its technology continued to gain attention and prominence worldwide, Parker Hannifin continued its research and development in the aircraft and missile fields. With the election of John F. Kennedy as president of the United States in 1960, Parker Hannifin was encouraged by the government's promotion of the space program.[2]

Yet, it was not only its Parker Aircraft Co. Division in Los Angeles that was undergoing rapid change. By applying an intensified marketing program throughout the late 1950s, Parker Hannifin's product lines were manufactured by Parker Fittings and Hose and Parker Hydraulics Divisions, Cleveland; Parker Seal Company Division,

Culver City, California; Hannifin Company Division, Des Plaines, Illinois; and a new International Division in Cleveland. To ensure that the growth of each division operated smoothly, 98 sales engineers worked in three separate selling organizations and were required to cover Parker Hannifin's broad market, including its industrial, aircraft, and missile fields.[3]

Gaining a Competitive Edge

As Parker Hannifin grew, it encountered competition from larger, more experienced companies. The initial push to gain a competitive edge occurred when the company began examining its hose business. To extend the company's reach, product inventory at distributors was imperative. If Parker Hannifin had a wide variety of its

The tenure of Parker Hannifin Corporation CEO Robert W. Cornell ran nine years from 1963 to 1972. *(Photo courtesy of Bill Pappas.)*

hose and tube fittings at distributors, it could provide replacement parts at a reasonable price in a timely manner. Dennis W. "Denny" Sullivan, one of the first four sales trainees hired in 1960, and who worked in the Fittings and Hose Division along with Allen N. "Bud" Aiman, sales manager, examined the issue. According to Sullivan:

There was more to this hose business than the big Clark Equipment [Company forklift hoses and fittings]. There's an aftermarket repair business that is really a different kind of business in that it's not price intensive. [But] we didn't have distributors. ... We had to develop them.[4]

The concept of using a distributor was new to Parker Hannifin, but other companies had been successful in utilizing distributors in the early 1960s. Sullivan and Aiman developed a network of warehouses in key cities to offer fast response to these customer requests.

"We could get inventory to these small distributors that we set up quickly, to build on them so that they could be competitive," said Sullivan, who would become executive vice president of Parker Hannifin's Worldwide Industrial and Automotive Products in 1993. Sullivan explained:

We opened warehouses in Des Plaines, Illinois, then Detroit, and soon after New Jersey and the East Coast. Out of these, we supplied smaller distributors that had been set up.

In addition to the industrial distributors, where Parker Hannifin was good at selling to the Ford Motor plants or the General Motors plants, there was a whole diesel engine–related aftermarket that had to do with backhoes and dump trucks and farm equipment. That was a wonderful repair business in addition to the OEM [original equipment manufacturer] business. There was a life to these hoses and you could test them and impulse them for 500,000 or a million cycles, but eventually the little wires would break and wear out, and you had to replace them. Right from the start, you'd begin having success [with the replacement business]. It became a wonderful network.[5]

Expansion Prompts Decentralization

Just as the concept of distributors had become important for Parker Hannifin's progress with its customers, so was the philosophy that the offering of an entire system could leverage the company's grasp on industrial and military markets. Robert "Barney" Barnd, whose company, Eaton Screw Products, was acquired by the then-named Parker Appliance Company in 1956, explained:

Instead of advertising ourselves as a seal company, as a fluid power company, or as a connector company, we took on the philosophy that Ghost Taylor started of making Parker a fluid systems company where fluid power products were not sold as individual products, but sold ... as an entire system together.[6]

While cohesiveness was the approach used when offering products to Parker Hannifin's rapidly growing customer base, this philosophy was difficult to apply to the management of the company's divisions. Because of the large geographical service and sales region within the United States and a newly developing overseas subsidiary

Spanco Brass Co., Otsego, Michigan, was purchased by Parker Hannifin in December 1960. This photograph shows the automatic screw machines.

DIVISIONS UNITE PARKER HANNIFIN

DURING THE 1960S, PARKER HANNIFIN GREW through acquisitions and dynamic structural changes within the company. Manufacturing operations were regrouped, some divisions were repositioned under group management, new divisions were created, and subsidiaries were added. The listings below show some of the development the company successfully navigated throughout the decade. The company prospered by maintaining its unique sense of culture that stemmed from its "decentralized" management philosophy.

In 1959, the manufacturing divisions included[1]:

- Parker Fittings and Hose Division
- Parker Hydraulics Division
- Hannifin Company Division
- Parker Seal Company Division
- Parker Aircraft Co. Division

In 1962, the divisions included[2]:

- Parker Aircraft Co. Division
  - Aerospace Components Division
  - Standard Components Division
  - Systems & Advanced Components Division
- Parker Seal Company Division
- Spanco Brass Co. Division
- Accessories Division
- International Division

- Industrial Products Group
  - Hannifin Cylinder Division
  - Hannifin Pneumatics Division
  - Hannifin Press Company Division
  - Parker Fittings and Hose Division
  - Parker Hydraulics Division

In 1963, the groups and divisions included[3]:

- Industrial Products Group
  - Parker Fittings and Hose Division
  - Parker Hydraulics Division
  - Hannifin Cylinder Division
  - Hannifin Pneumatics Division
  - Hannifin Press Company Division
- Parker Seal Company Division
- Spanco Brass Co. Division
- Aerospace Products Group
  - Aerospace Division
  - Systems & Advanced Components Division
  - Accessories Division
- International Division

Subsidiaries included:

- Parker Hannifin, n.v.
  - Schiphol (Amsterdam) the Netherlands
- Parker Hannifin NMF, GmbH
  - Cologne, Germany
- Parker Hannifin (CANADA) Ltd.
  - Toronto, Canada

in Amsterdam, the Netherlands (to handle warehousing, servicing, and sales of aircraft products in Europe), a decentralized management approach became necessary.

"The philosophy was of divisions as profit centers, and it was always to push that profit responsibility down as far in the corporation as possible," said Paul Schloemer, who was hired as a resident engineer in Parker Hannifin's Dayton office in 1957, and eventually became president in 1984. "Put someone in charge and give them the tools to succeed, the manufacturing facilities, the marketing support, whatever they needed to be successful."[7]

The idea of "decentralized divisions" with general managers guiding each division was a concept both Taylor and Cornell believed was essential for Parker Hannifin's progress. When asked by Schloemer how big a division should be, Cornell answered, "It should be no larger than the man running it and [what he] can understand."[8]

"What he was saying was that if you were making a simple product, it could be large in volume and number of parts produced and dollar volume. On the other hand, if it was a very technologically sophisticated product, it could be a much smaller operation," explained Schloemer. "The idea was that the manager had the responsibility to grow the business."[9]

With this responsibility came incentives. Based on a return-on-net-assets system, division general managers reported each month's sales numbers to Parker Hannifin's Cleveland headquarters.[10] Although hard work was required, general managers knew that their efforts would be rewarded.

"You had your own engineering, manufacturing, and purchasing. You had your sales through the sales organization. You had a forecast, your profit and so forth, which you reported every month," explained Duane Collins, who began at Parker Hannifin in 1961 as a sales engineer and eventually became CEO in 1993. "What [Cornell and Taylor] brought with them was the idea of decentralization, the single business unit or

The board of directors of Parker Hannifin, circa 1964, clockwise from front: H. R. Boyer, vice president, General Motors Corporation; C. C. Sigmier, chairman of Finance Committee; E. G. Peterson, vice president, Mitchell, Hutchins & Company, Inc; J. A. Weeks, partner, Thompson, Hine & Flory; S. B. Taylor, chairman of the board; R. W. Cornell, president; Col. Franklin C. Wolfe (U.S. Air Force retired); P. S. Parker, manager, Aerospace Division; and Mrs. H. M. Parker.

SBU. Within the groups, such as the Seal Group, there were divisions, and so forth.

"What the corporation did and continues to do is take the division's profit or results for the month, and add them up. [General managers] have a lot of visibility and responsibility. You feel like you're running your own business."[11]

While the decentralized culture of Parker Hannifin was firmly established in the 1960s, William "Bill" Armbruster recalled how he best came to understand the philosophy.[12]

"I remember a simile which was used by Aerospace Vice President Charlie Cleminshaw in 1963," said Armbruster, who began as a design specialist in 1955 at Parker Aircraft in Los Angeles. "His comment was, 'Parker is like having a whole bunch of pots cooking

different things on the cookstove, and it is management's role to keep going around to the various pots, stirring as needed.' "

"You work as a team. You build together as a team. You celebrate together as a team," said Frank Nichols, group vice president, fluid management and control systems.

This philosophy was utilized successfully during the company's many acquisitions in the following years.

Entering the Worldwide Market

With its team of general managers guiding the company's U.S. divisions, Parker Hannifin was poised for success throughout the early 1960s, and acquisitions became central to the company's growth. One acquisition was the Spanco Brass Co., Otsego, Michigan, in 1960, a small, family-owned company with 45 employees. Barnd was general manager until 1962, and under his guidance, his team turned the Spanco Brass Division into the leader of the brass fitting industry. After adding Gibbons Salem Machine Company in Sebring, Ohio, in 1963, international growth was also in the expansion plan that same year with the acquisitions of RJR Engineering in Derby, United Kingdom, and Kenmore Machine Products Company, which was located in the United States and Oslo, Norway.[13, 14] In 1964, another European presence was established in Watford, England, with the purchase of Presswork Hydraulics Limited.[15] These acquisitions were made to broaden the company's product line and to ensure a balance between the industrial and defense businesses.[16]

In 1962, Taylor and Chairman of the Board, Charles C. Sigmier, noted that the organization of a new subsidiary known as Parker Hannifin NMF, GmbH, in Cologne, Germany—more than 99 percent owned by Parker Hannifin—manufactured hydraulic devices complementary to Parker Hannifin products.[17] According to the year's Annual Report:

This facility, currently operating at a profit, should give us an excellent opportunity to manufacture for sale in the European Common Market hydraulic devices of our own proven design which cannot be exported on a competitive basis. Our Dutch subsidiary, Parker Hannifin, n.v., located at Schiphol Airport, Amsterdam, completed its first

full year's operation at a modest profit. It acts as the European marketing medium for our exported products and maintains service facilities and bonded warehouse.[18]

In 1963, Parker Hannifin made a contact in Peru that would eventually solidify its entry into the Latin American market. Maurice Castoriano was working in a shipyard that built and repaired boats for the country's fishing industry. One night he received an unexpected visitor:

Umberto Cancio came into my office. Very nice, perfect Spanish. He said, "Señor Castoriano, mucho gusto. I am with Parker Hannifin Corporation of Cleveland." He showed me the hose, the fitting. I said, "Man, this is very good." He said, "See, I have a big problem. I sold some hose to a company. They didn't pick up the bill. This stuff is in Customs and everything. It's a lot of money."

I think it was $4,000 or something like that. I said, "Well, I don't know. Listen, talk to the warehouse guy. He's going to tell you if we use this stuff."

Cancio worked late. He was in the office until about 9:30, 10:00. The guy from the warehouse came back. He said, "Hey, this stuff is just as good as Aeroquip."

Parker Hannifin extends its reach overseas with a Triple-lok tube-fittings facility in Derby, England, circa 1963.

According to Castoriano, the price Cancio quoted was about 30 percent cheaper than what he was previously buying. Castoriano was ready to purchase the fittings, but Cancio insisted on cash up-front. Castoriano refused. A few days passed and Cancio returned, stating that he had checked Castoriano's references and was ready to finalize the deal on Castoriano's terms.

At the time, the forecast for the Latin American market was between $12,000 and $15,000. Castoriano had purchased $40,000 worth of parts and became the main distributor of Parker Hannifin products in Peru.

In a 1963 *Cleveland Press* article, Parker Hannifin management predicted $50 million in sales for the fiscal year and noted that diversification had lessened the company's reliance on defense contracts.[19]

Consolidating Aerospace Operations

Changes were under way within Parker Hannifin's Aerospace manufacturing operations. It was during this time that the Aerospace Products Group was formed to combine all of the aerospace activities of the corporation. It incorporated the divisions of Parker Aircraft Co., headquartered in Los Angeles, and the Accessories Division with plant and offices in Cleveland.[20] The Aerospace Products Group, which now included the Aerospace Division, Systems & Advanced Components Division, and the Accessories Division, accounted for about 35 percent of total sales for the company.[21] Pat Parker, who was the general manager of its Los Angeles and Huntsville, Alabama, facilities from 1963 to 1968, was dedicated to its continued growth.

As part of Parker Hannifin's reorganization of the Aerospace Products Group and the Hydraulics Division during the mid-1960s, Armbruster saw firsthand Pat's indelible imprint on the industry.

"During this time period, we brought in talent from poorly managed competitors to climb the ladder of success against our adversaries," said Armbruster. "[By] bringing in key personnel from Sargent Fletcher, Weston, Adel, HydroAire, [we were] getting big 'bill-of-materials' on the C-5A

[heavy cargo transport airplane], the 747, DC-10, A-10 [Air Force aircraft], and others in a short period of time."[22]

Parker Hannifin's aerospace products had become increasingly important to the company as its work with NASA continued. Besides working on technologies useful to space exploration, Parker Hannifin also continued working with the government in supporting its military operations. For example, in January 1962, U.S. Army helicopter pilots ferried 1,000 South Vietnamese soldiers to sweep a National Liberation Front stronghold near Saigon, marking America's first combat mission against the Vietcong.[23] With America formally involved in the Vietnam War, Parker Hannifin would see a marked increase in military demands for products used on aircraft, submarines, ordnance vehicles, and weapons throughout the 1960s.[24]

This new market helped the company realize an increase in sales in 1964 of some $76 million. Coupled with the exponential growth that the company was experiencing—including a team of employees now 4,400 strong—Parker Hannifin went public, listing shares of the company on the New York Stock Exchange on December 9, 1964.

As Pat was meeting the increasing demands of the Aerospace Division, his personal life would experience another unexpected jolt. On August 17, 1965, his mother, Helen Parker, passed away suddenly. According to the 1965 Annual Report:

Wife of the late founder of the Parker Appliance Company, which became Parker Hannifin Corporation in 1957, Mrs. Parker had been associated with our organization as a director for more than 27 years. She leaves a heritage of outstanding devotion and service to all of us who enjoyed her friendship and had the privilege of working with her.[25]

December 9, 1964, Parker Hannifin became a publicly traded company, listing shares on the New York Stock Exchange. Just two years later, the company was named to the coveted *FORTUNE®* 500 list.

Acquisitions and Strife

As 1965 drew to a close, Parker Hannifin completed its share of acquisitions. In March, Parker Hannifin had acquired Tru-Flate, Inc., of Oakland, California, and Apollo, Pennsylvania, which manufactured pneumatic quick-disconnect couplers and other air system components used by automotive service organizations and gasoline retailers. Parker Hannifin also completed negotiations with R. E. Jeffries Pty. Ltd. in Australia. A pioneer in the production of fluid power components, R. E. Jeffries and Parker Hannifin began a joint venture for the production and sale of hydraulic and pneumatic products in Australia.[26] Other acquisitions included Z & W Manufacturing Co., and Cliff Manufacturing Corporation of Wickliffe, Ohio, and H. M. Meingast & Sons Ltd., of Owen Sound, Ontario, Canada.[27]

Z & W Manufacturing Co., and its subsidiaries based in California, Texas, Ohio, and Oregon; and Cliff Manufacturing Corporation of Wickliffe, Ohio, were purchased to further expand the company's Tube Fittings and Hose Products Divisions. In addition to providing machining equipment and employee skills needed to meet the increased demand for several Parker Hannifin product lines, both Z & W and Cliff also produced automotive air-conditioning system components. While these increased opportunities within the automotive original equipment manufacturer (OEM) and aftermarket clientele, the Z & W acquisition brought negative baggage: a strike from its employees. After the acquisition was finalized, a long-simmering union dispute caused the Z & W employees to walk out, leaving work in mid-production. All Parker Hannifin employees in the Tube Fittings and Hose Products Divisions immediately stepped in to continue production.[28]

"We all pitched in. I was putting together hoses," recalled Patricia "Pat" McMonagle, who was originally hired as an assistant in then Parker Appliance Company's Rubber Products Division in 1954 (she continued that role after joining what was then called the Parker Fittings and Hose Products Division in 1962). "We had presidents and vice presidents helping out. We went in and carried on for two months until the strike ended."[29]

Offering autonomy to Parker Hannifin general managers fueled the quest for quality product development in each division, a benefit Sullivan realized while general manager of the Hose Product Division, which

Parker Triple-lok tube fittings just keep improving with age

The old pros in pipe and tube fitting might remember when Parker introduced the flared fitting design. It was back in the twenties. And the pros of today agree that it's still the most reliable design.

Parker-Hannifin's modern manufacturing techniques keep Triple-lok flared fittings up to date. Quality con-

trol begins with careful analysis of the latest 316 stainless, brass, aluminum or steel. Contact surfaces are jewel-finished to pass the strictest profilometer tests. Male threads are rolled, to provide unlimited remakes.

A fail-safe fitting, Triple-lok cannot blow off as can a poorly assembled bite-type fitting. It's totally

reliable, even under extremes of pressure, vibration and temperature.

Parker-Hannifin offers the full range of fittings—flared, flareless, bite-type, compression—all good fittings. But for most applications, you can't go wrong with the granddaddy of them all—Triple-lok 37° flared fittings.

PARKER ☐ HANNIFIN
PARKER TUBE FITTINGS DIVISION
17325 Euclid Avenue, Cleveland, Ohio 44122

A Parker magazine ad from the mid-1960s speaks to the trade about the timeless design of the Triple-lok tube fitting. Invented more than 40 years ago, the ad states, "... And the pros of today agree that it's still the most reliable design."

had branched off from the Tube Fittings Division.[30] Well-versed in the range of hoses customers used—one of his first assignments had been to poll Chicago manufacturing companies and compile a list of reasons why customers purchased hydraulic hose—Sullivan knew changes were necessary.[31] While Sullivan was general manager of the Hose Products Division, Parker Hannifin was one of the largest purchasers of hoses worldwide. Its suppliers included Uniroyal, Gates Corporation, and B. F. Goodrich.

A pressing issue remained in that the company did not manufacture its own hoses. In 1969, the acquisition of D & G Plastic Company in Kent, Ohio, allowed Sullivan to initiate the production of truck airbrake

Eaton Screw Products Company, which became a wholly owned Parker subsidiary in 1950 and a division of Parker Appliance Company in 1956, suffered a catastrophic fire in 1965. *(Photo courtesy of* The Register-Herald*.)*

tubing to replace copper tubing. This addition to the Parker Hannifin product line was needed as the brass fittings the company produced were required for use with tubing. Now, Sullivan and his team could approach customers with a complete product.[32]

"We could tell the manufacturer that if you buy the tubing and fitting from the same place, if there's ever a problem, you have a lot less finger-pointing than if you were buying the tubing one place and the fitting another place," said Sullivan. "We had immediate success in doing this."

With expansion of both national and international divisions underway, the first business Parker Hannifin acquired experienced a serious setback. On June 17, 1965, a fire destroyed about half of the Eaton Screw Products building that housed Parker Hannifin's Tube

WAR EFFORTS PROMPT INNOVATION

WAR HAD ALWAYS BEEN A DRIVING FORCE behind the decades of product development at Parker Hannifin Corporation. The need to improve the defunct brakes of supply trucks used in World War I led to Arthur Parker's design of a pneumatic brake booster system, and the demands of World War II turned the Parker Appliance Company into a 24-hour-a-day, seven-day-a-week operation dedicated solely to supporting the U.S. military.[1,2] Even after its wartime commitment nearly destroyed the company, it aided troops during the Korean War with precisely engineered products, such as valves for aircraft fuel and hydraulic systems, components for jet engines, and newly designed refueling devices for aircraft.[3]

As conflict was building in Vietnam in the early 1960s, Parker Hannifin knew that its expertise would be needed to help support the country's war efforts. From its engineers to the founder's son, Patrick "Pat"

Parker, building a better product to ensure victory was always a priority.

An example of Pat's earliest interest in improving U.S. troop ability harkens back to his service as a naval officer in 1956.[4] Beginning his role as an Ensign, Pat was sent to the Navy's Aviation Supply Office in Philadelphia.

"The commanders and the captains liked their desks, so they sent Ensign Parker—a flunky, a gopher—out to the fleet to figure out why all this expensive equipment was crapping out," said Pat. "All I did was talk to the troops, the crew chiefs who were under the bellies of these airplanes cursing, swearing, and pulling [defective parts] out."

With an official commitment made by President John F. Kennedy to support the South Vietnamese in 1961, Parker Hannifin used its expertise to improve the country's military machines.[5] This was shown in how Parker Hannifin tailored its hydraulic and pneumatic systems to endure the rigorous beatings

Fittings Division.[33] Additionally, the fire damaged key machine tools used to manufacture steel and stainless steel fittings. Parker Hannifin rushed to repair the building, completing the construction of an addition that had been started before the fire. Contracts for reconstruction and repairs were signed immediately, and suitable machine tools were borrowed from other divisions or purchased used.[34] Although the plant was damaged considerably, within months the facility was producing steel and stainless steel tube fittings at about 80 percent of the rate prior to the fire.[35]

Government Calls

As the war escalated in Vietnam with the launch of Operation Crimp on January 8, 1966—the largest American operation of the war that deployed nearly 8,000 troops—Parker Hannifin's production of aerospace products intensified as well.[36]

"Even before the acceleration of military effort in Vietnam, our Government had planned to increase its aircraft programs as it changed from full reliance on ballistic missiles to a mixed complex of weapon systems," wrote Cornell and Taylor in the 1966 Annual Report. "Current commercial transport aircraft production schedules now are at an all-time high and are expected to continue for a number of years."[37]

To meet the growing demand, Parker Aircraft Co. Division expanded its Los Angeles plant by a long-term leasing agreement that added 58,000 square feet of space adjacent to the facility. Additional expansion occurred at Parker Hannifin's English subsidiary as a

---

experienced by the turrets mounted on tanks.[6] According to an advertisement by Parker Hannifin's Tube Fitting Division in the late 1960s:

The ride is rotten. And the turret takes a real beating. That punishment calls for reliability plus. Parker flareless tube fittings let you design extra reliability into your hydraulic and pneumatic systems. You can be positive that the fittings seal because the 'bite' can be checked visually during assembly. It's nice to know that extra margin of reliability is available when you need it.[7]

Parker Hannifin proudly offered a 216-page, free handbook detailing the improvements and modifications of products to demonstrate that they met new military specifications for tube fittings. The handbook detailed specification numbers related to fittings nomenclature, applications of various fittings, dimensional design data, Federal stock numbers for flared and flareless fittings, and conversion charts.[8]

Tank patrol may be a tube fitting's toughest job

In addition to supplying mass quantities of tubes and fittings, Parker Hannifin also lent its ideas to experimental applications. An example of this was the testing of Parker Hannifin's dual orifice fuel nozzle with integral flow divider valve, which was used on the U.S. Army's experimental vehicle, the Lycoming Advanced Tank Cannon's gas turbine engine.[9]

Parker Hannifin's Aerospace Hydraulics Division also added to the war effort by supplying hydraulic and pneumatic components for submarines and other underwater and surface vehicle applications.[10] According to a Parker Hannifin brochure, "Ship-to-ship refueling systems, designed and built by the Fueling Division, are now used by the U.S. Navy fleet and are being adopted worldwide by the NATO nations."

Parker Hannifin was successful in supplying the U.S. government with dependable parts for many vehicles and machines, tanks included, as seen in this 1969 advertisement.

PARKER HANNIFIN SUPPORTS *APOLLO 11*

IN 1969, WHILE THE WAR RAGED on in vietnam, Americans were looking to the sky for inspiration. Former President John F. Kennedy's space exploration goals had included "landing a man on the moon and returning him safely to Earth" by the end of the 1960s, and this was quickly becoming a reality.[1] The *Apollo 11* launch, a lunar spacecraft anticipated to perform the first manned moon landing, was planned for July 16, 1969. One million people crowded the highways and beaches near the Kennedy Space Center, Cape Canaveral, Florida, and more than 600 million tuned in via television to witness a Saturn V missile prepare to launch *Apollo 11* at 9:32 A.M.[2]

As *Apollo 11* entered the Earth's orbit 12 minutes later, employees of Parker Hannifin shared in the world's applause because they knew it was their equipment that had provided vital functions for all booster stages of the space vehicle, including the command service module and the lunar module.[3] Parker Hannifin had been making its mark in the aircraft and aerospace industry for more than five decades and had become the leading supplier of many systems and components to the National Aeronautics and Space Administration (NASA) since the organization's inception in 1958.

Wernher von Braun, the leading figure in aerospace research and the NASA Marshall Space Flight Center director, had given feedback to Parker Hannifin regarding its space technology.[4] Under his guidance, it was Parker Hannifin's Los Angeles facility that manufactured equipment essential to the *Apollo 11* mission, including ground support shutoff valves located in the launch pad complex. These directed liquid oxygen and fuel to the various systems on the spacecraft. Six-inch ball valves were used during the fuel and oxygen fill operations of the first stage, and 8-inch ball valves were relied on for the fuel and oxygen fill operations for the second stage.[5]

These propellant isolation valves were part of the reaction control system propellant feed system; the valve switches were cycled open and closed by the lunar module pilot immediately after landing on the moon's southern Sea of Tranquility on July 20.[6] In fact, the valves were galvanized in the annals of history when *Apollo 11* astronaut Harrison Schmidt commanded after touchdown to "cycle that Parker valve" instead of the rehearsed "switch to the ascent engines." The interplanetary plug was heard around the world via radio and television.

Neil Armstrong, commander, and Edwin "Buzz" Aldrin, lunar module pilot, became the first to land on the moon, while Michael Collins, command module pilot, remained in orbit. The next day, Armstrong and Aldrin made their descent to the moon's surface, spending 2 1/2 hours drilling core samples, taking photographs, and collecting rocks.[7]

Onboard the *Apollo 11,* Parker Hannifin's expertise was applied to the fluid systems, which relied

on specially designed seals and fittings to prevent leaks that could cause serious mission delays.[8] Critical sealing applications, such as those for the vehicle observation windows, also relied on the company's seals.[9] Precision engineering was employed through specifically designed tube fittings used in the vehicle to ensure leak-proof, dependable connections.[10]

Parker Hannifin parts were utilized by *Apollo 11*, from the beginning of its launch throughout the historic mission. Other examples of the applications included utilization of Parker fuel cell reactant supply modules from countdown to separation of the service module prior to re-entry, which controlled the flow of hydrogen and oxygen to the fuel cells that furnished complete mission electrical power.[11] To help the lunar module from its parking orbit and guide it to the lunar surface, a Parker Hannifin pressurization system was applied to its engine propellant tanks, which included a helium pressure-reducing valve, quad check valve, burst disc, and relief valve.[12]

Left: The *Apollo 11* at liftoff. (Photo by NASA/courtesy of nasaimages.org.)

Below: The *Apollo 11* used Parker Hannifin parts for a number of crucial sequences in its successful moon-landing mission.

Further applications included use of a quad check valve in both descent and ascent operations to prevent backflow that might allow mixing of propellants.[13] The astronauts were affected directly by Parker Hannifin parts by use of a suit loop pressure switch. This switch, used when the lunar module is unpressurized and the space suit umbilical cord is used, assured maximum safety should the suit be torn or umbilical cord cut.[14]

After returning to Earth on July 24, the *Apollo 11* crew was welcomed as heroes, and Parker Hannifin employees celebrated their own participation in a successful mission.

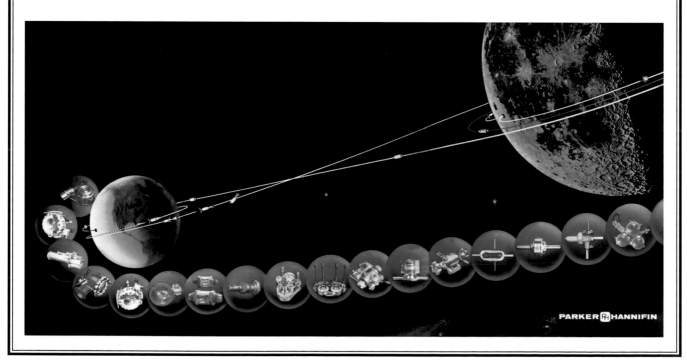

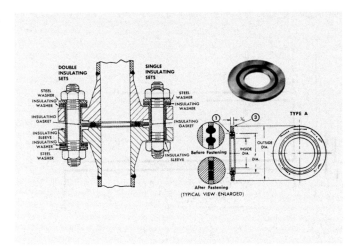

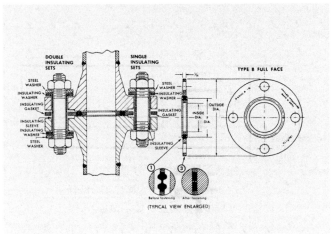

new plant began operations in a facility twice as large in Derby, England. Growth continued with construction of a new hydraulic cylinder plant in Owen Sound, Ontario, Canada, and expansion of the Grimsby, Ontario, plant. This resulted in the formation of Parker Hannifin (Canada) Ltd. To cap off 1966, the company also entered into a joint venture contract in Mexico to manufacture seal products, adding Parker Seal de Mexico S.A. to its portfolio.[38]

Fame and Fortune

With plants located in 34 U.S. cities encompassing 10 states, Canada, Mexico, England, West Germany, Norway, and Parker Hannifin SpA in Milan, Italy, which handled warehousing and sales of industrial and refrigeration products marketed in Italy, Austria, and Switzerland, Parker Hannifin was establishing its presence as the leader in hydraulic, pneumatic, and fluid system components. Featured products from the company came from the Systems & Advanced Components division in the Aerospace Products Group, which developed ship-to-ship refueling between fleet tankers and navy destroyers by using a probe and receiver fueling system for marine fuel transfer at rates of up to 6,000 gallons per minute.[39] The Aerospace Products Group also designed and manufactured special helium valves for the lunar excursion module of the *Apollo* Spacecraft for vehicle attitude control and for descent and ascent propulsion systems.[40]

As production and progress marked 1966, Parker Hannifin also added a milestone by cracking the *FORTUNE*® 500 listing of top companies. In the June 1966

Parker Seal Company Division's Pocket Catalog from 1966 described and promoted the various seals the company offered.

issue of *FORTUNE*® magazine, the listing showed Parker Hannifin with sales of $130.7 million, ranking it 498th— a first for the company.[41]

Parker Seal Company Division was showing its strength as it also aided in the exploration of space by incorporating a variety of its products into the two-man *Gemini* space vehicle, including Gask-O-Seals for the large window hatches. Products from the Seal Company division were the common leakage prevention denominator for all fluid systems, whether used in industrial, aerospace, automotive, refrigeration, or other applications.[42] As the seal products gained prominence in 1967, Pat became president of the division in Culver City, California, in addition to his position as general manager of the Aerospace Products Group.[43]

In 1967, the Seal Company division produced approximately 3 million O-rings, accounting for two-thirds of the dollar volume for the division.[44]

"Applications of O-rings are legion, ranging all the way from medical and surgical equipment to the power steering unit in your car," said Cornell in his address to the Boston Security Analysts Society on March 2, 1967.

O-rings were of particular interest to Franz Kaspar, vice president marketing services, Europe. There was no industrial standard throughout Europe. When an O-ring was needed, each customer would create a drawing specifically for that usage and have it produced individually.

"We started to push for a standard," said Kaspar. "We were successful particularly with large companies such as Fiat. They like to have a standard because then they could just apply these seals out of a catalog instead of making a drawing, which is, of course, more expensive."

This idea of standardization was also used for other Parker Hannifin parts, such as cylinders. Kaspar's intentions were to have a catalog that customers could reference and order parts from, instead of designing parts every time one was needed. The venture proved very successful, according to Kaspar, and manufacturing locations for cylinders were established in Germany. Locations soon followed in Italy, France, and the United Kingdom.

As growth occurred in all divisions, the Cleveland plant remained the center for many products. One example was the production of jet engine fuel manifolds by the Accessories Division. As one of the world's largest producers of jet engine fuel nozzles, it was a logical step to manufacture the manifolds on which fuel nozzles are mounted prior to installation on an engine.

"The manifold rings are completely manufactured at the Cleveland plant. A great deal of modern manufacturing technology and Parker know-how is put into each manifold," reported a November 1967 internal Parker Hannifin newsletter, *Jet Set.* "At the present time, manifolds are being manufactured for the Avco/ Lycoming T55 Turbo Prop [sic] Gas Turbine Engine. The engine powers some of this country's most powerful helicopters, such as the Boeing 'Chinook' and our most versatile fixed wing airplanes."[45]

A new 36,000-square-foot plant was planned for the Industrial Hydraulics Division in Otsego, Michigan. The facility was completed in September 1968, and cost more than $500,000.[46] Yet, growth continued throughout 1968 as Parker Hannifin acquired seven additional companies, although it was the first time in many years that the market for fluid power components did not increase.[47] Using a total of 72,000 shares and $1,630,798 to make these acquisitions, Cornell and Taylor stated that, at current levels, the acquired companies would produce approximately $8.7 million in annual sales.[48]

"With the addition of our acquisitions, however, we were able to more than 'hold our own' in an increasingly competitive marketplace," wrote Cornell and Taylor in the 1968 Annual Report. "We feel we have improved our share of this market and can continue to improve our position during the coming year. We are confident that labor-saving equipment should sell well in periods of rising costs, and most of our products are used on such equipment. For this reason, we are planning to provide productive capacity for an approximate 10 percent increase in volume during fiscal 1969."

Turning Tide

As 1969 approached, the country was reeling from the assassinations of Robert F. Kennedy and Martin Luther King and the continuing war in Vietnam, and Parker Hannifin maintained its momentum.[49] The company had again been listed by *FORTUNE®* magazine as one of the 500 largest American industrial corporations, moving up to 447th position (as determined by sales volume).[50]

With a decade of vast change under its belt, Parker Hannifin was about to modify its landscape again. At its board of directors meeting December 18, 1968, two major changes were announced. Taylor officially retired from his position as CEO, and Cornell was elected chairman of the board and CEO on December 31. A pivotal change came with the election of Patrick S. Parker to company president.

Popularly known as 'Pat,' he previously served as president of the Parker Seal operation in California. Earlier he had been with Parker Aircraft in 1957 as production planner, later becoming sales manager and then division manager before transferring to Parker Seal. A native Clevelander, he earned his undergraduate degree from Williams College and MBA from Harvard University.

A new era awaited Parker Hannifin, and Pat Parker was ready to lead his father's company.

Parker Hannifin had a strong presence at the Hydraulics and Pneumatics Show in Philadelphia, circa 1974.

CHANGE THROUGH UNCERTAINTY

1969–1977

1969 Sales: $197.3 Million | 1977 Sales: $590.0 Million

I'm not a detail guy. I'm seeing the big picture, and I allow the detail to be handled by a lot of the folks that report to me.

—Patrick S. Parker

AS THE 1960S CAME TO A CLOSE, Parker Hannifin proudly proclaimed in its Annual Report: "Parker makes more fluid power products for more people than any other company in the world."[1] Much of this success was attributed to "the creation of efficient production and distribution methods to provide rapid delivery ... of over 1 million different product items to customers worldwide."[2] Parker Hannifin's line of products was becoming increasingly diversified with additional acquisitions such as The Hose Accessories Company in Philadelphia, further fueling the Fluid Connectors Group and its Tube Fittings Division. Yet the company was not immune to the impending inflation, recession, and high unemployment of the 1970s.[3]

Businesses across the country were caught in a serious slump as 1970 began. "Seldom has the transition from buoyant optimism to spreading doubt come so abruptly for such a large cross section of manufacturers," reported the February 1970 issue of *Time* magazine. "As a result, businessmen are paying new attention to costs and gaining added respect for the old-fashioned virtue of thrift."[4]

With dramatic cost-saving measures implemented by companies such as Boeing, which saved $100,000 a year by turning out unneeded lights and reducing its payroll by $75 million in 1969 through the elimination of more than 14,000 jobs, it was clear that the upcoming year would be challenging.[5]

In explanation as to why the company entered the counter-cyclical automobile aftermarket sector—a market from which the company has since withdrawn—Pat Parker offered the following: "As we suffered through the recession of 1970, we were also planning on what we could do to lessen these cyclical swings. It dawned on us that our tiny acquired sector that was servicing the world's most

President Patrick S. Parker had the difficult task of leading Parker Hannifin through a recession, photo circa 1969.

popular piece of capital equipment—the automobile—was relatively immune to these business cycles. A new goal was then established—to become a major factor in the auto replacement parts business. This goal would have to be accomplished through acquisition in this mature market, so we set ourselves to task."[6]

Tapping the Automotive Aftermarket

When Pat was elected president in 1969, one of his goals was to double the company's annual sales of nearly $200 million to $400 million by 1974.[7] Even with the deteriorating economic climate that affected all industries, the automotive repair and maintenance—or aftermarket industry—seemed to be the answer to stopping Parker Hannifin's cyclical business swings. Yet, this market was more difficult to crack into than anyone at Parker Hannifin had anticipated.

"It turned out that we weren't anywhere near in tune with what you have to do to exist in that business," said John Zakaria, who had begun his role as an accountant in Parker Hannifin's Hydraulic Division on Euclid Avenue in 1966. "[The most difficult thing] was signing up franchise distributors only to have our competitors come in and buy out our entire inventory, replace it with theirs … you'd find our parts all over the place. [Conversely,] you took a heavy hit when you signed up a new distributor by replacing the entire inventory he had."[8]

Because of the intense competition in the automobile aftermarket industry, it became difficult for the company to make money. The key to establishing the company in this market came with the 1971 acquisition of Ideal Corporation in Brooklyn, New York.

"Equally important [to this acquisition] was its long-time chairman, Philip Rauch," said Pat. "Phil was also the son of the founder, but he took the helm of the family business under drastically different circumstances than I did. Phil's father died in 1932, and Phil took over the business doing a volume of $80,000 annually, at the ripe age of 21."[9]

When Ideal merged with Parker Hannifin, Rauch had grown his father's company into a $40 million enterprise. Ideal and Rauch spearheaded the growth of Parker Hannifin's automotive aftermarket effort.[10] As a manufacturer of worm drive hose clamps for the automotive aftermarket, the plumbing and construction

In 1971, Parker Hannifin acquired Ideal Corporation, a manufacturer of stainless steel automotive and aviation hose clamps. Ideal's president, Philip Rauch, would become chairman of Parker Hannifin's board of directors, circa 1974.

industry, and in-plant maintenance, the merger was a perfect fit.

"There were a couple of businesses that were good for us, [like] Ideal clamps," recalled Zakaria, who eventually became vice president/controller for Parker Hannifin's Worldwide Industrial Business and vice president of Procurement. "We made money on that."[11]

While the automotive aftermarket was picking up momentum, the company was making other strides. Two acquisitions established Parker Hannifin's presence in the European tube fittings and valves market in 1970: B. Appleton Co., Inc., of Hewlett, New York, which made a range of polyurethane seals, strengthening Parker Hannifin's Seal Group; and Compagnie des Raccords et Robinets, S.A., of Annemasse, France.[12] As a result of the acquisition in France, Condor Werkzeuge und Steverungen in Germany, and the purchase of the remaining 50 percent of P-H Australia Pty. Ltd., in Sydney, Australia, Parker Hannifin's foreign operations led all others in percentage sales growth. In 1970, international

business accounted for more than 10 percent of total corporate volume.[13]

"The rapidly growing demand for fluid power components overseas, and the wide acceptance of Parker Hannifin as a major full-line supplier, has necessitated expansion of three of our European manufacturing facilities," wrote Pat, with Robert Cornell, chairman of the board, in the 1970 Annual Report.[14]

Economic Concerns

As 1971 began, President Richard Nixon's worries about a recession became an unwelcome certainty for the United States. In January, the U.S. Department of Labor announced that unemployment had risen from 5.8 percent in November to 6 percent in December, which was the highest jobless rate since December 1961.[15,16] Under increasing public pressure because of the lagging economy and the United States' continued presence in Vietnam, President Nixon tried to reverse the economic tide in 1971 by ending the convertibility of the U.S. dollar into gold. This ended the Bretton Woods international economic agreement and caused the U.S.

dollar to fall in world markets. Nixon also implemented Phase I of his economic plan, which included a 90-day freeze on all wages and prices above existing levels. In November of that year, Phase II entailed mandatory guidelines for wage and price increases to be issued by a federal agency.[17]

Even with these national efforts, the sale of Parker Hannifin products for the year ending June 30, 1971, declined to $194 million from more than $211 million the previous year. All Parker Hannifin's domestic operating groups experienced lower sales because of the softness of the U.S. economy. The substantial reduction in capital goods buying had a serious impact on many of Parker Hannifin's major customers.[18]

According to Pat Parker and Robert Cornell, in the company's 1971 Annual Report:

The reduction in profits was caused, in part, by inherent characteristics of our business. A high degree of vertical integration is required in our manufacturing processes, and this necessitates a large fixed capital investment. During the year, we operated our facilities at a production rate lower than our current sales level, in order to reduce inventories. This also substantially reduced profits. However, net income for the year reached our forecast and, at the same time, we were able to accomplish our objectives for reducing inventories, accounts receivable, and corporate debt.[19]

Parker Hannifin's growth spanned the globe in the 1970s. Below is the company's plant in Annemasse, France.

Parker Hannifin's Tube Fittings Division manufactured the Hyferset, a pre-setting tool, in the mid-1970s. It was marketed as an efficient, dependable device for pre-setting Ferulok ferrules (the piece that connects the nut to the body die) on tubing of steel, stainless steel, and Monel, through a hydraulic operation in the Hyferset's hand pump.

To make certain that Parker Hannifin's books fell in the black, the responsibility of each general manager was increased throughout the recession.

"We had slow periods and had what they called 'Black Fridays,'" said Zakaria. "If your sales were down 10 percent [on the Friday that results were reported], you had to cut 10 percent of your people by the end of the day."[20]

Yet, even through Black Fridays, Pat recognized that the way the company was going to succeed was to retain good people and treat them well. When he stepped into the role of CEO in 1971, he remained loyal to these ideals.

"My legacy was to build the team … promoting from within and developing a team of young people, many right out of college. And, finally, not managing the business but letting the upcoming people lead it," Pat said. "It was developing the talent, then getting out of the way and letting the good players play."[21]

Getting the Job Done

Parker Hannifin became known for handpicking talented college graduates, and one of the best examples was Donald E. Washkewicz. After noticing a job posting from Parker Hannifin's Hose Products Division in Wickliffe, Ohio, on Cleveland State's Fenn College of Engineering's bulletin board, Washkewicz applied. His senior year design project, which studied noise in automotive air-conditioning systems, interested the division's general manager, Denny Sullivan. It eventually led to Washkewicz's hiring in 1972.[22]

"The first project I was given was to work on the development of a new product line—thermoplastic hoses,"

said Washkewicz. "Back in those days we didn't make any hydraulic hose. We made the metal fittings and purchased the hose from large rubber companies, whether it was hydraulic rubber hose in all various pressures or thermoplastic hose. We would buy the hose, make the fittings, and sell the package to our distributors and to original equipment manufacturers [OEMs]."[23]

After an unsuccessful joint venture with a local supplier of thermoplastic hoses, Parker needed to find a way to make its own hydraulic hose.[24]

"The interesting thing was I didn't know anything about thermoplastics. We never learned anything about thermoplastic or elastomeric materials in engineering school," recalled Washkewicz, who began as an engineer, followed by roles such as laboratory director, research and development (R & D) manager, and later general manager of the Thermoplastic Division, named "Parflex."

"I worked in that area for about six months, then I was moved to another project. We had quality issues on heavy-duty, tractor-trailer trucks regarding an air starter hose assembly, a product we had purchased. We made the assemblies and supplied them to [this] truck builder."

When the trucks were started, the adhesive wasn't strong enough to hold the inner tube, causing the tube to be sucked into the starter motor. Because Washkewicz had worked on cars to support himself through college, he was charged with replacing the hoses on the more than 280 trucks that were affected. After arriving at Jones Motor Freight in Richfield, Ohio, Washkewicz was given 20 minutes to change each truck's hose and get it back on the road.

"I'm looking down [into the truck] between the frame rail and the engine block. You could barely get your arm down in there, but then the hose fitting had to be loosened. The engine was extremely hot, having just exited the highway. It was like mission impossible," Washkewicz said. "This was a real challenge for me because I had to figure out how to get the thing apart

without melting my arm, and there was no way I could do it in 20 minutes."[25]

To carry out his mission, Washkewicz welded special wrenches together for leverage to help break the nut loose. To combat the intense heat and steam coming from the trucks, he used buckets of ice water and wrapped rags around his arm. With this method, and caked in grease, Washkewicz changed each truck's hose within 30 minutes. After three months of this work, he still had not heard from his boss or anybody from the Hose Products Division. Washkewicz then received a call to attend an important meeting to update Parker Hannifin executives on the state of his thermoplastic hose project—a project he had not worked on in months.[26]

"There's a big, long table, probably 25 senior executives around it, stacks of paper, and patent attorneys. I tried to clean as much grease off as I could," said Washkewicz. "When asked for a progress report on the thermoplastic project, I explained, 'I've been working on another project. I've been working on changing these hoses on trucks for the last five or six months.'"[27]

Denny Sullivan, who was the division general manager at the time, was shocked that Washkewicz had been sent to change hoses rather than concentrate on thermoplastic hose development. Washkewicz immediately—and gratefully—returned to Wickliffe, Ohio, to continue his work in thermoplastics. This eventually led to his promotion to R & D manager where he oversaw the entire thermoplastic project.[28]

"I had probably finished two-thirds [of the trucks' hoses]. It was a learning experience," said Washkewicz. "As the R & D manager, I was put in charge of coming up with products that would be produced in a new facility that was being built in Ravenna [Ohio]. Early in the R & D process, Sullivan allocated several hundred patents to each executive to read and understand the state-of-the-art in hose design."

Two of the first products launched at the Ravenna plant were air brake tubing for trucks and the liquid refrigerant line on automotive air conditioning systems.

By expanding way beyond these initial products, Washkewicz, along with Sullivan and Duane Collins, who were both intimately involved in Parker hose efforts, developed what was to become the Parflex Division.[29] Later, his commitment to developing products for the Hose Division led him to lead an R & D effort to develop and manufacture a complete line of rubber hydraulic control hose.

"The decision was made by Sullivan and Collins to develop our own rubber hose to give Parker a better competitive position relative to the competition," said Washkewicz.

This R & D effort resulted in several trade secrets, as well as a number of technology patents.[30]

"I was very fortunate to have worked with a great R & D team, made up of extremely talented employees. Some of them were recruited from the industry like Denny Delbane, Tom Bergeron, Isaac Shilad, Wayne Grosse, Jack Tooill, John Greco, and Harold Belofsky," said Washkewicz.

"We were reading chemistry books trying to figure out how to bond different thermoplastics together," said Sullivan. "We figured out how to make it, and it became a huge business for Parker."[31]

As Parflex became successful, Sullivan proposed another idea to Parker Hannifin executives—drilling for oil on the Ravenna facility's property. It was a $100,000 bet, but one both Parker and Sullivan were willing to take.

"We hit gas, so we were energy efficient for the rest of the time at that plant," Sullivan recalled. "It was a real advantage."

With its growth, the Hose Products Division set its sights on expansion, planning a new rubber hose plant

In 1972, Parker began researching the possibility of manufacturing rubber and thermoplastic hose like that pictured here. Prior, the company produced only the fittings and couplers and purchased the hose from outside suppliers.

DISTRIBUTING SUCCESS

Parker Hannifin supported its distributors by encouraging customers to seek out their wares.

As A CRITICAL BUSINESS AND MARKETING TOOL, distributors make their impact working as middlemen between manufacturers and retailers. Since Parker Appliance Company first used distributors following World War II, it has viewed them as partners as well as an extension of the company.[1,2]

S. B. "Ghost" Taylor tapped into the use of distributors to bolster sales of Parker Appliance Company products after he joined the company as president in 1945.[3] Taylor initiated the concept—an idea he brought to Parker Appliance Company after leaving Reliance Electric, a Cleveland manufacturer that served as a primary supplier of motors to the military during World War II. Reliance had used a "sales

department" of knowledgeable employees to help it become a timely supplier of industrial motors and emphasize the applied engineering aspect of the business. Yet these representatives did not just sell products—they also investigated customer needs and made equipment recommendations.[4] At the time, it was the perfect model.

"For Parker, it was a time of struggle for its very existence," said Bill Webster, who was hired as an engineer in 1950. "Mr. [Art] Parker was gone, all government orders were gone, and there were few, if any, contacts with potential users of industrial products such as tube fittings. Reliance Electric had used distributors for industrial sales, so [Parker Appliance] set out to develop similar distribution."[5]

The United States had the only remaining first-class economy in the world, creating a perfect opportunity for war veterans to form businesses, with many capitalizing on industrial distribution.[6]

"These guys were ready to work," said Webster. "Distribution start-ups sprang up all over the nation. If the company would support them with service, they would work hard to promote the company's products. It was 'win-win.'"[7]

In 1951, Parker Appliance reached more than $12 million in sales. Fueled by its acquisition of Eaton Screw Products, Parker was also building its network of sales engineers as it expanded across the country.[8,9] Organized by the leaders of the company's earliest divisions, including Scott ("Scotty") Rogers and T. J. ("Tommy") McCuistion of the Seal Division and Don Manning of the Fittings Division, distributors were becoming a loyal and effective group.[10] In the 1970s, they remained central to the company's success, due in part to its 30-plus acquisitions.

"We are always very sensitive to the distribution network so that with each acquisition, you not only get a unique product offering, but you also get a unique set of distributors representing those products," explained Jeff Weber, who started at Parker Hannifin as an inside sales coordinator in 1967 and eventually became group advertising promotions manager for the Hydraulics Group. "We always tell distributors that they are the backbone of the interface with this company and its customers. We will maintain you as our representatives."

This individualized attention set Parker Hannifin apart from others in the industrial manufacturing business. Distributors received the same training as in-house sales teams and access to the relevant range of Parker Hannifin products.[11] In addition to forming a distributor advisory council to address concerns, Pat Parker visited distributor sites.[12]

"Before I knew it, Pat Parker walked into the office and spent two or three hours giving me an update on where Parker was growing, what they were doing, and just stimulating me to keep going," said Carey Rhoten, president of The Hope Group, which became a Parker distributor during the 1960s. "He just popped up and [would] get you all excited—[he really] shared the vision."[13]

As Parker Hannifin grew overseas during the 1970s, with subsidiaries in Brazil, Mexico, Japan, and Singapore, its distributors increased in number as well.[14]

"They really have been loyal to distributors," said Randy Gross, CEO of RG Group, York, Pennsylvania, which was a Parker Hose and Fitting distributor in 1964 and has grown to represent hydraulics, pneumatics, connectors, instrumentation, refrigeration, motion control, and electronic solutions with Parker Hannifin's products. "We live in the markets and touch more customers than a factory direct-sales force can ever touch. We provide value in solution selling as a team with Parker. We try to look at what their strategic plans are and sometimes get ahead of them in terms of how we think; we bring their products to the marketplace and have one face to the customer."[15]

Parker Hannifin and its distributors continue to anticipate the needs of its customers. A central responsibility for Parker Hannifin group presidents has been selecting distribution channels for specific product lines and providing ways these distributors can offer added value. For example, the ParkerStores® retail concept, launched by Don Zito, who retired from Parker as Fluid Connector Group President, and Bill Eaton who retired as Fluid Connector Group Vice President Sales and Marketing, involves a suite of stand-alone stores—some as far away as Australia and New Zealand—offering a complete hose and fittings inventory. Another successful concept is the Hose Doctor, a premier mobile hose service program using Parker Hannifin products and offering 24-hour, seven-days-a-week on-site service.

In 2007, there were more than 12,000 distributor locations worldwide, serving original equipment manufacturers (OEMs) and the maintenance, repair, and overhaul (MRO) of the working machinery market. The distributors were credited with possessing local market knowledge and also bringing a sense of "strong pedigree" to their geographical areas.[16]

"Our distributors have undergone an evolution. They are the envy of the industry," Weber said.[17]

Visible "bite" insures bone dry hydraulic connections—that's reliability!

The Ferulok "bite", or grip, on a tube can actually be inspected before the connection is made, insuring leakproof performance.

That's why many major machine tool builders select Ferulok flareless tube fittings.

Parker Ferulok tube fittings are designed for heavy or standard-wall tubing, and are available in steel, stainless steel and Monel. They are machined from barstock and forgings to assure maximum strength and reliability.

Check the Yellow Pages for your Parker-Hannifin distributor or write: PARKER TUBE FITTINGS DIVISION, 17325 Euclid Avenue, Cleveland, Ohio 44112.

Parker Ferulok tube fittings

PARKER PH **HANNIFIN**
pneumatics   hydraulics

65-TF-1

This advertisement explains the importance of the Ferulok tube fittings and the quality of the Parker Hannifin design.

the Kansas plant just under the deadline of December 31, 1979. For Parker, this mission was similar in scope to President Kennedy's mandate for the United States to land a man on the moon and return him safely to Earth by the end of the 1960s.[33]

"As a result of these early R & D efforts, Parker has a global hose business today in excess of $1 billion. Without the leadership of Denny Sullivan and Duane Collins, none of Parker's success would have been possible," said Washkewicz.

According to Pat, an executive's job is to create change, not stability.[34] Washkewicz became very good at this, and 28 years later he became the company's president and chief operating officer and, eventually, its chairman and CEO.[35]

"There must have been 10 of Parker's top executives that came out of Tube Fittings and, eventually, Hose Division. They all came from the same pack," said Sullivan. "I think it had to do with the kind of work ethic or product strategy that everybody bought into."[36]

The Hose Products Division represented opportunity for growth, according to Syd Kershaw, who began at Parker Hannifin in 1968 as a chief manufacturing engineer and then served as the general manager for the division in 1973.

"I think it was a very good growth market. There was a lot of automation," said Kershaw. "We made a lot of good decisions over the years and became more vertical in manufacturing a hose, and that made the division a real leader."

Difficult Climate

By the end of fiscal 1973, Parker Hannifin had increased its fiscal sales by 24 percent from 1972—the

for Manhattan, Kansas. This was Parker's first large venture in the manufacturing of rubber hydraulic hose.

"Our goal was to make the first production run of rubber hose [in the new plant] by the end of the seventies," Washkewicz recalled. "We were trying not only to develop the hose, but then to develop the process to make the hose. If you don't have the right recipe, if you don't know all the little tricks in the manufacturing process, the [hose] doesn't perform very well. It's one of the most complicated things I've ever undertaken."[32]

With this asset-intensive project looming over his head, Washkewicz led the charge for hose production at

highest in the company's history. The company's ability to generate cash allowed it to grow its business through strategic acquisitions. In addition to Roberk Company in Shelton, Connecticut, a manufacturer of aftermarket automobile components, and Pathon Manufacturing in Medina, Ohio, Parker Hannifin had also acquired its second filtration manufacturer in 1972, Tell Tale Filters, Ltd., of the United Kingdom. This solidified the company's entry into this key business.[37]

While 1974 progressed, and the United States remained entrenched in the Vietnam War and saw President Nixon resign that August, Parker Hannifin faced its own dilemmas.[38] Operating during a period of stringent price controls coincident with rising costs, followed by a period of both cost and price instability; when federal controls proved inadequate, the company experienced reduced profits for fiscal 1974.[39]

Like other companies across the country, Parker Hannifin faced a shortage of capital to finance growth and a continued lack of energy sources. Only two acquisitions were made in 1974, including Phillips-Precision and the purchase of the remaining 40 percent of Ideal International, and the country decided to use coal as its primary energy source to meet the increasing electrical demands.[40] This was advantageous due to OPEC's (Organization of the Petroleum Exporting Countries) announcement in 1973 that it would no longer ship petroleum to nations supporting Israel, which included the United States and Western Europe. This announcement, combined with OPEC nations' agreement to raise prices 400 percent resulted in the 1973 world oil shock. This forced factories to cut production and lay off additional workers.[41]

"A full-time engineering staff is working with our factories to improve the efficiency with which energy is utilized," Pat Parker and Robert Cornell assured stockholders in the 1974 Annual Report.

Even with tighter financial guidelines and energy conservation efforts in the mid-1970s, Parker Hannifin maintained plants in 44 cities in the continental United States, and 25 facilities in foreign locations. Part of the company's success involved nearly 1,700 technically qualified distributor organizations that worked with customers in product selection, application, and service.[42] Parker Hannifin also established its official headquarters in Spain, Parker Hannifin España, in August 1974.[43]

Dual Applications

As rapid change was occurring throughout Parker Hannifin, including the drive to manufacture and sell a "total system," Parker Aerospace moved its main plant from its original location on Century Boulevard in Los Angeles to Jamboree Road in Orange County.[44] The new facility allowed for the design and development of new products, featuring extremes in size and weight.

Still working closely with NASA, Parker Aerospace was producing a wide spectrum of products, including the smallest shut-off valve used in the space program. At less than 1 inch long, $^{3}/_{8}$ths of an inch in diameter, and $^{1}/_{50}$th of a pound, it was nicknamed the "peanut valve." Its role was crucial for collecting soil samples from the moon and Mars.[45]

"These little valves would drip tiny amounts of nutrients onto Martian soil samples. We were looking for microbiological life," recalled Bill Webster, general manager of the Gas Turbine Fuel Systems Division at that time. "We teamed up with NASA's applied physics laboratory to build the device. Those little devices would dispense [something like] two microliters per shot."[46]

The peanut valve was also being tested by R & D on an insulin pump for people with diabetes.

"We used what they call 'pulse width modulation,' which means if the pump can output five microliters every time you give it a signal, if you have it pump every second, it will deliver 60 times five, or 300 microliters. The flow rate would be the distance between the pulses," Webster said. He explained further:

After testing, we worked with a group of doctors to make a pump that would be attached on the outside of humans. I had reported to the corporate board of directors in Cleveland that we were partially in this medical field and that we ought to concentrate on Aerospace or really go at it. Pat Parker was so interested in all kinds of things. He was just interested enough to create a biomedical division ... we did some good work with pumps and found that there was a great interest in home care for cancer treatment and chemotherapy.[47]

In comparison to the peanut valve's applications, Parker's largest airborne disconnect device was also under

RESCUE FROM SPACE

TWO DAYS AFTER THE LAUNCH OF the third American-manned lunar-landing mission planned by the National Aeronautics and Space Administration's (NASA) Apollo program, *Apollo 13* suffered an explosion that endangered its crew's lives—and the possibility of returning to Earth.[1] As oxygen and electrical power was lost to the service module portion of the *Apollo 13* command/service module, the crew was forced to use the lunar module as its "lifeboat."[2] With the loss of 50 percent of the spacecraft's oxygen supply, and severe constraints on power, cabin heat, and potable water, the crew raced against time to reenter the Earth's atmosphere and return to Earth.[3]

From the moment that John L. Swigert, command module pilot, uttered, "Okay, Houston, we've had a problem here," considerable ingenuity was required from the astronauts and NASA flight controllers to ensure a safe return.[4] While this story is familiar to many, what is not known is that experts from Parker Hannifin were called upon by NASA to assist the crew through the crisis.[5]

Parker Hannifin had designed and manufactured more than 120 components and assemblies used on *Apollo 13,* including products on the three booster stages, the command service module, and the lunar module of each Apollo mission.[6] After a heater in one of the *Apollo 13* oxygen tanks shorted, the oxygen ignited. The resulting explosion destroyed the tank and blew a hole in the command module's equipment bay.[7]

The lunar module's oxygen control assembly, which was built to perform vital pressure control, was a Parker Hannifin product. This assembly controlled the oxygen used to pressurize the lunar module cabin, the astronaut suits, and the backpacks used by the astronauts during lunar exploration. The oxygen control assembly received high-pressure oxygen from the lunar module supply tanks and regulated the pressure to a usable level.[8]

As soon as the crisis occurred, NASA, Rockwell, and Grumman Aeronautical Engineering Company experts immediately involved Parker Hannifin to determine how to utilize efficiently the remaining oxygen to sustain the three astronauts, and how to execute the critical reentry maneuver.[9] The lunar module, the command module, and the backpack oxygen were the only remaining sources of oxygen. Parker Hannifin experts were asked to perform a series of tests on the oxygen control assembly to ensure that the equipment could convert the available oxygen to the required pressure for use in the cabin. They also had to determine a rationing plan for the remaining resources to offer sufficient life support for the anticipated duration of the flight back to Earth.[10]

"The Parker team worked around the clock," Bill Swift, a Parker Air & Fuel Division team leader, stated. As one of the team of experts responsible for the development of the oxygen control assembly, Swift explained how Parker Hannifin employees had moved to a facility in a remote area of the California desert to test the highly explosive oxygen.[11]

Communicating hourly with NASA, the team developed mission scenarios and "what-if" possibilities, providing real-time data from the *Apollo 13* crew

Pᴀʀᴋᴇʀ Hᴀɴɴɪғɪɴ'ꜱ ᴛᴇᴀᴍ ᴏғ ᴇxᴘᴇʀᴛꜱ ғᴏᴜɴᴅ a way to provide sufficient oxygen to the crew of the *Apollo 13*, enabling the astronauts' safe return to Earth. Parker Hannifin's *Apollo 13* Team included:

- Dan Bora
- Ken Bragg
- Jimmie Hart, Jr.
- Erwin Johnson
- Bob Jones
- Dick Kenyon
- Jim Lowes

- Leroy Miller
- Jim Rasnick
- Bill Swift
- Jack Ulanofsky
- Maer Walter
- Art Warner
- Pete Young

and relayed telemetry information to establish testing parameters to fully evaluate all circumstances.[12] One assignment included calculating the minimum oxygen consumption rate of the astronauts versus the amount of oxygen onboard.

"Our first test indicated that, under normal conditions and assuming anticipated crew oxygen requirements, it was highly unlikely that the astronauts would survive," stated Maer Walter, Parker Hannifin's former laboratory director and a member of the remote site testing team. "That's when we really got to work to change the outcome. I don't think anyone on the team closed their eyes for more than 15 minutes for over two days."[13]

"We were all very concerned about the lives of those astronauts," Swift stated. "When we realized that our equipment was the most crucial factor in the return of the *Apollo 13*, we became even more determined that we would do whatever it took to bring them back safely."[14]

To bring the crew back alive, the Parker Hannifin team ran test after test, with the goal of reducing the amount of oxygen used in the spacecraft. As tests proved how oxygen could be saved, the parameters were forwarded to NASA's mission control team, who relayed the information to the *Apollo 13* crew for implementation.[15]

"Once the spacecraft reached Earth orbit safely we were ecstatic," said Jim Lowes, Parker Hannifin's Space Division general manager, and later the Aerospace Group's vice president. "Unfortunately, the problem was not yet behind us. To reach the optimum perigee—the point in orbit nearest the Earth—for reentry, the spacecraft needed to jettison the lunar module and make two Earth orbits in the command module."[16]

While the jettison went well during the first orbit, there wasn't sufficient oxygen for another pass around the Earth. Time was limited and the crew was instructed to reenter, even though the perigee was far from favorable.[17]

"There was great concern that the spacecraft could burn up as it entered the Earth's gravitational field," Lowes later stated. "It was a great relief when they made it."[18]

The *Apollo 13* astronauts—Lovell, Jr.; Haise; and Swigert, Jr.—visited Parker Hannifin's Irvine, California, facility to thank its employees for a job well done.[19] At the National Design Engineering Show 2000, Chicago, Lovell acknowledged the role Parker Hannifin employees took in helping to keep the astronauts alive.[20]

Apollo 13 astronauts Fred Haise, John Swigert, and James Lovell are shown here during the press conference following their ill-fated mission. *(Photo courtesy of NASA Marshall Space Flight Center [NASA-MSFC].)*

development for the Space Shuttle in 1975. This stainless steel and aluminum component was 17 inches in diameter and connected the jettisonable liquid hydrogen fuel tanks with the shuttle. A unique mechanism was developed to avoid wear on the critical cryogenic seal by lifting the flapper directly off its seat.[48]

Being Pat's responsibility for many years, the Aerospace Group continued to match his energy and enthusiasm with its products. Paul Schloemer, who worked as vice president/general manager of the Air and Fuel Division, became vice president of operations and finally president of the group in the 1970s.[49]

"The biggest sale drivers were mostly the fuel system components, such as fuel level control valves and in-flight refueling equipment. That was the start of the whole [aircraft] hydraulic business for us, which is now the biggest part of Aerospace," said Schloemer. "It was hard to follow Pat [as general manager of Air and Fuel Division, and later CEO and president of Parker Hannifin], everybody looked up to him. Not just because his name was Parker, but because of what he did and the fellow he was. He was a really good businessman. He had a good vision."[50]

Charting Worldwide Expansion

While Parker Hannifin's growth in industrial, automotive, and aerospace components was reaching new heights in the United States throughout the 1970s, its reach abroad was expanding further. In 1975, Parker Hannifin had acquired 34 percent of Stig Eklund A.B., in Sweden, and 49 percent of Parker Fittings de Mexico S.A., Mexico.[51]

Parker Hannifin's seal business grew in Germany, and from its earliest beginnings, Heinz Droxner worked tirelessly to ensure its success. Hired as the second sales engineer for the group's Germany operation in 1972, Droxner soon became the sales manager of Germany, Austria, and Switzerland—a natural fit for a native of Germany.[52]

"Pat Parker opened a seal business [in Germany] with about 45 people two years earlier," said Droxner, who would become president of the Seal Group in 2002. "We always say that Germans have to run the German operation; the Italians, the Italian; and the Chinese, the Chinese. It's a very good fit."[53]

As 1975 ended, overseas penetration—in the form of increased acceptance by foreign customers of Parker Hannifin's "Total System" concept—also contributed to the company's substantial growth.[54] At this time,

Parker Hannifin navigated the 1970s under the strong leadership of Chairman Robert W. Cornell, left, and President Patrick S. Parker.

the system concept was defined as offering all the components a customer needed.

According to Cornell, retired chairman of the board; Rauch, chairman of the board; and Pat, president, in the 1975 Annual Report:

As the useful labor saving fluidpower devices penetrate more and more overseas markets, smaller manufacturers are desirous of having a single supplier responsible for system function. Parker Hannifin is the only company able to supply such a service on a worldwide basis. In Europe, our most important overseas market, sales increased 21.6 percent to $58 million in the past 12 months.

In the 1990s, the term "systems" evolved into meaning complete packages engineered and assembled for the customer. To formalize the systems strategy, a mobile systems team was formed in 2000. According to Kjell Jansson, vice president, Global Mobile Systems, Sales, and Marketing and a key impetus behind the company's progression into engineering and sales of these complete packages, before the systems concept evolved, the company's various divisions functioned independently for the most part.

"We introduced the system engineering teams," he said. "[Prior] there was nobody who could tie together products from several divisions and groups. ... The whole thing started on our watch."

As the United States celebrated its bicentennial in 1976, Parker Hannifin added a domestic acquisition that marked the beginning of the company's climate business: Refrigerating Specialties of Broadview, Illinois, a manufacturer of valves and regulators for ammonia control in refrigeration units. Yet, the company's reach

In 1975, a new Parker Hannifin logo was introduced, replacing one that had been in existence since 1957, when the then-named Parker Appliance Company merged with Hannifin Manufacturing Company. This new logo continues to be used today.

around the globe continued as well with Parker Hannifin Japan, Ltd., a market that would require trial and error.[55]

"In the late 1970s we had very little in Asia—we had just begun in Japan—there was nothing there," said Joe Vicic, who began with Parker Hannifin in 1967 as a sales management trainee, then after a four-year military hiatus, took a position overseas with the Fluid Connectors Group. "We had a guy with a telephone, maybe a secretary, and a catalogue. My job was to educate distributors and make it easy for them to promote our connector product line."[56]

Although worldwide expansion was hindered by inflation in most foreign economies and political pressures that affected the worldwide capital goods market, in 1977 Parker Hannifin generated a 5.6 percent return on sales compared to 4.9 percent the previous year, representing a 14 percent gain.[57] Allen "Bud" N. Aiman, president and chief operating officer, and Pat, praised management for achieving growth that was almost entirely financed through internally generated funds.[58] To cap off 1977, Parker Hannifin also passed the half-billion-dollar mark in sales, almost doubling the earnings the company reached five years prior.[59]

Parker Hannifin was ready for 1978—a year that would bring further change and strategic acquisitions to prepare the company for the upcoming decade.

A forging press in use at Parker Hannifin's Tube Fittings Division in Lewisburg, Ohio, circa 1978.

MAKING STRIDES

1978–1980

1978 Sales: $695.7 Million | 1980 Sales: $1.0 Billion

A great deal of our rapid but controlled growth has occurred within the last 10 years. What may the next 10 years hold for Parker? Undoubtedly, continued growth. We are poised to enter the 1980s as a billion-dollar company.

—Patrick S. Parker, from the
"Cleveland Dinner" speech, October 4, 1979

As 1978 BEGAN, THE ECONOMIC CLImate of the United States was suffering from soaring interest and inflation rates, in addition to rising unemployment.[1] Contributing to this financial difficulty was an energy crisis instigated by oil shortages.[2] Businesses reacted to this slowdown by searching for innovative ways to cut costs. Parker Hannifin began developing energy-saving products to maintain its reputation as the leader in the fluid power market and to offer its customers products appropriate to their needs.

Meeting Market Needs

As the 1970s progressed, the need for less expensive fluid control systems for smaller machines was becoming increasingly apparent. Mechanical drivers usually powered these smaller machines, and the drivers used sprockets, chains, and gears to link the working tool to a power source. The power source—usually a gasoline engine—was required to operate continuously at full throttle, even if the machine's load was light. Because of the rising cost of fuel, these mechanical drivers were becoming more expensive to operate.[3] Parker Hannifin created prototypes for a low-cost hydraulic control that could replace the cumbersome and costly mechanical drivers.[4]

In addition to manufacturing a product that offered customers energy savings between 15 and 50 percent, the new fluid power system could be applied to machines, such as earth borers, a form of auger for boring into the ground.[5] Koehring Co., Milwaukee, was a big producer of earth-moving equipment, and the company worked closely with Parker Hannifin to integrate the more efficient hydraulic system into its earth borer.

Leaders of Parker Hannifin included, from left to right (circa 1978): Allen N. "Bud" Aiman, president and chief operating officer; Patrick S. Parker, chairman and CEO; and Philip Rauch, chairman of the executive committee, chairman of the board (retired).

Parker Hannifin plants throughout the United States remained small, yet extremely effective in their ability to react quickly to customer needs. This combination prevailed in plants such as those in Batesville, Mississippi, and Lyons, New York, circa 1975.

Benefits of the new system included design flexibility, which allowed Koehring to separate the boring head from the engine to lower it into a hole, and a comparatively inexpensive price. The design included a feedback-control loop built from two sliding valves, with one valve that senses the load on the working tool and transmits its reading of this pressure to a second valve. These valves activate other valves on the hydraulic pump and on the engine to vary the engine's speed as well as the power it delivers. Not only was this design efficient, it offered the ability to use a smaller and lighter engine and was made entirely from standard hydraulic hose, valves, couplings, and other off-the-shelf parts. This offered even further cost savings to the customer.[6]

"Within seven years, our annual market [for the new fluid power system] should reach tens of millions of dollars," Pat Parker predicted in 1975.

At the end of 1978, Pat's forecast was becoming a reality. In addition to servicing Koehring and other manufacturers of lift trucks, commercial lawn mowers, farm machinery, and other types of mobile equipment and machinery in the U.S. market, Parker Hannifin's international fluid power capabilities were increasing. For example, a crawler excavator manufactured by the United Kingdom's J. C. Bamford Excavators Ltd., carried Parker Hannifin filter caps, oil level gauges, strainers, pressure filters, directional control valves, and special fittings.[7] Parker Hannifin's industrial segment was rising to meet economic and energy challenges with zeal and confidence.[8]

Big Goals in Small Towns

While each of Parker Hannifin's groups was growing, it remained central to Pat that the company's primary objective—excellent service for each customer—was adhered to meticulously. Even after he was named chairman of the board and CEO in 1977, with Allen N. "Bud" Aiman taking over as president and chief operating officer (COO), Pat remained dedicated to this goal.[9]

"He just loved customers," said Nickolas W. Vande Steeg, who began his career at Parker in 1971 and served in a number of management positions, including president of the company's Seal Group, corporate senior vice president and operating officer, and then president and COO. "He loved to find out what they wanted and needed, and then to satisfy that need. Early on, when I was division manager, I said, 'Pat, it's kind of lonely out here,'" Vande Steeg recalled.

Pat told him to get a dog if he was lonely—and reminded him to satisfy his customers and grow the business.[10]

One way in which Pat felt the company could more effectively offer personalized service was through a network of small plants established in rural areas. By balancing internal growth with acquisitions, Pat believed fervently that plants should be small and manageable, according to Don Washkewicz, who was appointed president and CEO in 2001.

"Pat wanted them to be under 350 employees so plant managers would know everyone on a first-name basis," Washkewicz said.[11]

Parker broke into Latin America via this approach that created modest operations in rural regions by incorporating the help of entrepreneur Maurice Castoriano,

a Frenchman whose family emigrated to Peru during World War II. After more than a decade of brokering deals with the likes of hydraulics component manufacturers Vickers and Aeroquip, and developing contacts throughout South America, Castoriano forged the start of a lucrative relationship with Parker Hannifin Corporation.

According to Castoriano, in 1963, a Parker Hannifin sales representative for Latin America was in need of a local buyer of some $4,000 worth of hose and fittings that another buyer reneged upon. The shipment was impounded in customs. Castoriano agreed to purchase the materials, and within months, subsequent regular purchases nearly tripled Parker's meager Latin America sales, and won Castoriano exclusive rights to Peru.

By the late 1960s, Parker Hannifin Argentina—an O-ring plant housed in a small, old building—was established, and in the mid-1970s, another modest plant was set up in São Paulo, Brazil.[12, 13] Castoriano was instrumental in the creation of both operations. Regardless of their physical size, Pat never underestimated the importance of these South American plants.

"During April 1978, Pat Parker visited us for the second time, seven years after his first visit to Argentina," wrote Miguel Rey Fortes, a general manager for the São Paulo plant. "Along with Henry Sutcliffe, general manager of Parker Seal Mexico, and Bob Davies, mentors of the Seal plant installation in Argentina, he came to see the first Parker Hannifin O-ring plant in South America.

"In 1978, Parker Argentina, taking advantage of the government's economic policy, open importation, and the peso-versus-dollar stability, started manufacturing hose fittings and tube fittings, importing hydraulic hoses [rubber and Parflex]," Rey Fortes recalled. "We reached 156 employees between the two divisions: Seal and Fluid Connectors."[14]

Because many of the companies acquired by Parker Hannifin as well as the plants it constructs are based in small towns, the size of the businesses in these locations are extremely important to the communities.

"There were several small towns [where] we're the only employer in town or the biggest employer in

---

Research and Development was integral to Parker Hannifin's success. This was demonstrated by "The Atomization of Liquids," authored by Harold C. Simmons, director of engineering, Parker Aerospace. He researched its application for fuel injection devices used for gas turbine engines. This image shows Simmons' application in two types of air-blast nozzle; at the time of publication, the "ejector-air-assisted design" was used on almost all new engines.

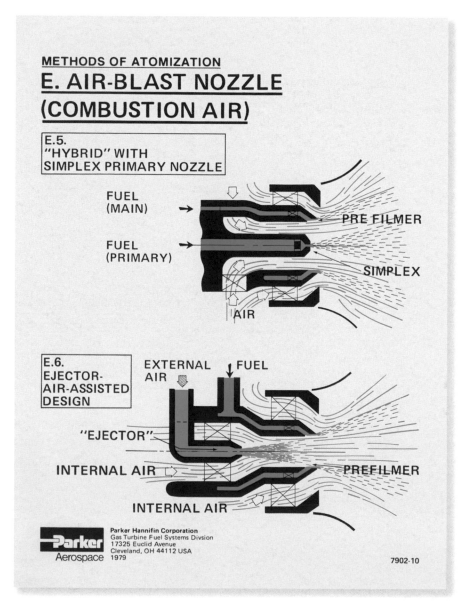

REALIZING THE AMERICAN DREAM

IN THE MID-1970S, THE U.S. ECONOMY WAS FACING A period of stagflation, a term coined to describe financial stagnation and price inflation.[1] As high interest rates and a recession dominated the country, some businesses not only continued to survive, but thrived—especially those in Irvine, California. In 1960, the city of Irvine was created by The Irvine Company in association with the University of California Campus at Irvine in Orange County.[2] It was one of the nation's first and largest planned industrial parks.[3] Built on thousands of park-like acreage, the Irvine Industrial Complex attracted local and national companies, including Bertea Corporation, Philco-Ford, Beckman Instruments, Allergan Pharmaceuticals, and Parker Hannifin Corporation.[4]

While business was thriving in Irvine as 1976 began, workers were finding it difficult to attain the American dream of home ownership as the area's popularity and high interest rates drove housing prices up.[5] In response to a growing need for an affordable solution, Charles E. Cleminshaw, senior vice president of Parker Hannifin's Aerospace Group, led the Greater Irvine Industrial League in the building of moderately priced homes in Irvine.[6] Working with The Irvine Company to develop a workable program to help moderate-income employees buy affordable homes, Cleminshaw, along with Irvine and University of California–Irvine officials, planned and created Woodbridge Village Homes.[7]

Just as in the earliest days of Parker Hannifin, when founder Art Parker made certain his employees were helped in finding convenient and reasonably priced housing after moving the company from a small loft on Cleveland's West Side to its new East Side plant on Euclid Avenue in 1936, Cleminshaw looked after Parker Hannifin's Aerospace employees.[8] After months of planning, Cleminshaw and the Irvine Housing Opportunities board, along with The Irvine Company, unveiled the sale of 85 moderately priced townhomes. Two models were available: the two-bedroom "Poplar" model was offered at $31,500, and the three-bedroom "Elm" model was offered at $33,000.

town," said Patti Sfero, who started her career with the Parker Hannifin Tube Fittings Division in 1964 and held several different positions before becoming human resources manager in 1991. "We encourage our plant managers and our human resources people that are local to get involved in the community. It's not unusual to see them riding in the [town's] Founders' Day Parade on a tractor."[15]

"There's always been a strong, kind of cultural element to be close to the product, be close to the customer, and it's hard to do either one of those if you run a highly centralized business [that is] growing and handling as many products as Parker," said Lonnie Gallup, who began at Parker Hannifin in 1972 as a territory manager trainee and would later become vice president and general manager of the Hose Products Division. "One of the reasons it's worked at Parker is the management at higher levels have all come through the business, and they understand the importance of being close to the customer and product. There's a lot of satisfaction that comes from this."[16]

Aerospace Expansion

Just as Parker Hannifin cultivated plants in South America, Mexico, Japan, and Singapore, the company remained focused on its domestic market—more specifically, the aircraft industry. With its earliest

An aerial view of the Irvine Industrial Complex, home to Parker Hannifin's Aerospace Group and the Bertea Corporation, which merged in 1978.

Built in the Village of Woodbridge, a subdivision of Irvine, the townhomes were offered to local families, with total income determining possible buyers' eligibility. The townhomes were for sale to those whose maximum annual income was less than $20,000. With more than 2,000 families interested in purchasing the 85 homes in August 1976, the Irvine Housing Opportunities board offered a fair solution:

... [we needed] to offer everyone who has expressed interest in buying an equal opportunity to do so. To do this, a public drawing, similar to the ones held for the other products in the Village of Woodbridge, will be held to establish the order in which you may purchase a home.[9]

After qualifying through an income eligibility and loan application process, prospective buyers filled out cards for a public drawing held September 19, 1976. With a secured lottery box holding the entries, officials from Coopers & Lybrand, an accounting firm, monitored, drew, and announced the winning tickets.[10] After a review of each winning appli-

cation ticket by the Irvine Housing Opportunities board, Housing Urban Development officials, and United California Mortgage, 85 families were granted affordable housing in the flourishing area of Irvine.[11]

With so many young couples and families working for Parker Aerospace and other growing businesses at the Irvine Industrial Complex, Woodbridge Village Homes was a solution that many welcomed—and could not have been realized without Parker's Cleminshaw and the Irvine Housing Opportunities Board.

connections established by Art Parker's friendships and camaraderie with prominent aviators—such as Charles Lindbergh—aviation had long been a priority.[17] Parker Hannifin's Aerospace Group initially housed its facilities on Century Boulevard in Los Angeles. Throughout the Korean War and the 1960s, Parker Aerospace outgrew this location and moved to a new facility in Irvine, California, in 1971.[18]

Just as Parker Aerospace was growing, so was one of its contemporaries, the Bertea Corporation. A company that designed, built, and serviced hydraulic equipment and flight control systems for commercial and military aircraft, Bertea had become the major supplier of electrohydraulic flight controls, producing nearly

65 percent of controls steering U.S. commercial airlines in the late 1960s.[19]

With significant bills of material on the Douglas DC-10, Lockheed L-1011, and Boeing 747 aircraft, among others, Bertea was stretched beyond capacity, leading to the construction of a 42,000-square-foot building in Irvine. Even after production demands for the DC-10 and L-1011 declined in the mid-1970s, demand for single-aisle 727s and 737s increased. In addition, Bertea was awarded significant development contracts on the Hughes Apache helicopter, the McDonnell Douglas F-18, and the Sikorsky Black Hawk helicopter.[20] Yet, with a 12-month backlog of orders, it needed to take a different course of action.

"By early 1978, production capacity was below near-term demand and the company faced a shortage of machinists and other skilled production workers due to a combination of competition for production workers from the oil tool industry and high Orange County housing costs," wrote Ivan Marks, group vice president of finance and controller for Parker Aerospace during this time. "In June 1978, Parker Hannifin Corporation made a tender offer to acquire Bertea in a tax-free transaction to Bertea's shareholders, which was approved and accepted and closed in July."[21]

Ten years after its shares went public in 1968, Bertea Corporation, with annual sales of more than $46 million and a net income of $2.4 million, joined Parker.

"This was not an easy decision. Bertea was becoming more dependent on fewer but larger projects," said Richard "Dick" Bertea, president and CEO of Bertea Corporation during the acquisition, who later became senior vice president and chairman of Parker Hannifin's executive committee. He explained further:

The McDonnell Douglas DC-10 was new and just getting under way. [Parker Hannifin] saw this program was going to have a major impact on the company and needed a full manpower commitment from Bertea. Another major customer, Boeing, also needed a heavy workforce to work on their equipment, particularly engineering.

I think [Pat Parker] particularly appreciated two or three assets in Bertea Corporation. One was the technology and the engineering strength of the company—the fact that the electrohydraulic flight controls were substantially more advanced and involved larger portions of major aircraft programs."

The Parker acquisition allowed the company to participate on a much larger scale in major programs like the McDonnell Douglas DC-10, the Boeing 757 and 767, military helicopters, and the McDonnell Douglas/Northrop F-18. I recognized a trend for major aircraft builders to go to subcontractors that could provide larger components of an aircraft and have the financial depth to cover the development phase of new programs.[23]

It also had become apparent to Bertea that being acquired by Parker Hannifin would be not only beneficial, but an amiable venture as well.

"The acquisition went unbelievably well," explained Bertea. "Our two cultures fit very well and there was a lot of personal value in opportunities stressed on both sides with Parker management meetings, coming and speaking to all of our employees and knowing our company quite well."

Not only was Parker Hannifin a strong ally for supporting Bertea's interests and those of the newly acquired Vansickle Industries in 1978, a leading manufacturer of replacement wheels and brakes for lightweight private aircraft in Avon, Ohio, it had also been finely tuning its marketing efforts.[24] As a supplier to American Airlines for its DC-10 planes, which were being built by McDonnell Douglas in the 1970s, Parker Hannifin had firsthand experience with the importance of customer support.

"American Airlines [representatives] came into our office to talk about the DC-10, for which we were

Paul G. Schloemer (left), president of the Parker Hannifin Aerospace Group, is briefed on quality control procedures by Richard Bertea, chairman of Bertea at the Irvine, California, facility of Bertea Corporation. Parker Hannifin acquired Bertea in 1978.

building fuel valves and hydraulic valves. They said, 'You guys do a horrible job of providing spare parts for the airplanes that have to go into service,'" said Bill Webster, who served as vice president of marketing for the Aerospace Group during that time. He recalled:

The truth of the matter is, up to that moment, we used distributors. All of the missed deliveries, or whatever [went wrong], we [mistakenly] got credit for. American Airlines said, "Either you guys have to step up and do a better job on your spare parts support and product support, or we're going to recommend that Douglas not use your product on the airplane."[25]

As a result—and within minutes of American Airlines' directive—Aerospace created the Product Support Division, which would become the distributor of all Aerospace products. Although the Product Support Division struggled to report a financial gain during the first 12 months, as the inventory grew so did the profit margins.[26]

Additional reinforcement for the division would also come from its first manager, Ken Waltz, a by-product of the Bertea acquisition.[27] Webster explained:

[Bertea] had its own Product Support Division. With the help of Ken Waltz, we folded that all in together so that we had a unified division. Then, we created a Repair Division, which Bertea had done, that all became part of the overall so-called aftermarket. We went from a 1 on a scale of 1 to 10, to a 10 once the airplane went into service. We got high marks [from American Airlines].[28]

The focus on customer support also led to the Aerospace Group's decision to sell "systems."

"The Aerospace Group certainly led the way for Parker in developing complete systems," said Steve Hayes, who started with Parker Aerospace in 1972 as a division accounting manager and eventually became president of the group in 1993. "That was a major move. ... We could go to customers and say, 'We'll give you a whole system. You don't have to deal with 15 different companies.'"[29]

In addition to gaining Bertea's product support expertise, the acquisition also positioned Parker Hannifin

to be awarded a multimillion-dollar contract in early 1979 to supply primary flight control actuators for Boeing's wide-body 767 commercial airliners.[30] The contract called for 300 sets of 17 actuators to activate and precisely position the aircraft's ailerons (hinged controllers), elevators, and rudders on its wings. In addition, fuel injection nozzles for the General Electric CF6-80A engines that were to be used on the 767 were to be supplied by the Gas Turbine Fuel Systems Division in Cleveland.[31]

"This business is exciting for Parker since initial involvement in the program positions us well for a continuing partnership with Boeing in this new generation of aircraft for the next 20 to 25 years," said Pat.[32]

Aviation, space, and marine sales for fiscal 1979 rose 26 percent to $162 million at the end of 1979, from $129 million the previous year. While earnings were up just 11 percent because of absorbing start-up costs on several programs for the new generation of commercial aircraft and business jets, these broad-based programs and the replacement parts business were projected to generate profitable business flow throughout the upcoming decade.[33] The Aerospace Group gained more strength through the acquisition of Aremac Associates, Inc., Pasadena, California, which gave Parker Hannifin machining capability and a highly skilled workforce. Adapto, Inc., in Goodyear, Arizona, was also acquired in 1979 to provide a well-equipped, numerically controlled facility.[34]

"Demand for upgraded, fuel-efficient aircraft is at crescendo pitch," wrote Pat Parker and Allen N. "Bud" Aiman in the 1979 Annual Report. "This pent-up demand is currently exceeding the industry's productive capacity. As a major supplier to the industry, Parker is expanding to keep pace with this accelerated demand."[35]

Some Prosperity in Spite of "Misery"

Throughout President Carter's first three years in office, he was unable to reduce soaring interest and inflation rates or lower unemployment rates effectively. This resulted in an unprecedented escalation of the country's "Misery Index," an indication of economic well-being that averaged 16.27 during Carter's presidency. A 40-year high, the measurement was not favorable for the president or the country's business climate.[36] Yet,

Parker Hannifin had faced this type of financial turbulence before, and because of its precise planning, it was able to survive.

The recession of 1971, which caused the company's profits to tumble, led to the creation of a strategic plan called "cycle forecasting." Devised by Tommy McCuistion, vice president of Corporate Planning, the forecasting plan was based on the premise that each industry followed its own cyclical rhythm for a period that lasted from three to four years. This period includes six phases: growth, prosperity, warning, recession, depression, and recovery. The entry into each phase, marks the beginning of a specific set of business goals.[37]

Under cycle forecasting, during the growth phase the company anticipates prosperity by expanding the workforce and speeding up its training programs. In accord with its acquisition philosophy, it also looks for new manufacturing sources. In the prosperity phase, executives plan for the months of warning by curbing expansion. Superfluous companies are sold during this period of peak earning power. The key contributor to making cycle forecasting successful is the strategy of strict inventory control, which allows for heavy manufacturing activity during depression periods, before the demand of the growth phase increases production costs because of overtime wages.[38]

"Changing economic conditions have impacted the four sectors of our business at different times during the past fiscal year, with differing degrees and even in differing directions," wrote Pat Parker and Allen N. "Bud" Aiman in the 1980 Annual Report.

While Aerospace remained strong, with sales up 22 percent over 1979, Pat noted that some softening of general aviation orders and shipments and cutting of some commercial airliner production schedules were affecting the group. Yet, even as Aerospace experienced some positive news, the Automotive Group was hit hard by fuel prices, difficulties faced by U.S. automakers, and interest rates and credit restrictions. These conditions caused a 2 percent decline in sales and a 37 percent drop in operating profits for the Automotive Group.

Although the Misery Index was living up to its name for some Parker Hannifin markets during 1980, the company's domestic industrial business increased by 13 percent, even amid recession-induced plant closings, layoffs, and the resultant decrease in industrial production. In addition, Parker Hannifin's worldwide efforts were showing increasingly positive results. In the late

From left to right, Donald S. Manning, senior vice president and president, Fluidpower and Refrigeration Components Group; Patrick S. Parker, chairman and CEO; and Paul G. Schloemer, president of the Aerospace Group, circa 1979.

had reached as far as its Singapore operation, which was created in 1976.[41]

The beginning of 1980 saw sharp declines in industrial orders, and layoffs and plant closings by most of Parker Hannifin's major original equipment customers. Mobile and farm equipment builders and heavy-duty truck manufacturers were also suffering, and Parker Hannifin continued to rely on its cycle forecasting. This strategy allowed the company to boast sales figures that same year that passed the $1 billion mark for the first time. [42, 43]

Pat praised the company's accomplishments and contrasted its stellar progress to its humble beginnings:

A company with assets, facilities, people, and products around the world. ... An almost unimaginable achievement for a corporation, which saw its total assets go over a hillside but a few decades ago.[44]

1970s, the strength of the European economy and Parker Hannifin's focus on areas of high growth and profit potential helped improve performance.[39] With its international marketing efforts, the company had positioned itself as the supplier of all quality products to operate a reliable fluid system.[40] This optimistic trend

As the only full-line fluid power systems component manufacturer serving the global marketplace, with more than 20,000 employees, 110 plants, 64 sales forces, and more than 90,000 products used in 300 industries, Parker Hannifin was poised to enter the 1980s.[45]

Pat Parker, chairman of the board, left, and Paul Schloemer, president and CEO, observe Parker Hannifin's Compumotor microstepping motor controls in action. These helped to produce the Multi-Vapor lamps that lit the Statue of Liberty in 1986.

DRIVING THE WORLD'S MOTION

1981 – 1989

1981 Sales: $1.1 Billion | 1989 Sales: $2.4 Billion

Invention comes from keeping your ears perked and your eyes open.

—Patrick S. Parker[1]

As THE 1980S BEGAN, ALLEN "BUD" Aiman was guiding Parker Hannifin as its president and chief operating officer while Pat Parker continued in his role as chairman of the board and CEO.[2] Together, they were responsible for Parker Hannifin's progress, including keeping its products up-to-date with the evolving technological needs of industry. According to Pat, "Nearly every machine built uses some of Parker's components, sub-assemblies, or systems to fulfill its mission."[3]

Despite the widespread acceptance of Parker Hannifin products, the company was facing economic challenges. The recession of the early 1980s was stubborn. As U.S. industries struggled, Japan's industrial growth surpassed that of all other free-market industrialized countries.[4] The Japanese achieved impressive results by applying stringent efficiency standards and technological output, a combination that trumped most American companies.[5]

International production techniques influenced American manufacturers in designing, buying, fabri-

cating, and assembling products, and Parker Hannifin was ready to adapt. Aiman, who had led the company for four years, retired on July 1, 1981, because of ill health. Pat maintained his role of chairman and CEO, while Donald Manning became vice chairman, and Paul Schloemer was appointed president.[6]

"As the clock ticked away in 1981, I had not lost sight of my responsibility to ensure change and rejuvenation at Parker," said Pat. "Fortunately, my problem was greatly simplified because of the great depth of the management team, and because I had worked very closely with Paul Schloemer since, literally, the day he joined Parker. For example, during the early sixties Paul was the

Allen "Bud" Aiman started with Parker in 1954 as a salesman for the Seal Division and would become president and chief operating officer in 1977. Aiman retired from Parker Hannifin on July 1, 1981, due to ill health.

Eastern region manager for Aerospace, and I was running several manufacturing divisions in that Group. His responsibility was to get the business—I had to price it and make money at it. This can be tough, as there is a natural conflict in those two assignments. But I can say that Paul didn't lose many orders, and Parker Hannifin didn't lose any money."[7]

"I always felt that if I was successful, did the right thing for the business, that the opportunity would be there for me," said Schloemer, who began at Parker Hannifin in 1957 as a resident engineer and held several different positions at Parker Aerospace, including president of the group. "[The Aerospace Group] was well versed in computer-aided design and manufacturing, which we thought we needed to take to other areas of the corporation on the industrial side of business. That was one of the things that I was trying to do."[8]

Prior to Schloemer's presidency, Pat initiated a new internal organizational structure. In response to a weak economy, the heads of the company's four operating sectors became part of the Office of the Chief Executive. These included Alfred Lindstrom, International; Paul Schloemer, Aerospace (eventually replaced by Robert Rau); Dennis Sullivan, Industrial; and John Wenzel, Automotive.[9]

Further change within Parker's International Sector included the purchase of Ermeto Armaturen GmbH, of Bielefeld, Germany, a successful manufacturer of hydraulic fittings and valves. This acquisition, completed in December 1980, helped Parker register gains in sales and operating income for its European operation by the last public stock offering at the end of 1981.[10]

Further acquisitions in 1980 were made by the Seal Group, which purchased J. B. L. Systems, a major supplier of high-volume seals to the electronic and electrical industry in the United States.[11] That December, the Fluidpower Group acquired HydraPower, which manufactured rotary hydraulic actuators.

An employee at Parker Bertea Aerospace is shown working within its modern facility, which offered computer-integrated manufacturing and computer-aided process planning.

This product complemented the Fluidpower Group's strong position in linear actuators. Following these developments, Fluid Connectors Group acquired Deerwood Products to gain a precision, high-production machining facility in central Minnesota.[12]

Automotive Afterglow

The early 1980s were a time of growth in Parker Hannifin's Automotive Group. Even though the company had not intended to become a predominant automotive original equipment manufacturer (OEM) supplier, it knew that it could fill an important niche within the OEM and automotive aftermarket.[13]

"Why would Parker stay in the [automotive business]? There is so much to be learned by being an automotive OEM vendor. Automotive companies, whether they're wonderful or not, do an awful lot of pioneering in different aspects of business," said David Rudyk, who began his career in Parker Hannifin's Automotive Group in 1979.[14] "Electronic order management came largely from the automotive marketplace. Quality systems were really launched, if not in Aerospace, in Automotive. It was an early training ground for Parker."

This pioneering spirit within the Automotive Group was encouraged by Pat. The Euclid Avenue headquarters was equipped with a prototype shop where vehicles were brought in as test beds for analysis and research. Pat was a contributor to this in-house automobile laboratory.[15]

"Pat was very comfortable operating a lathe, and on one particular day he was down in the [automobile] lab with a lab coat on, working on a project. I was escorting several executives from Honda through our facilities," recalled Rudyk. "These Honda execs had a chance to meet our then-CEO of the corporation, lab coat on, hands all messed up with oil from working the lathe. I think it impressed the heck out of them that our CEO was somebody that was a hands-on kind of person, not just a person in a mahogany row behind a desk."[16]

Despite a sluggish economy, Rudyk and others in Automotive enjoyed an encouraging 26 percent increase on sales by the end of 1981.[17]

Parker Makes Parts

This trend would continue for Parker Hannifin throughout the 1980s as the dollar lost value against the Japanese yen, and the West German mark also lost substantial value. Reducing the price of U.S. technology and products made them competitive in Japanese and European markets—it was cheaper to produce components for foreign machinery in America than to import them for assembly.[18] This advantage, in concert with the fact that two of the largest industrial companies in the world were Japanese automotive manufacturers—Toyota Motor and Nissan Motor—positioned Parker Hannifin to offer OEM and aftermarket products, meeting a growing demand for automotive components.[19]

Individual Opportunity

As the U.S. economy grew in response to President Ronald Reagan's supply-side economics, the cutting of taxes, spending, and regulations by Congress, Parker Hannifin employees were also thriving within a culture of opportunity.[20] Throughout the prior decade, Parker Hannifin had grown into 59 autonomous profit centers under the direction of eight Groups and a small, strategy-oriented corporate staff.[21] This deliberate strategy served

This corporate photo, taken in the 1980s, shows a range of Parker Hannifin components and touts the company's business in a straightforward manner.

many markets with a wide product line and maintained elevated employee morale.

At the time, Dana A. Dennis was offered a position as a financial analyst with Parker Hannifin.

"I said 'yes' [to the position] because Parker offered opportunity for the individual. The environment is conducive to people development. They let you do your job. They're not always over your shoulder," said Dennis, who held several positions before becoming vice president and corporate controller in 1999. "Pat Parker always had time for you and that flowed down to people caring and the team environment."

A team environment became invaluable to Robert W. "Bob" Bond. After working for his family's Canadian business, which was a Parker Hannifin distributor during the 1960s and 1970s, he took a position with the Fluid Connectors Group in 1977. Following the completion of the company's management trainee

program in Canada, Bond worked at an order desk and became familiar with Parker Hannifin products and customers. After he took over as general manager at Parker's Fluid Connectors' Minneapolis Quick Coupling Division, he realized the order desk was the ideal place to have learned about the business.

"Connectors are certainly the start of the company," said Bond, who held several positions in the Fluid Connectors Group including vice president of Operations; and Group president. "When I started with Connectors, we were nowhere near being No. 1 [among competitors]. It takes diligence on behalf of not just the group, but the

Parker Hannifin offered a full line of pneumatic valves for controlling gas turbine engine bleed air, specializing in butterfly and coaxial valves, along with a variety of actuators.

corporation and its management [to become No. 1]." He continued:

Duane Collins used to always say that it's a long game. It's not going to be over at the end of the next twelve months or the next quarter. It takes organic growth. It takes product development. When you go from being that far back, it takes strategic and opportunistic acquisition. It takes customer relationships and all the things you would expect, but it takes doing that every day, every week, every month, every year, for a long, long time. It's sticking to what it is that we do.[22]

Yet making strides in the early 1980s was not easy. Inflation in the United States had begun to slow from double figures in 1982, but interest rates remained high, and unemployment was the highest in 40 years.[23] In this difficult environment, Parker Hannifin's overall fiscal

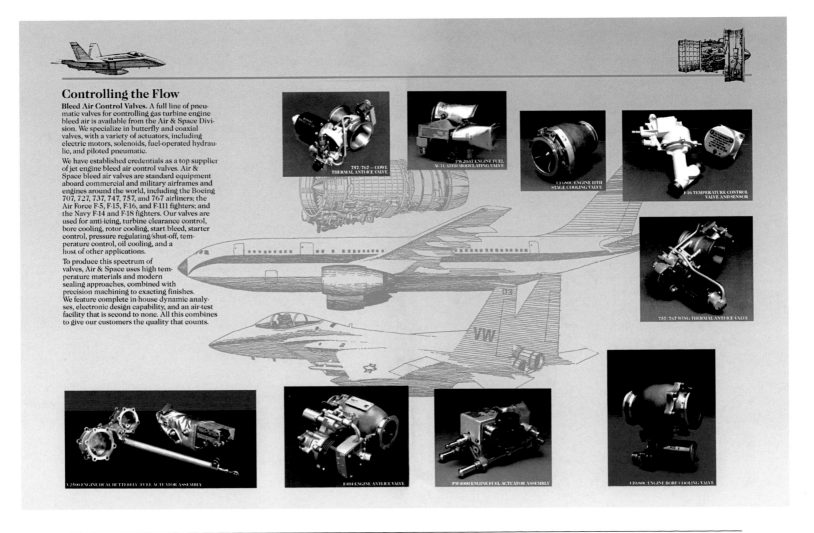

Controlling the Flow

Bleed Air Control Valves. A full line of pneumatic valves for controlling gas turbine engine bleed air is available from the Air & Space Division. We specialize in butterfly and coaxial valves, with a variety of actuators, including electric motors, solenoids, fuel-operated hydraulic, and piloted pneumatic.

We have established credentials as a top supplier of jet engine bleed air control valves. Air & Space bleed air valves are standard equipment aboard commercial and military airframes and engines around the world, including the Boeing 707, 727, 737, 747, 757, and 767 airliners; the Air Force F-5, F-15, F-16, and F-111 fighters; and the Navy F-14 and F-18 fighters. Our valves are used for anti-icing, turbine clearance control, bore cooling, rotor cooling, start bleed, starter control, pressure regulating/shut-off, temperature control, oil cooling, and a host of other applications.

To produce this spectrum of valves, Air & Space uses high temperature materials and modern sealing approaches, combined with precision machining to exacting finishes. We feature complete in-house dynamic analyses, electronic design capability, and an air-test facility that is second to none. All this combines to give our customers the quality that counts.

sales for 1983 declined 10 percent from the previous year, and its industrial segment, which included the Fluid Connectors Group, labored through the worst economic recession in decades within its primary markets.[24] Sales for Parker Hannifin's industrial segment fell 16 percent from the previous year, severely affecting earnings.[25]

While economic pressures placed some Fluid Connectors plants on shortened workweeks, reduced workforces, and caused other plants to close or consolidate because of slowed demand, the Industrial Segment managed to maintain its positive position. In addition to making significant progress in vertical integration of its product lines and penetrating existing and new markets as a low-cost producer, Parker Hannifin acquired The Roto-Actuator Corporation of St. Clair Shores, Michigan, a rotary actuator company, to broaden its fluid power product offerings. Overall, Parker Hannifin responded to the available market demand with the capacity, capability, and products for on-time delivery at competitive prices.

The Roto-Actuator Corporation was the sole acquisition in 1983—but this sluggish trend would soon change.[26]

Positive Change

As Parker Hannifin prepared to acquire promising and compatible organizations and product lines, it maintained a philosophy fueled by the importance of gaining excellence through outside sources.[27]

According to Pat:

Our acquisition philosophy would be strongly oriented toward continuing to seek out small- to medium-sized companies with a successful record. ... We prefer to acquire companies with clearly defined product-market strategies, as opposed to those with diverse disciplines. We need experienced management. In any significant acquisition we would have to be convinced that capable management was in place and committed for at least two years.[28]

Duane Collins, president of Parker Hannifin's International Sector, helped the sector achieve record sales in 1988, as it expanded into new markets. *(Photograph ©Mort Tucker Photography.)*

The economic recovery of 1984 led Parker Hannifin to acquire Uniroyal Hose Divisions in Missouri and Iowa; Keith Products, Texas; G. N. P., Inc., Illinois; K-Lon Corporation, Florida; and Towler Hydraulics GmbH, Germany. An increase in Parker Hannifin's domestic industrial business during that time made these acquisitions possible and enabled the company to serve its markets globally.[29] That same year, Parker Hannifin acquired W. H. Nichols Company. With headquarters in Waltham, Massachusetts, and operations in Portland and Gray, Maine, and Sturtevant, Wisconsin, W. H. Nichols was a world leader in gerotors and gerotor pumps (precision pumping units) for fluid transfer. Its president, Jack E. Chappell, was brought over and named corporate vice president of Parker's Nichols Group.[30, 31] This newly created Group operated within all three Parker Hannifin business segments—automotive, industrial, and aerospace—and helped all three grow during the 1980s.[32]

While Parker Hannifin supported the promotion of senior management from within through increasingly autonomous responsibility, a parallel philosophy was incorporated when retaining talent through acquisition.[33] The acquisitions were also part of a "three-leg" strategy that included organic growth and customer relationships. These two areas were directly affected by the crux of most acquisitions—the employees that were integrated into the Parker Hannifin workforce.

"If we lose a key manager, we feel we have failed. We don't just buy the assets," said Dana Dennis. "We buy the people, their knowledge, their expertise, and their management, and we want them to stay."[34]

Perhaps one of the best examples of acquiring expertise occurred in 1985 with the purchase of Racor Industries in Modesto, California. Prior to the acquisition, Parker Hannifin had a small filtration operation, which

included a company in Detroit called Rosaen Filters, acquired in 1968, that targeted a specific portion of the automotive market, and Tell Tale Filters, Ltd., of the United Kingdom, in 1972. It became clear to Jim Mockler that anyone using filters, would need Rosaen Filters. The market was wide open, and Mockler wanted to tap into its huge potential.

"It became pretty apparent that [filtration] was a lot different in many respects than hydraulics and pneumatics," explained Mockler, who retired as president of the Fluidpower Group in 1993. "Spinning filtration out as a separate group really gave it the emphasis it needed."

Adding Racor was the right move at an opportune time. An international leader in manufacturing innovative diesel fuel filter/water separator systems, Racor catapulted growth in the Fluidpower Group.

"Racor is probably the most successful acquisition in Parker's history," said John K. Oelslager, who began with Parker Hannifin in 1966, and became general manager,

Filter Division, under the Fluidpower Group. Oelslager held several positions in Parker Hannifin before eventually becoming the Filtration Group president in 1997.[35]

"Racor was a fun acquisition, too, because the guy we bought it from, I think he had previously been a stockbroker. He had invested in this company and built it up nicely, had no real experience in that area, but he had very good people working for him," said Mockler. "I still remember the day we were trying to figure out who would replace him as the general manager. We looked through our organization to find somebody, and looked outside, and just couldn't find the right person. We kept going back to him, and asking, 'Who do you recommend?' He said, 'I keep telling you. You want Peter Popoff' [appointed to president of the Filtration Group in February 2008]. As it turned out, he was loved by everybody in the organization, and they would do anything he wanted."

Financial success for the Fluidpower Group in 1985 was attributed primarily to the Racor acquisition, and the group's operating income increased more than 20 percent on a 14 percent sales increase.[36] The following year, Parker Hannifin purchased Schrader Bellows and acquired its leading line of pneumatic equipment and automation systems for world markets. It was a perfect fit for Parker Hannifin's Pneumatic and Cylinder Divisions and the largest acquisition by Parker Hannifin at the time. In purchasing Schrader Bellows, the company could reach markets outside of hydraulics, including factory automation, robotics, electronics, and food processing.[37] Further complementing the purchase was the acquisition of Finite Filter, which provided an exceptional line of filters for pneumatic applications.[38] Later in 1985, Parker Hannifin acquired existing subsidiaries of Schrader Bellows in Brazil, France, and Mexico, in addition to Metal Bellows in California and Massachusetts.[39]

Parker's ventures into filtration and pneumatic technologies were directed by analysis of the current state of business. Hydraulics was losing money because of the recession, and, at the time, Parker was 85 percent hydraulics.

This advertisement, which showcases the longevity and innovation of Parker Hannifin components, was published in the mid-1980s.

1986
CLEVELAND NATIONAL
AIR SHOW

Burke Lakefront Airport
Aug. 30, 31, Sept. 1
Souvenir Program
$3.00

Don Zito, vice president of operations of the Fluid Power Group at the time, who retired as president of the Connectors Group in 1997, said entering the filtration market was the next logical step for the company. According to Zito:

I noticed that filtration was everywhere. I mean filtration was a ubiquitous industrial function, and I thought to myself, "You know, why do we have to confine ourselves to industrial hydraulics? Why can't we become more broad-based?" ... I presented to the board of directors some thoughts with respect to making this potentially a group.

While the board's initial reaction to the idea of the new group was indifference at best, Zito's years of persistence paid off.

"Now it's a billion-dollar organization," Zito said. "It's one of my dreams come true."

In addition to the strategic moves in acquisition, in the later part of the 1980s, there was a shift in manufacturing processes to simplify machinery and facilitate

As Honorary Chairman of the 1986 Cleveland National Air Show, Pat Parker provided invaluable assistance, particularly in efforts to market the show to the business community. *(Program cover reprinted by permission of the Cleveland National Airshow.)*

the production of complicated parts. Donald Smrekar, who retired in 1998 as group vice president of Manufacturing Technology, oversaw the creation of the CNC multiple spindle screw machine.

"At one time, it was the most advanced screw machine in the world," said Smrekar. "Today, there are a lot of machines out there that are doing the same thing as the precision nocam. That's what we called it. It was a numerically controlled screw machine, and we only built them for Parker."

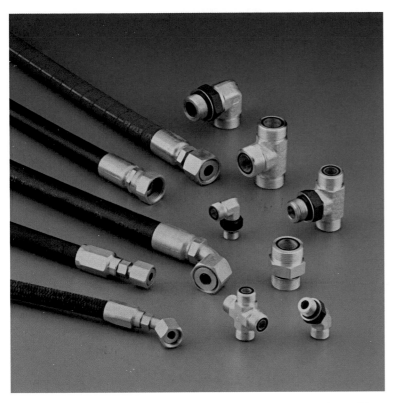

Since 1924, Parker Hannifin has served the marketplace with dependable fluid power technology. The Seal-Lok fitting (O-ring face seal) is one of a broad line of tube fittings and adapters.

The main difference in the machines was the ability to make program changes in the machine instead of manually setting up parts. The machines were quicker, more accurate, and able to produce difficult products more efficiently.

"In fact, there are still machines running in the Ohio facility making that same type of part," said Smrekar.

The distribution network also received attention, and the current distribution network was a direct outgrowth of the industry's efforts to downsize and cut costs. There was an emphasis to streamline operations as much as possible, and this was seen directly in the way Parker Hannifin distributors approached customers. Distributors began functioning more proactively to meet customer needs. This shift from having distributors act simply as order takers into offering a complete solution to a customer began in the 1960s and progressed throughout the 1980s.

"Parker was the leader in moving [toward systems integration], but our distributors have really undergone an evolution, and our distributors are the envy of the industry," said Jeff Weber, group advertising promotions manager, Hydraulics Group. "Our competitors would love to have our distribution network."

INVESTIGATING A TRAGEDY

PARKER HANNIFIN HAS BEEN INVOLVED WITH America's space program for many decades, an association that has included the Mercury, Gemini, and Apollo programs. The company experienced many successes, including assisting NASA with the safe return of the *Apollo 13* astronauts to Earth. Parker Hannifin also continued its support when the Space Shuttle program began in the 1970s. This involvement, however, became part of a tragic incident that shocked the world about 15 years later.

On the cold morning of January 28, 1986, the Space Shuttle *Challenger* lifted off from Cape Canaveral, Florida. The mission had been affected by a number of delays and had the distinction of including a civilian crew member, a teacher from New Hampshire. Yet just 73 seconds after liftoff, the shuttle disintegrated in the sky, producing great plumes of gray smoke. All seven crew members perished.

A Presidential Commission investigated the incident for four months, eventually releasing an exhaustive report that focused on an O-ring, the material for which was manufactured by Parker Hannifin, in one of the solid rocket boosters (SRBs), which provide thrust for liftoff.[1] A number of factors were considered in both the Commission investigation and outside investigations, including the unseasonably cold temperatures that manufacturing documentation advised would adversely affect the O-ring's performance, and

However, maintaining inventory was a constant struggle, Zito said. Plants were constantly using up certain parts and always reordered manually.

"Somebody figured out that having those plants go through their inventories all the time and constantly trying to replenish thousands and thousands of parts of inventories that they needed all over the country was driving everybody crazy," explained Zito. "It would be much smarter if we had a central computer keeping track of the inventory."

As a result, a "push" inventory system was initiated, which allowed a central facility to notice that another warehouse would soon be low on a certain product. Parts would be shipped automatically to distributors on the next truck that left the main manufacturing facility.

"It significantly reduced the cost of order fulfillment, internal order fulfillment, and it simultaneously improved customer service significantly. Before the manager of the satellite facility ever had to realize he was out of parts on one item, those parts were on their way to him or already sitting in his loading dock ready to be put back into his stock," said Zito. "That was a major, major change."

Information technology was rapidly evolving into an effective means of communication. To gain access to the

In October 1989, Culver City, California, employees of the O-Seal Division hold what they believe is the largest one-piece Gask-O-Seal ever produced. *(Photo by Hartzel Studio Photography.)*

a lack of communication among NASA officials who were under time pressure to launch.[2]

Parker Hannifin Seal Group manufactured elastomeric seal cord for Morton Thiokol, a NASA contractor. The Seal Group produced 12-foot sections of cord—meeting the exact specifications requested by Morton Thiokol—at its Berea, Kentucky, plant, and subjected the cord to rigorous testing.[3] The testing included tensile strength, heat aging, compression set, oil testing, and low temperature performance.[4] The cord was sent to Hydra Pak, Inc., in Salt Lake City, where it was spliced together to form the O-ring. Morton Thiokol then used the O-ring when manufacturing its SRBs for NASA.

Following the incident, Pat Pastryk, then president of Parker Hannifin Seal Group, assisted representatives from Morton Thiokol in searching through archival records documenting the seal production process

dating back to 1977.[5] According to NASA's Accident Analysis Team Report, the O-ring was ultimately found to be composed of "one of the acceptable formulations used by Parker Seal Co. Samples of O-ring material from this batch have been tested at MSFC [Marshall Space Flight Center, Huntsville, Alabama] for requirements of MILR-83248 [a type of O-ring] and found to be in compliance."[6] Parker Hannifin was never implicated in the failure of the O-ring, as the material the company provided was within the established parameters.

Parker Hannifin continues its support of America's space programs today, and is integral in supplying sealing, heating, and cooling elements for the International Space Station.[7] It remains a customer of NASA to this day. Its parts have been used in every space shuttle program, and some have been in use without replacement for more than 20 years.[8, 9]

best technology, Parker Hannifin began a targeted acquisition strategy.[40] In a speech just three years earlier, Pat had detailed the acquisition process itself, which was quickly becoming standard:

Given these challenges and constraints [of the differences between fluid system controls and electronics], the decision was made to embark upon an extensive and long-range acquisition program to achieve our goals. The parameters we set for ourselves were simple, but demanding:

- *We would only acquire components companies in our field of expertise.*
- *We would only acquire well-managed, successful businesses.*
- *We would use our own equity wherever possible to tie the previous owner-manager to Parker's future success.*
- *It is a clear cut, simple program, but so is sailing around the world. I guess my philosophy has always been that plans and ideas are fine and necessary, but that execution is really the heart and soul of any business venture.*[41]

The company also purchased Compumotor, a California-based operation, moving Parker Hannifin into the growing electromechanical controls business. Compumotor designed, manufactured, and distributed a line of electronic components and systems used in tasks ranging from semiconductor manufacturing to fiber optics; producing precision bearings for aircraft; video-disc manufacturing; production of steel belts for tires; and telescope positioning controls.

Compumotor products also included a low-cost compact microstep motor/drive/indexer series and an industrial control microcomputer, which complemented the use of personal computers in the scientific, engineering, architectural, and construction fields.[42, 43]

Parker Hannifin never believed that electric motion would power heavy-duty machinery or even flight controls, but predicted that servomotors would be an appropriate fit for the technology. The Compumotor acquisition was a means to achieve this goal and enter the new market by gaining different components, including actuators and cylinders.[44]

Highlighting International Presence

The late 1980s offered promising trends in the automotive industry for Parker Hannifin, with a major increase in the sales of gerotor pumps for 1987 model cars in its Parker Nichols Group. At the time, the group was the leading supplier of these precision pumps for engine-oil, transmission fluid, and gasoline tank applications. It was also a profitable time for the Aerospace Group, which reached sales of $553 million, an increase of 20.9 percent over the previous year. In addition to a strong military market for Parker Hannifin's components and systems, the group's Biomedical Division released the Parker Micropump—an invaluable drug-infusion system for the application of continuous chemotherapy.[45]

Although Parker Hannifin continued to grow throughout North America, Pat felt certain that it could make its presence known anywhere. With international plants achieving record sales in 1987 due to increased demand in Latin America—notably Brazil and Argentina —Pat reviewed the importance of Parker Hannifin parts to members of the Brazil business community in 1988:

I emphasize users of machinery—whether you're washing clothes, cooling this room, or flying down to Rio, you're wearing out Parker parts. Over 50 percent of our business comes from users—the replacement market. It has been our dedication to this user market that I contend has differentiated Parker from other components' suppliers and has enabled us to become a worldwide leader in motion control.[46]

While the Latin American market helped increase Parker Hannifin sales in the late 1980s, this was offset to some degree by a flat demand and softness in some European markets. With sales affected by the weaker U.S. dollar, Parker Hannifin took the initiative to improve its international operations. In 1987, the company improved efficiency and cut costs by expanding facilities in West Germany; building a new Schrader Bellows plant in France; and expanding warehouses and distribution facilities in Norway, Finland, and the Netherlands. Service to Schrader Bellows customers was improved in Australia, and Italy opened a new, enlarged plant, which included a new sales and service center.

Yet Pat admitted the road ahead would not be easy for the International Sector.

"The industrial world has staggered from one crisis to another. Interest rates have seen the most violent fluctuations in history," Pat remarked in 1987 at the Harvard Business School Club of Cleveland. "The dollar exchange rate for the world's major currencies has fluctuated a mere 100 percent up and down in this period. Unemployment has hit double digits in all of the industrial European countries and the United States, and we have racked up a cool trillion dollars in government debt. Isn't it terrific to try and run a manufacturing business scattered all over the world in these tranquil times?"[47]

But, as Duane Collins became president of Parker Hannifin's International Sector in 1988, he stressed the positive:

We had two huge advantages that I kept saying to our people that we had to exploit. One, we spoke English. The world business language is English. Two, we had the dollar, and the world's currency was the dollar. I kept saying to our International [Sector], "We've got to exploit these advantages."

I went to visit one of our hose competitors in Italy, and he said, "Mr. Collins, we've been watching Parker from here for the last 10 years. You have grown unbelievably. You are now number one [in the U.S. market]. I keep telling my people that there's a big fog offshore that's going to be rolling in one day." I said, "Well, we'll see ..."[48]

We grew very rapidly because we had the dollar, we had the language, and we had the support. Pat was very international [in his] thinking. We had tremendous support from the company.[49]

One initiative Collins stressed was the enhanced communication between the 18 European countries Parker Hannifin served. By establishing one platform that could communicate among all, Collins could simplify operations and produce an economy of scale.[50]

"We put in place [a computer system] during the time I was in International that allows us today to know what we did in Finland yesterday. We can tell you by part number, by customer, by profit, by sales," said Collins. "When we started to put that in place, when we opened our first plant in Poland, we could plug our general manager into the Parker system through a telephone line. Instantly, he is world class. We really bring economies of scale to the program."[51]

While Collins invigorated worldwide communications for Parker Hannifin, the International Sector achieved record sales in 1988 through increased market penetration and entry into new markets. With sales 23.2 percent higher than the previous year, the company marked notable growth in European pneumatics, cylinder, and packing products businesses. Construction also had begun in Korea on a hydraulic hose fittings plant of Hwa Sung Parker Co., a joint venture. China also continued its joint venture with Parker Hannifin in the operation of a hydraulic seal manufacturing plant.[52] Parker Hannifin was becoming the world force that Pat envisioned.

Preparing for the Next Decade

On its 70th anniversary in 1988, Parker Hannifin reached more than $2 billion in sales. Highlighted by seven acquisitions that year, the company continued to take advantage of industrial and aerospace acquisition

In April 1989, Parker Packing Division employees hold a large-diameter seal, typical of those used in tunnel-boring machinery.

PARKER AND THE WORLD OF ENTERTAINMENT

Parker Hannifin was instrumental in creating the stunning technological visual effects in the movie *Jurassic Park*.

As the world's leading diversified manufacturer of motion and control technologies and systems, Parker Hannifin's efforts are usually hidden within better-known products. While its expertise such as tiny O-rings aid a watch's stem and Parker Hannifin pumps are vital to a car's fuel system, these products are seamless in their function and rarely noticed. But in the mid-1970s, Parker Hannifin's ability to harness motion control would be seen and admired as it debuted in the world of entertainment.[1]

Parker Hannifin's involvement in entertainment dates back to 1975, when it provided the clenching bite of the shark in the film *Jaws*.[2] The Parker Servo Valves used in the great white shark controlled the amount, pressure, and direction of the fluid flowing through its body, helping it move.[3] Parker Hannifin technology would create an even more spectacular special effect for the film *Titanic*, released in December 1997—the sinking of a great ocean liner.

Greg Paddock, entertainment engineer and hydraulic territory manager for Parker Hannifin's Hydraulics Division, Pacific Region, was approached by the movie's special effects coordinator, T.R.I.X. Unlimited. Paddock had 10 weeks to complete the detail work, design, and construction, as well as travel to the set in Rosarito Beach, Mexico, where he managed the hydraulic lift system's installation and operation.[4] The film's ship was a 775-foot long structure, about 90 percent of the original *Titanic*, and Parker Hannifin had to move and submerge the enormous

vessel. The $1.3 million lift system weighed 1.4 million pounds, with eight separate lift axes. It was 10 times larger than anything Paddock had ever designed, and would tip the massive scale model.[5] It included eight Parker electrohydraulic valve and feedback cylinders to raise and lower the set into the water.[6] The director then asked if the *Titanic* could be broken in two. Parker Hannifin obliged.

"Pat made four or five visits to the [*Titanic*] site," said Steve Camp, Hydraulics Group regional manager. "It was a fast-track deal. We did the engineering, installation, and delivery from start to finish in a short period of time. We have the best delivery of customer service in the business."[7]

Parker Hannifin's reputation contributes to the respect it receives from the movie industry. Parker Hannifin's Servo Valves controlled alligators in *Eraser* (1996) and two large snakes in *Anaconda* (1997). Jet fighters in *True Lies* (1994) were moved with Parker valves. In *Batman* (1989), Parker hydraulics were used in the Bat cave to move a 97,000 pound telescope and motion base. Parker Hannifin valves, cylinders, and pumps were combined to control *Jurassic Park*'s (1993) terrifying dinosaurs, while *Godzilla*'s (1998) tail was propelled by Parker hydraulic pumps, cylinders, valves, and filters.[8] Other movie

productions have benefited from Parker Hannifin's ingenuity, including *The Perfect Storm* (2000), in which precision Servo Valves operated at 100 gallons of water per minute to create waves fierce enough to torment the *Andrea Gail*, and *Pearl Harbor* (2001), which used custom-designed VOAC valves to simulate the trajectory of the deadly torpedo. In *Minority Report* (2002), the motion of the Plexiglas prisoner tubes was controlled by Parker electrohydraulic valves and cylinders, and in *Master and Commander* (2003), custom cylinders and manual lever valves rocked the mighty clipper ship. [9, 10]

Parker collaborated with Disney Studios in the production of *Pirates of the Caribbean: Dead Man's Chest* (2006). To develop an actual floating motion base for the three ships used in the film, Parker Hannifin, in conjunction with Controlled Motion Solutions, a Parker hydraulic technology center, developed a complete system to create the effect of 18th-century ships foundering in heavy seas. Parker Hannifin engineers created a system to manipulate the world's first floating-base gimbal, a mechanical device that allows the rotation of an object in three dimensions. [11]

"You can control motion pneumatically, electromechanically, or hydraulically. Parker's got all three," said Camp, who started at Parker in 1979. "From a Parker scope, about 10 percent of movies are done electromechanically, 15 percent are done pneumatically, and 75 percent are done hydraulically due to big structures. Hydraulics [systems are] the most flexible and have the highest horsepower." [12]

Pat Parker always championed the company's involvement. Pat took his son, Streeter, to visit the *Titanic* set numerous times. He was also personally invited to be a movie extra. [13]

"Pat was invited to a 'Bit Party' and was cast as an extra to jump off the boat, but he thought his insurance wouldn't cover it [if anything happened]," said Camp.

Along for the Ride

Parker Hannifin's hydraulic expertise is also used in theme park rides and live stage productions. From Disneyland's Magic Mountain, in Anaheim, California, to attractions at Universal Studios in Orlando, Florida, and Disneyland Resort Paris, Parker products are at work. [14]

"Since the ride industry got rolling, Parker was involved," Camp said. "When Disneyland came along, rides required more motion control and evolved motion simulators. Parker's always there with servo hydraulics and servo systems. We have a flexible network that can [support varied projects]." [15]

Pat also made his presence known in Las Vegas. On a visit to "the Strip" for a golf convention in the early 1990s, Pat and Streeter were walking by the newly constructed Bellagio Hotel and Casino. While it was only 6:00 A.M., Pat noticed that a crew was working to repair the Fountains of Bellagio. [16]

"[Pat] climbs over the rope [toward the fountains]. Guys start yelling, 'Hey, hey, get back!'" said Streeter. "He said, 'I'm just checking it out. What's the problem?' The foreman told him that the guys [had] built it all wrong. [Pat] said 'Here's my card. This is my company. You call this guy, and he'll be down here tonight, at the latest tomorrow morning. By tomorrow, you'll be working on replacing the system, and it'll be half the cost of this one. I'll guarantee it.'" [17]

The Bellagio engineer recognized the Parker Hannifin name and called the number. Within 24 hours, the fountains were being equipped with Parker Hannifin controls, which provided motion, brass fittings on the air-purging system to keep the electronics dry, and special hoses that connected the water pump to the gimbal heads. Polyurethane tubing and 1,110 cylinders completed the system that allows the more than 1,000 dancing fountains to perform a "water ballet." [18]

Also in Las Vegas, a Parker cylinder moves the stage for the legendary Cirque du Soleil acrobatic show. Parker's hydraulics also control stage movement at the historic Hanna Theater in Cleveland, Ohio.

Parker Hannifin's success in the entertainment industry matches Pat's mantra: Have fun.

"Pat made sure you mixed business with fun. Have fun first, then the business comes along," recalled Camp. "At the end of the day, Pat wanted to make sure that people were maintaining a balance." [19]

opportunities. By bringing in Gull Corporation, Parker Hannifin obtained essential airborne electronics capabilities to service the systems and subsystems contractors for aircraft in the coming decade. Waterman Hydraulics brought hydraulic control valves for fluid power applications, and Stratoflex broadened Parker Hannifin's aerospace, automotive, and industrial market coverage through its highly regarded fluid connector manufacturing.[53]

Yet, as 1989 progressed, the decision was made to sell Parker Hannifin's three automotive aftermarket component divisions to an investor group headed by the president of the Parker Automotive Group.[54]

"The automotive business turned rotten," explained John Wenzel, who retired as president of the Automotive Group. "It became very difficult."

After weathering this market's turbulence, with continuing consolidations among component manufacturers and changes in marketing alliances, the move to sell the three divisions helped Parker Hannifin prepare for the 1990s. The company received $80 million and was able to

Donald Manning, Pat Parker, and Paul Schloemer toasted longtime employees of Parker Hannifin at the company's "Old Timer's Dinner," held in the fall of 1988.

focus on the manufacture of original equipment for the automotive market.[55]

With more than 800 product lines for hydraulic, pneumatic, and electromechanical applications spread throughout the world, Pat emphasized the five essentials for success: people productivity, production throughput, quality, cost reduction, and customer service.

To instill his belief in the importance of total performance, Pat and Parker Hannifin management launched "Parker Targets" in 1989.

"This was ahead of its time and led to Parker's culture of continuous improvement and employee empowerment," said Executive Vice President and CFO Tim Pistell.

This unique corporate initiative included a Targets Council of 22 managers from across the company to

gather, evaluate, and introduce productivity technology and the best manufacturing practices worldwide; to provide training; to measure productivity; and to ensure long-term, permanent support and participation by senior management in the improvement process.

"Parker Targets was an introspective program in the broad series of self-appraising questions into your operation," explained Don Zito, who retired as president of the Connectors Group in 1997. "How are you doing in this regard? How are you doing in that regard? Here are some tools to use. There was some pretty extensive training that was held at the managerial levels throughout the corporation to incorporate this philosophy, different philosophies in terms of improved customer service, better asset management … into your operations and how you could go about doing that. It was a pretty extensive program."

"In the 20 years just passed, our business as measured in both sales and profits has grown fifteen-fold," Pat said. He continued:

But, of even more significance, this decade of the eighties has seen dramatic deterioration in the ability of the old management structure to meet the needs of the marketplace and has provided dramatic rewards for those companies that have been able to use technology, training, and communications to push the decision-making capability right down to the person at the phone, at the production machine, at the computer. That is what "Targets" is—making every member of the team his own manager and giving him or her the tools and training to do it right the first time.[56]

Pat encouraged the manufacturing divisions to commit extra hours, leadership, and hard work to meet customer service, quality, and pricing requirements during the next decade.

Parker Hannifin's progress during the 1980s was filled with significant accomplishment. With $1.8 billion invested in research and development to generate new products and manufacturing processes, 40 acquisitions, and the purchase of advanced manufacturing equipment and facilities worldwide, Parker Hannifin was ready to embrace the decade ahead.[57]

Bill Eaton, vice president of Distribution, Connectors Group, and Hydraulic Group, said: "Parker is a big business obviously … but we're organized and operate as a number of small businesses. We still have the entrepreneurial business, and we're focused on either a market or a product, which gives us the opportunity to really become good at what we do with that respective division."

"In the big league of world manufacturing, the U.S. Yankees have occupied the cellar for the season of the eighties. Out of shape, off their timing, complacent after some 30 years of no strenuous competition, our team has been kicked around and abused, and for lots of good reasons," wrote Pat in a *Cleveland Plain Dealer* guest editorial:

The big difference a tough decade has made, though, is that instead of bemoaning the lack of a "level playing field" the American team is aggressively pursuing these opportunities.

So, from my view at Parker Hannifin, as a supplier to all the world's industrial teams, the Yankees are going to be the class of the league for the nineties. You won't go wrong betting on the Yankees in the world's manufacturing league for the upcoming decade. We are going to be winners.[58]

Communications and IT infrastructure challenges necessitate new locations for Parker's headquarters in Europe and the United States. Early in the 1990s, Parker's European headquarters moved to a new home in Hemel Hempstead, England (pictured above). Later, in 1997, the company's world headquarters was also relocated, to a new building near Cleveland, Ohio, to carry the business into the 21st century.

GLOBALIZATION THROUGH OPPORTUNITY

1990–2000

1990 Sales: $2.5 Billion | 2000 Sales: $5.4 Billion

As Parker enters more markets worldwide, globalization is increasing. Both acquisitions and new facilities are helping the company serve customers in over 120 countries from our operations in 38 nations.

—Duane Collins

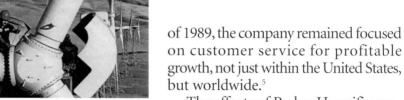

AT THE END OF 1989, THE IDEA OF global capitalism was becoming a reality following the dismantling of the Berlin Wall.[1] With the collapse of the Soviet Union and the end of the Cold War, the stage was set for rapid economic growth both in Europe and the United States.[2] The period had also been characterized by the popularity of personal computers, few foreign wars, and the conclusion of a tenacious economic recession.

With Paul Schloemer as president and CEO, the company began organizing for the new decade. In addition to selling its three automotive aftermarket components divisions the previous year, Parker Hannifin also divested its small Biomedical Division in January 1990. While the Biomedical Division had sales of about $4 million in 1989, the sale of this division and the automotive parts business allowed the company to concentrate on its core motion control markets—aerospace and industrial.[3,4]

People Power

Even as Parker Hannifin was experiencing record sales, net earnings, and earnings per share at the end

of 1989, the company remained focused on customer service for profitable growth, not just within the United States, but worldwide.[5]

The efforts of Parker Hannifin employees were essential to reaching this goal. Hiring the right people, providing the best tools, and preparing employees for promotion according to their ability and individual motivation were all important factors. The fact that Parker Hannifin products were in demand added to the sense of growing optimism.[6]

"When Pat took over, [he] started Parker as a people organization, recognizing that the way the company was going to succeed was to have good people, treat the people well, and retain the people," said John Zakaria, who began at Parker Hannifin in 1966, eventually becoming vice president/controller and director of purchasing, North American Industrial.

This 1994 wind turbine employs Parker hydraulic tube fittings, hose, and hydraulic power units, to generate 350-405 kilowatts of power at the Altamont Pass Windplant™, which is 70 miles east of San Francisco.

and it's really those groups then that, along the way, try to be—what would you call it?—nice competitors. In other words, Parker always took the idea that we're going to have the best customer service. We're going to have the best products. We're going to spend the money so that when I'm out there, I can explain to you why my hose is better than your hose and really have some features and test reports to back it up. And the highest price. We're usually 10 percent higher on price than most other competitors. You had to be able to justify the higher price.

Schloemer had similar sentiment, adding that the decentralized corporate philosophy at Parker empowered employees throughout the chain of command. According to Schloemer:

The philosophy of divisions as profit centers [allowed decentralization to work] and it was always a philosophy to push the profit responsibility down as far in the corporation as we could, put somebody in charge of that division. We always had incentives in the sense

Maintaining the decentralized culture of the company was also key, said Denny Sullivan, executive vice president, Industrial, and a Parker veteran who started with the company in 1960. According to Sullivan:

Those of us who started with Bob Cornell … learned how well [decentralization] works if you just let people who know what they're doing do it and don't interfere with them too much, and give them a good incentive system so that if they do it, they can really do well and their team can do well. We just saw it work.

Over time, there have been different ideas of centralizing things. You do have to centralize stuff like legal and finance and so forth, but as far as the products, if you have people who are really expert in their field … they're the ones who have all the friends in the industry. They're the ones who have all the contacts,

Right: In the early 1990s, the Fluidpower Group produced and stored parts in more than 60 manufacturing plants and warehouses worldwide.

Below: Donald A. Zito, corporate vice president and president of the Fluid Connectors Group, joined Parker in 1962 as a sales engineer. He has held various positions with the company, including materials manager and product sales manager for the Tube Fittings Division, and general manager of the Industrial Hydraulics Division.

of financial incentives for our people, but I think there were other incentives, too. Anyone running an operation knew if he was successful he was going to have the opportunity to take on more responsibility, and then the financial incentives that came with promotion were always there.[7]

Don Zito, who retired as president of the Fluid Connectors Group in 1997, explained how the company's employee incentive plan worked:

[Parker Hannifin] had a profit sharing based on return on net assets employed at the time, and it impressed me that when I became president of Connectors, I tried and I think I successfully sold the concept to extend the plan globally. I think that's when it went corporate-wide … .

Parker Hannifin's management expertise was usually cultivated from within—its executives typically had at least 20 years of service, such as Schloemer. However, in the early 1990s the company needed to seek outside talent. To keep pace with its competitors, Parker Hannifin relied heavily on its 30,000 employees to generate the more than $2.5 billion in sales it was projecting for 1990, but recruiting skilled engineers to fill its ranks became more challenging.[8] Between 1983 and 1990, the number of students enrolled in U.S. engineering programs declined sharply, and Parker Hannifin, among others in the industry, was feeling the results of fewer skilled engineers available for hire.[9]

Parker Hannifin, however, offered endless opportunities, and this proved beneficial as the company sought established talent from its competitors. For example, Lee Banks was working for the Copeland Corporation in Chicago, training with the world's largest manufacturer of hermetic and semi-hermetic compressors for refrigeration and air conditioning, when the company decided to transfer him to Sidney, Ohio. Banks refused the transfer and instead called Larry Hopcraft, vice president of Automotive and Refrigeration at Parker Hannifin. The two had met when Banks caddied for a Parker Hannifin manufacturer's representative—a representative that Banks was also working for, selling Parker Hannifin products just a few years earlier. Banks took a gamble, spoke with Hopcraft in 1991, and asked about opportunities at Parker Hannifin.[10]

"Larry said, 'Lee, we've got a job for you in Chicago—a national sales manager for the Refrigeration and Air Conditioning Group,'" said Banks, who held many different roles at Parker Hannifin before becoming president of its Worldwide Hydraulics Group and eventually executive vice president and operating officer. "[During that time] in that industry, not the fluid power but the refrigeration industry,

At NASA's Marshall Space Flight Center in Huntsville, Alabama, engineers from Parker Hannifin's O-Seal Division and NASA inspect a prototype 72-inch diameter seal that uses a tongue-in-groove design for possible inclusion in a space station's module-to-module interface.

[Parker Hannifin] had a very small market share and was trying to develop technology and become a big player."

Although the Refrigeration Group, which was combined with the company's remaining automotive segment, slowly struggled through a flat market of air conditioning and refrigeration in the early 1990s, the effort paid off.[11] With Banks' expertise and guidance, Parker Hannifin made strides. As his career advanced, holding positions as manager of the Fluidex Division in Madison, Mississippi, and then general manager of the acquired Skinner Valve Division in Hartford, Connecticut, Parker Hannifin's refrigeration business also flourished.[12]

"Parker wanted to expand its line in the general purpose solenoid valve line. They hired some engineers with this experience, and designed a complete line of general purpose solenoid valves, moving them to the recently established Fluidex Division," said Banks. "That was about a $20 million business. And then, over three years, we bought the businesses from Honeywell, and we had very quick organic growth. That business today is probably a $200 million worldwide business."[13]

Tapping the Worldwide Market

As new markets were tapped in the United States during the early 1990s, Parker Hannifin focused on globalizing its product groups, and, in 1993, the board of directors

elected then president of International Duane Collins, to CEO, replacing Schloemer, who retired after nine years in the position and 36 years with the company.[14]

In his role with the International Group, Collins had traveled throughout the world, rarely stopping in the United States. During the early 1990s, Parker Hannifin acquired Polar Seals in Helsingor, Denmark; formed a subsidiary in Venezuela; and created a joint venture of Uniflex-Parker Co., in Thailand. In January 1992, the company formed Parker Hannifin Taiwan and concluded the Parker AMC joint venture in Japan.

Global travel became commonplace for Parker Hannifin executives, and the company was in need of its own aircraft rather than continually scheduling chartered aircraft. Years before, Pat had purchased a Turbo Commander 980 from pilot Al Maurer.

"We sat down and punched [the agreement] out in about two hours," said Maurer, who would become Parker Hannifin's pilot in 1986, traveling around the

Right: Chairman Emeritus Pat Parker was on site to accept Parker Hannifin's new Learjet in 1999. The Learjet 45 was the 2,000th aircraft manufactured at Bombardier's Wichita, Kansas, production facility, a customer of Parker Hannifin since the 1960s. At the time, Parker Hannifin operated a fleet of Learjets, including a Learjet 45 and a Learjet 31A.

Below: In 1995, Dennis "Denny" Sullivan (left), executive vice president, Industrial and Automotive; Duane Collins (center), president and CEO; and Pat Parker (right), chairman, visited one of several Parker Hannifin exhibits at the Hannover Fair in Germany, the world's largest industrial exhibition.

globe throughout the 1990s. "Shortly after, Pat decided we should have a Gulfstream [aircraft] to service our West Coast customers, the Aerospace and Seal Group, like a shuttle going back and forth. We did that, out and back to California three days a week. We were the highest-time operator in the world for probably two years. We flew 1,500 hours a year."

As Collins began making his mark, Parker Hannifin's Fluid Connectors Group was busy expanding. Successful growth was seen through the acquisition of hose production facilities in Hoogezand, Netherlands, in 1992, and by purchasing Germany-based Polyflex in 1995, which was a European market leader in thermoplastic hoses.[15]

The business in Europe was carefully structured so each country would have its own national trading sub-

sidiary or sales offices run by personnel native to the area. Each had specialized sales forces organized by market, including industrial, mobile, distribution, and automation, similar to North America's efforts. With this organization in place, differences between the United States and Europe were appearing in Parker Hannifin's overseas efforts.[16] Throughout the 1990s, it was apparent that more of the European market was derived from original equipment manufacturers (OEMs) than through distribution, as had been the case in the United States.[17] Yet Parker Hannifin's global business continued its downward cycle in 1993, with flat sales and earnings. Sales decreased and restructuring charges, primarily in Europe, added to the financial downturn.

Parker Hannifin remained positive. Its carefully planned cycle forecasting, implemented during

DUANE COLLINS GETS THE TAP

Duane Collins' career with Parker Hannifin began in 1961 and spanned 45 years. From 1994 to 2000, he grew company sales by 140 percent and earnings by 610 percent, as well as increased earnings per share by 588 percent.

DUANE COLLINS SERVED PARKER HANNIFIN in 10 different roles during the 32 years prior to becoming CEO in 1993, including general manager of the Hose Products Division, president of the Fluid Connectors Group, corporate vice president, and president of the International Sector. As head of International, he had traveled extensively throughout the world and had tremendous knowledge about the global market. Collins' international experience was great training for the direction in which the company was about to embark.

During Collins' tenor with International, for example, the company's European territory comprised 18 countries, with 18 tax authorities and 18 languages. Creating a viable economy of scale under such diverse business conditions was tremendously challenging.

"Each country was essentially a market to itself," Collins said. "The borders were high, the barriers were high. Our challenge was how do we get to the French market and the German market, and so forth."

the 1970s recession, would aid the company as the world economy recovered from the recession of the 1980s.[18]

According to the company's 1993 Annual Report, in spite of the restructuring, Parker Hannifin registered a notable improvement over the previous year's perfor-

mance. Industrial operations in Europe and Brazil were successfully reorganized to counteract the global recession, and Aerospace operations had been scaled back in response to a reduced demand from military and commercial industries. There were significant new efficiencies, as well as debt reduction and positive cash flow.[19]

Collins' solution was to implement new business systems, including treasury and payroll systems, that worked universally throughout the continent, beginning with a single computer system.

Every country had its own computer system, none of which talked to anybody [else], not even within the country to each other. ... So a lot of emphasis was spent there ... . Today, if you want to know what we did yesterday in Finland, we can tell you by part number, by customer, by profit, by sales.[23]

It was this building of International via these types of strategies that not only helped catapult sales of the sector from $300 million annually to the nearly $5 billion it realizes today, but also reinforced Pat Parker's decision to put Collins in charge of International to begin with, and would become the impetus to promote him to CEO.

Although it was no secret in 1992 that Paul Schloemer, president and CEO since 1984, was likely close to retirement, Collins said he was content at the time to continue running International.

"Then I got a call from Pat," he said. "He asked me if I would like to become the CEO of the company."

It was agreed during that conversation that nothing about the succession would be made public for a year, and after a short stint as vice chairman, Collins took over as CEO of Parker Hannifin in 1993.

According to Collins, the company was underperforming during the early 1990s, which meant he had to hit the ground running.

The first order of business was to try to get the company back to making the kind of earnings that we had been doing traditionally. ... The longer range was one of making the groups global, because

up until '92, when I became the vice chairman, we were regional. I was in charge of all international, and I had a counterpart in charge of all North America. So the first thing we did was to make it global immediately. That was in June of 1992. That was the transition year.

Although highlights of Collins' career include the design of Parker Hannifin's global groups concept and global IT infrastructure, as well as the development of the Asian market, he says one of his most important accomplishments, especially early on as CEO, was hammering home the importance of customer service. He maintained that customer service and financial performance are directly related, adding that he had the quantifiable data to prove it division by division throughout the company.

According to Collins:

I went around to our operations ... and the first thing I talked about was customer service. And what I found out was that if, in fact, we weren't serving the customer, if they wanted to name one person who was at fault, it was Duane Collins, because 1) the employee didn't get the message, so they didn't understand that was the emphasis [or] 2) we didn't give them the tools to do it. Because what I found out was that once they understood the message and if, in fact, they had the tools to do it, they did things way beyond anything I could even ask them to do. I would get letters from customers telling me about what a wonderful employee we had or phone calls telling me what great people we had who were then serving the customer. But the people had to have the tools to do it. It's easy for me to say, "Do it," but then if you don't give them the wherewithal to do it, they can't do it.

Parker Hannifin added strength to its North American and European Industrial operations with the acquisition of the Ross hydraulic motor and hydrostatic steering controls business, an added benefit for the Parker Nichols line of hydraulic motors. Purchased from TRW in a cash transaction in 1993, the acquisition provided Parker

Hannifin with plants in Greeneville, Tennessee, and TRW's hydraulic motor assets in Germany.

Additional growth was occurring in Parker Hannifin's Latin America market as well. Lynn Cortright, president of Parker Hannifin's Latin American Group, began recruiting for staff. In 1992, he hired Ricardo Machado,

who was a native of Brazil, as Targets manager for Parker Hannifin's Jacareí, São Paulo, Brazil, facility. He was responsible for incorporating the newly launched Parker Targets program to instill productivity, best manufacturing practices, training, and support from senior management as standard practices in the facilities.[20]

"Two months after [I began], I got a phone call and [Cortright] said, 'Come to the United States. I want to show you some plants.' When I was here, he said, 'I want you to start a fluid connector business in Brazil. We have been trying for many years,'" said Machado, who held several positions, including general manager of Brazil's Fluid Connectors Division in 1994. "He sent me to a Targets seminar. I came back and started Connectors, which was shared with pneumatics.

"[Cortright] was a visionary, in terms of knowing connectors would fit very well in Brazil. I had the official division, which was the pneumatics, but I also [added] some hydraulics. … From the first day, it has been a fantastic experience," said Machado, who was named president of Parker Hannifin's Latin American Group in 2000.[21]

As the Latin American market became viable and the company formed Parker Automotive de Mexico and Parker Fluid Connectors de Mexico in 1994, Parker Europe grew again that year by acquiring the leading Scandinavian filter manufacturer, Finn-Filter Oy.[22] Finn-Filter produced hydraulic filters, diesel filters for marine and automotive applications, vehicle-cab air filters, and particle separators, and had plants in Urjala and Hyrynsalmi, Finland. It also held a Swedish sales subsidiary called Swedab Finn-Filter Svenska A.B.

With all the experience Parker Hannifin had gained through its numerous acquisitions, a certain way of approaching the acquired company was established. Parker Hannifin developed a light, but effective touch. According to Ursula Sawyer, vice president of Information Technology, Climate and Industrial Controls Group:

[Parker Hannifin was] very conscious of the people and how they felt about this big corporation grabbing them. I think [Parker Hannifin] finally realized that the greatest opportunity for change is at the beginning, in the first 100 days when people are expecting change to happen. So if you're going to do it, do it then. You go in there, and the biggest thing is listening to people.

Don't say, "It's our way or the highway." It doesn't matter whether it's their systems you're changing or the customer service or the marketing or what you're doing on the floor. It's kind of the same thing. It's listen to them, and then say, "Okay, here's Parker. Now let's sit down together and figure out how we're going to put this together."

Left: In the early 1990s, many Parker Hannifin aerospace components were used in commercial and military aerospace aftermarket capacities and other related high-tech industries.

Above: The Applied Technologies Group invested in product development, especially gerotors. Three new units in the electromechanical controls segment were created to increase international business, and products were marketed through both international and domestic distributors.

Additional ground was covered in Europe with the acquisition of the Electro-pneumatic Division of Telemecanique in France, a manufacturer of actuators, valves, and air-preparation components for industrial pneumatic applications. Atlas Copco Automation Division, a Swedish manufacturer of pneumatic components for a variety of automation markets, was also added to the European portfolio in 1994. Two years later, Parker Hannifin purchased VOAC (Volvo Atlas Copco) Hydraulics to revive its mobile hydraulics market presence.

"Even though the mobile hydraulic market was volatile, [Parker Hannifin] needed to get back in there," said Kjell Jansson, who was president of VOAC North America in 1996 when it was acquired by Parker Hannifin.

Jansson, who continued with Parker Hannifin to become vice president of sales and marketing, Global Mobile OEM, credited the mobile hydraulics growth to redirecting Parker Hannifin's focus on selling solutions. He continued:

We'll go out to the customer and say, "I'm going to sell an entire system for your machine." Parker helps you design the machine and sell everything on it and take responsibility for the function rather than just selling some product.

VOAC was really the cornerstone in reentering that market. [Parker] sales in the mobile market were, at the time VOAC came in 1996, only $50 million. Today mobile hydraulics sales worldwide are probably around $1.3 billion—a massive change in 10 years.[23]

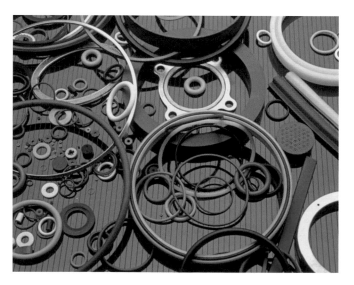

Right: Kjell Jansson, vice president of Sales and Marketing, Global Mobile OEM, helped grow global mobile hydraulics sales from $50 million in 1996 to more than $1 billion today.

Below: The Seal Group experienced competitive pricing pressures in the 1990s, but worked diligently on new products and designs.

In the mid-1990s, Parker Hannifin turned its attention to the Asian market, and Joseph Vicic was tapped to grow this segment of the business. As the Asia Pacific Group president, Vicic was stationed in Hong Kong in 1994, with a staff of 65 employees for the entire region— 15 of these in export services—and approximately $20 million in revenue.[24]

"It was daunting, but being ignorant of the facts, you don't know what you can't do," said Vicic, who began in 1967 as a sales management trainee. "The good thing was I worked for Duane Collins. Duane had a vision. He could always see a little bit more over the horizon. He basically gave me the responsibility to get the job done. He gave me a lot of latitude. It was more strategic planning than fiscal planning. He let me hire great people."

Vicic's first job was to expand the distributor network in the Asian market, which he approached by managing these distributors as partnerships. Vicic recalled:

[Collins] always imparted the fact that if you can't be of influence in Japan, you're probably going to miss out on a big piece of the market. At first, he pushed both China and Japan, but to Mr. Collins, Japan was the Gordian knot [difficult puzzle]. Figure that out, you've got a lot of horsepower behind you. Number two, go for growth—take the high ground. Build a "Parker Fort," and make it difficult for other guys to come in under market penetration. Keep the bad guys away. Get Japan involved because they are the 500-pound gorilla in Asia.[25]

As 1995 ended, Parker Hannifin's businesses in the Asia Pacific region enjoyed significant growth. With strong sales of mobile equipment, semiconductor fabrication, and construction, Korea and Japan provided active and growing markets. The growth was attributed

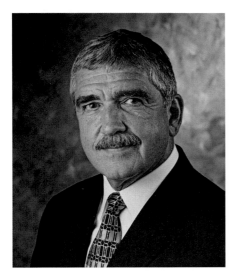

to several investments, including new information systems, additional technical personnel, and employee training programs. Parker Hannifin's Korean hose and fittings and air conditioning joint ventures also received welcome capital improvements.[26]

With only a year under his belt, Vicic's successful contributions in Asia were proof of the type of ambitious leaders Parker Hannifin supported.

Amplified Expansion

Alongside the global growth, the executive team leading Parker Hannifin's United States operations was also expanding.

"I promoted Nick Vande Steeg to be head of the Seal Group, and my controller was John Zakaria, who was my right-hand man. We pretty much ran the industrial part of the business. We had a great team," said Sullivan, who served as executive vice president, Industrial and Automotive, in 1996. "I had fun doing what I was doing."[27]

The Industrial and Automotive team had impressive results, with fiscal 1996 showing increases in sales and global penetration for the Seal Group. With four new plants in the Czech Republic, Denmark, Italy, and Mexico, the Group also benefited from investments in facilities and technology, as well as employees' efforts to improve efficiency. When Vande Steeg became president of the Seal Group of North America, the O-Ring Division, which had been one of the most profitable divisions at the company, was losing ground. Things were not looking well, as Vande Steeg explained:

Left: Joe Vicic retired as Asia Pacific Group President in 2008 after more than 41 years of service at Parker.

Center: Dennis Sullivan, who started with Parker Hannifin in 1960 and held positions including president of the Fluid Connectors Group and president of the Fluidpower Group, retired as executive vice president of the company in 2003.

Right: Upon his promotion in 1996 to president of the Seal Group, Nick Vande Steeg had by 1998 returned the lagging group to one of the highest performing in the company.

The first board meeting I went to, one of the board members, Allen Ford said, "Nick, I find it interesting that you'd be willing to become the president of this Group. They're not doing well, and I think we ought to sell them." I said, "Would you wait for a couple of years and let me take a run at this?" He said, "I don't know if you've got that kind of time."

Vande Steeg dove in and began learning all he could about the business, including identifying what was not being done correctly. His efforts paid off immensely.

"We brought it back. Today, the O-Ring Division is once again one of the highest performing divisions in the corporation," said Vande Steeg, who would go on to become president and COO of Parker Hannifin.[28]

In 1998, the Seal Group reported record worldwide results, with sharply higher revenues reflecting market share gains in North American automotive

and industrial markets. Kurt Müller, European Seal Group president, reported higher sales volume due in part to the rebounding German economy and expanded market share in hydraulic and pneumatic sealing system applications. With 21 manufacturing plants and more than 200 distributors worldwide, as well as joint ventures in Mexico and China, the Seal Group successfully regained its lead.[29]

While the Aerospace Group had seen downsizing and restructuring in previous years, it was finally headed in a positive direction. Having spent more than 21 years with Parker Aerospace, Steve Hayes, appointed president of the Group in 1993, had seen significant growth throughout the past two decades. But he admitted that

---

According to Pat Parker, the company's components were omnipresent—they were used in every man-made device that moved. Parts functioned in applications ranging from watches and fuel systems to controls in commercial airlines.

when taking over, there had been a downturn.[30] There was a concerted effort to bring the Group's performance up. Hayes explained:

During my tenure as president we made the largest acquisition that Parker had ever made. In 1996, we acquired a company called [Abex] National Water Lift, headquartered in Kalamazoo, Michigan. It was called NWL, and it was in hydraulic pumps and flight controls.[31]

Seen as an investment for growth, Abex NWL would allow for continued expansion of Parker Hannifin Aerospace system capabilities in hydraulics and flight control actuation, providing an edge when compared with component-only suppliers. Parker Aerospace established record sales volume in 1998, with commercial transport, business jet, and general aviation segments reporting strong figures.[32]

The economy also favored the Fluid Connectors Group. With Jack Myslenski as its president in 1998, Fluid

DISTRIBUTORS: CORNERSTONES OF BUSINESS

PART OF PARKER HANNIFIN'S evolution into a multibillion dollar global corporation involves its network of distributors. By providing these companies with the highest level of service, support, and training, the Parker ethic of high-quality products and top-shelf service trickles down and is delivered through these agents to the end customer. In addition to distributor training programs, Parker created a Distributor Advisory Council (DAC) in 1997, which meets twice a year to assist distributors with issues outside the fundamentals covered in regular training.[1]

The JetStick, a water jet propulsion system in which the steering and the motion of the boat are controlled by a joystick, was developed by Parker Hannifin and one of the company's distributors, The Hope Group, for the Hinckley Company.

Following are testimonials from company distributors about how their organizations function as extensions of Parker Hannifin.

"We found [Parker Hannifin] to be a good company to work with," said David Parks, executive president/division head of Hydradyne Hydraulics, a $140 million distribution company based in Harvey, Louisiana. "We have similar philosophies of business about providing a full motion control solution to the customer, and Parker affords us that opportunity."[2] About 70 percent of Hydradyne's product offering comes from Parker Hannifin, but there are challenges. Parks explained:

The challenge a distributor has with a manufacturer is that we always have the challenge of helping them to be better at what they do. How good they are at what they do is going to have a direct impact on how good we are at what we do. ... Parker's training programs are the best in the industry. They're very proactive on training and recognize the importance of having people in the field who know and understand the products and know how to apply them. They're pretty serious about making sure that those standards are met and maintained.[3]

"One of the great strengths of Parker is its people," said Gustavo Cudell of Gustavo Cudell, Lda., in Oporto, Portugal. "They are enthusiastic and trustworthy people, and they are very familiar with the local culture of our country and also with other countries. They also have a full product range in hydraulic equipment, and it's increasing ... it's becoming more and more complete."[4]

Randy Gross, CEO of the York, Pennsylvania–based RG Group, a $35 million industrial distribution and small manufacturing business, explained how his company functions almost as a representative of Parker Hannifin:

We provide value in solution selling as a team with Parker with all their products and their engineering experience, and we're an extension of Parker. Communication coming out from Parker on new products, and the dedication to introducing new products is pretty strong.[5]

Because Parker Hannifin is composed of autonomous groups and divisions, sometimes the distribu-

tors' responsibility is to provide solutions' packages to customers. In this manner, the distributors allow customers one relationship—instead of working with multiple contacts—for all their product needs.

"We're supposed to know how to get that done, and that's what we promote in the marketplace," added Gross. "We're a 'relationship guy' with lots of technical [products], and if we don't have them, we can get them."

"They encourage companies like ourselves to provide systems solutions," added Carey Rhoten, president of The Hope Group in Northboro, Massachusetts, which is a distributor of Parker Hannifin products. "The Sorenson Systems portion of Hope is about a $7 million business providing custom solutions utilizing principally Parker components. We perform this consulting role with the customer, and once you do that, you really are in a strong position for both retention and expansion with the customer."[6]

Kohler GmbH, a distributor based in Germany, gains 70 percent of its machine tooling business through Parker Hannifin components. The company works with five Parker Hannifin groups, and Klaus Kohler was also the first president of the DAC.

"Parker fits our strategic goal, and naturally, I'd say that very often the leaders are not the cheapest ones," said Kohler. "They are relatively expensive, and we have to be innovative with distribution systems, special supplying, special products … lots of kitting."[7]

Aside from being innovative with product, Kohler added that as Parker Hannifin grows through acquisitions, he can increase his company's business, depending on new products. If the acquired company offers products that haven't been available previously, another line is opened for distributors.[8]

According to Luis Antonio Frade of Louritex, Lda., Lourinha, Portugal, his company manufactures machinery that shears and bales scrap metals using Parker Hannifin parts. His machines have a cutting power between 400 and 1,300 tons.

Completing the System

Parker Hannifin has had a unique position in participating in the design of the JetStick, a water jet propulsion system in which the steering and the motion of the boat are controlled by a joystick, for the Portsmouth, Rhode Island–based Hinckley Company. It's a perfect example of how Parker Hannifin has worked to support its distributors—in this case, The Hope Group—and its customers seamlessly, meeting everyone's needs.

"One of our bigger customers is Hinckley, and we have designed and built a [hydroelectric] control module for its JetStick controls. It's 100 percent Parker, 100 percent designed and built by us, and we build about 100 systems a year," said Rhoten.[9]

According to Edward A. Roberts, vice president of marketing for the Hinckley Company, the reliability of Parker Hannifin products was a primary factor in collaborating with the company. Parker Hannifin's alliance with Hinckley began in 1994; the JetStick was incorporated in 1996. "There was a fair amount of developmental work done together," Roberts explained. "You literally control the boat with three fingers, and you can make it do anything you want."[10]

Taylor Machine Works in Louisville, Mississippi, has been using Parker Hannifin parts since the 1960s. According to Mike Boyles, director of engineering, the company builds 1,000 vehicles per year, including 110,000-pound capacity forklifts.

"We make all kinds of mobile material handling equipment: mid-range and large forklifts, empty and loaded container handlers, cranes, all kinds of specialty vehicles," Boyles explained. "We buy the components, and then we control the system design on our end. Parker Hannifin does an outstanding job for us. We believe in [relationships when] marketing our products. We like and respect that from our suppliers as well. They have some great people who really understand the different applications of hydraulics."[11]

Parker Hannifin's Racor Division, acquired in 1985, produces fuel/water separators that filter out contaminants that could harm marine diesel power systems.

Connectors acquired Temeto A.B., a leading Swedish distributor of hydraulic components, and Extrudit, a successful British tubing company. The Group also prided itself on its quick-response service for customers, an accomplishment attributed in part to the global network of ParkerStores®, that started out as walk-in hose and fitting outlets that offer 24-hour service and stock more than 3,000 different items.

"The ParkerStore® program and Hose Doctors program were two of the big thrusts from the Hose Division that were eminently successful," explained Don Zito, who was president of the Fluid Connectors Group at the time.

Stores were owned and operated by the distributors. Zito recalled how the idea was successful from the start, with one East Coast distributor adding more stores to the six he already had.

"It was, I think, an entrepreneurial distributorship, and [that distributor] made the investment, got it profitable, and then made another one. It was really quite phenomenal," said Zito.

LARRY HOPCRAFT: A REMEMBERED COLLEAGUE

LAWRENCE "LARRY" HOPCRAFT JOINED PARKER Hannifin in 1973 as vice president, controller, with responsibility for the Fluid Connectors and Automotive Air Conditioning Products Groups. He earned many promotions and was eventually appointed corporate vice president in 1990, a year after being promoted to president of the Automotive and Refrigeration Group. This new position included global travel. On September 2, 1998, Hopcraft and his wife Pauline ("Polly") boarded Swissair Flight 111 at John F. Kennedy International Airport in New York City and headed to Cointrin International Airport in Geneva. Less than two hours after departure, the plane crashed into the ocean off the coast of Nova Scotia, killing all 229 people aboard. Hopcraft's career spanned more than 20 years with Parker Hannifin.

ParkerStores® were so successful that new locations grew by 50 percent in 1998. Customer satisfaction was also enhanced through Parker's Kitting Service, which offered preassembled packages of connectors and related components that were shipped and invoiced as a single unit.[33]

The Hydraulics Group also had success in 1998. Its president, Don Washkewicz, posted double-digit results in the United States and Europe, while Automation Group President John Oelslager increased his group's volume modestly despite a volatile market. Filtration remained solid, with a continuation of double-digit growth and U.S. volume strong due to major activity in energy, automotive, food and beverage, agriculture, and diesel engine markets.

Part of Parker Hannifin's strength in filtration came from its acquisition of Racor Industries in 1985. Craig Maxwell, who started with Parker Hannifin's Racor Division in 1996, and eventually became corporate vice president of Technology and Innovation, explained his introduction to the company:

When I came to Parker to interview at the Racor Division, my wife was with me. To this day, she still says [that] the thing she noticed was everyone was smiling. When she visited me [at my previous employer], nobody was smiling. Everyone had their head down, just charging forward. Every single year since 1985, the Racor Division had grown 18 percent, both in sales and earnings.

When I got there in 1996, we celebrated that the division had reached $70 million in sales. It was clear to me that they had such a wealth of talent there, such a deep bench. They were growing, but we could grow a lot faster if we got them focused on really big projects.[34]

Parker Hannifin launched its first external home page on the World Wide Web in April 1996. The Web page featured rotating images of Parker products, which illustrated its breadth of product lines.

On the Home Front

Plans were already in motion at Parker Hannifin's corporate headquarters in Cleveland as the new millennium approached. In 1997, because the existing headquarters were not sufficient to take the company into the 21st century, contractors were busy raising steel for a new headquarters on the site of an old golf course in nearby Mayfield Heights, Ohio. According to Washkewicz, while clearing the property, a golf ball with a Frank Sinatra logo was found that was estimated to be almost 40 years old. The 200,000-square-foot

Parker NEWS network

Inside This Issue
• Duane Collins shares Parker 2000 vision
• Tornado strikes O-Ring

MAY 1996

NEWS AND INFORMATION FOR PARKER EMPLOYEES

News Scan

HYDRAULIC FILTER EXPANDS

The Hydraulic Filter Division, Metamora, Ohio, broke ground last month on a 28,000-square-foot plant expansion that will improve manufacturing flexibility, production throughput and quality. A major portion of the expansion will be devoted to manufacturing filter elements in an environmentally controlled area. Existing office space will be refurbished to accommodate a training room, R&D lab, and employee lunchroom. Completion date: October 1996.

PARKER IMPROVES FORTUNE 500 RANKING

Fortune magazine recently unveiled its annual list of the 500 largest publicly-owned companies in America. Parker ranked 386th on the 1995 list, up from 437th a year ago. Overall rankings are based on annual revenues. In other rankings, Parker was 292nd in profits, 402nd in assets, 343rd in stockholders' equity and 337th in total return to investors.

PNEUMATIC DIVISION ANNOUNCES CHANGES

To improve the Pneumatic Division's (Richland, Mich.) position in the marketplace, Larry Reinhart, General Manager, has announced the following promotions and organizational changes, effective immediately: Larry Ryba, National Sales Manager; George Peletis, Engineering Manager; Jaime Beingolea, Cuyahoga Falls, Ohio, plant; and Mike Leffler, Product Sales Manager-Controls. **P**

Parker launches Web site

Parker's home page on the World Wide Web as seen when accessed with Netscape Navigator software. The product pictured on the center of the page transforms into another product every three seconds, illustrating Parker's breadth of product line.

Parts that perfect the whole.
Welcome to Parker Hannifin Corporation

Parker has entered a new frontier—cyberspace.

On April 19, Parker launched its official home page on the World Wide Web at the address http://www.parker.com. The site contains corporate information including recent news releases and financial highlights, organizational information, a products and services summary, and literature request and e-mail correspondence sections.

(Continued on page 2)

Customer Service

Listening to the customer

What is premier customer service? The voice of the customer provides the only true direction for any organization, states the Parker Targets Strategic Objectives. This means that we must first determine what the customer needs and wants. How do we find out?

"To provide premier service, we knew that we had to do the things that were the most important to our customers. We decided that asking them what they wanted would be the best way to find out," says John Fairhurst, Operations Manager - United Kingdom, for the Pneumatics Division in Cannock, England.

So the Division developed a questionnaire and sent it to its top 50 customers. The survey asked them to rate the Division's delivery performance, professionalism and attitude of staff, range and quality of products, distribution, overall rating, and four specific future suggestions.

(Continued on page 3)

Abex acquired

Aerospace organization changes announced

Parker completed the acquisition of the aerospace assets of Abex NWL Division of Pneumo Abex Corporation April 15 for $201 million. Parker now has the industry's most complete hydraulic line, notes Steve Hayes, President of the Parker Bertea Aerospace Group.

"With our new market segments in engine-driven pumps, thrust-reverser actuator systems, and electrohydraulic servovalves, Parker now will be able to meet the increasing desires of our key customers to work with a limited number of suppliers who provide a wide range of products."

Abex recorded sales of about $200 million in calendar 1995 and has 1,290 employees worldwide. It has operations in Kalamazoo, Mich., Dublin, Ga.,

(Continued on page 2)

Stephanie Streeter elected to Parker Board of Directors

Streeter

Parker has elected Stephanie A. Streeter, Vice President and General Manager of Avery Dennison Brands for Avery Office Products, to the Parker Board of Directors. Avery Office Products, based in Diamond Bar, Calif., is an $898 million sector within Avery Dennison Corporation, a $3 billion Fortune 500 company.

(Continued on page 4)

facility was designed to accelerate administrative operations and to meet the technological requirements of the information system needs of a global company.[35] This pivotal business and demographic change for Parker Hannifin was led by Syd Kershaw. A Parker Hannifin employee since 1968, Kershaw was the vice president of manufacturing in charge of moving the company from its factory on Euclid Avenue to 34 acres in Mayfield Heights. Kershaw made certain that the new, modern building would have allotted infrastructure, including video at each desktop, a full-service cafeteria, and a fitness center.[36]

The impending move was also of great interest to Pat, who remained entrenched in Parker Hannifin's daily business as chairman of its board—an involvement of which Kershaw was keenly aware.

"I was getting ready at corporate headquarters, and we're having all these meetings. Pat liked to sit in on some of them. For some reason, I forgot to invite Pat to the meeting," said Kershaw. "I went in [to Pat's office] and said, 'Pat, we had the meeting. I forgot to invite you.' He said, 'Syd, that's a problem. Anytime you forget my name, just go outside and look up on the building. You see the sign?' He had a good sense of humor."[37]

As Parker Hannifin moved 500 employees into its new headquarters in late 1997, it had become officially prepared for the 12 acquisitions it would make in 1998.

Parker purchased Skinner Valve and Lucifer, a solenoid valve business from Honeywell, as well as purchasing Dynamic Valves, Inc., and Veriflo Corporation in 1998. Global additions would follow in 1999 through an alliance with Kuroda Precision Industries in Tokyo and the purchase of Nylaflow in the Netherlands.

Larry Zeno, who retired in 2001 as corporate vice president, Office of the President, emphasized that having the right equipment was helpful, but that success was unattainable without the efforts of the company's employees.

"You can buy all the nice machines and build all these beautiful buildings, but if you don't have the people to get the job done, none of that makes any difference," explained Zeno.

Zeno said that about half of his time in the Office of the President was spent in tasks that ultimately expanded the capabilities of Parker Hannifin employees.

Pat Parker hired Lawrence Gipe to paint "Pointing the Way to the Future," which hung on the wall in the fourth-floor lobby at Parker Hannifin's Euclid Avenue headquarters. The painting cost $30,000—paid for by Pat—and was donated to the Cleveland Historical Society when Parker Hannifin moved to Mayfield Heights in 1997. *(Printed by permission, courtesy of Lawrence Gipe.)*

"In the Parker spirit, leaders have substantially different qualities," said Pat. Pat retired in 1999 after serving 46 years. He continued:

First, someone who is really leading, listens. Not because you're told to, not because you want to be polite or wait your turn to advance your ideas, but because you want to—and you need to—really understand what is happening. A second quality is the ability to come up with ideas. These are the engines that propel the Parker force. Good idea people, like good listeners, are not born. They are made.

In addition, a leader needs a sense of humor, or rather a sense of proportion. Look, [stuff] happens. More than anything else, your Parker teammates, up and down the line, will judge you on how you handle the crises you create for yourself and those around you.[38]

With the year 2000 approaching, Parker Hannifin looked with pride at its contributions to engineering throughout the previous 70 years, the most significant being the first-in-the-industry integration of hydraulic, pneumatic, and electromechanical technologies.[39]

"Combining these three technologies has given us a unique niche in engineering," Pat said. "There probably is nowhere in the world that you can go and not be touched by a Parker product that is somehow improving the standard of living.

"We've worked hard to build an organization with innovation, technical excellence, superior product quality, and premier customer service as our core competencies.

In 1998, Chairman Pat Parker, right, stands in front of Parker Hannifin's new Mayfield Heights, Ohio, corporate headquarters with members of the Office of the President (left to right): Vice President Lawrence Zeno, Executive Vice President Dennis Sullivan, and President and CEO Duane Collins. The 200,000-square-foot building was constructed in 1996 and 1997 from precast concrete, steel, and glass.

We are in business for the long-term, and our strategy remains to pursue attractive opportunities that beckon from many markets of the world."[40]

ENGINEERING YOUR SUCCESS.

Parker Parker Hannifin Corporation Annual Report 2007
The Premier Diversified Motion & Control Company

Parker Hannifin crossed the $10 billion mark in net sales for the first time in fiscal year 2007, topping $12.15 billion in fiscal 2008.

WINNING FOR THE FUTURE

2000 AND BEYOND

2000 Sales: $5.4 Billion | 2008 Sales: $12.15 Billion

If you listen to the customer and do what the customer wants, you'll never go wrong. Don't do what's best for Parker, do what's best for the customer. … Organize around the customer's needs, because the customer pays the bills. Our new brand promise reflects this—that partnering with our customers to increase their productivity and profitability will ensure our long-term success.

—Don Washkewicz, CEO

FROM ITS BEGINNINGS IN 1918, Parker Hannifin has focused on innovation, stemming from Art Parker's idea of a pneumatic braking system. Throughout each decade, the company drew from both hardship and success to strengthen its culture of hard work, collaboration, and product quality.[1]

As the 21st century approached, Parker Hannifin was even more driven to provide precision-engineered solutions for the commercial, mobile, industrial, and aerospace markets. Under the leadership of Duane Collins, president and CEO since 1993, sales more than doubled—and earnings quadrupled. At the end of 1999, Collins was named chairman, replacing Pat Parker. Don Washkewicz was promoted to president and chief operating officer (COO).

A Winning Strategy

When Washkewicz took over as president and COO at Parker Hannifin corporate headquarters in February 2000, he admitted the company's success was laudable, yet its operating performance had remained static, mostly in the "middle of its peers."[2]

"As I assumed responsibilities as the COO, I knew I needed to find a way to take the company to new heights. I'm in the corner office. I can do nothing, or I can decide to do something transformational," said Washkewicz, who at the time was a 28-year veteran of Parker Hannifin. "The business was running well, but the broader question was where do we want to take it from here? I could see the potential of Parker and its hardworking employees."

By building on Collins' goals of premier customer service, financial performance, and profitable growth, Washkewicz started devising ways to achieve these objectives and succinctly communicate them to all employees around the world. "The ultimate objective was to drive operational excellence and growth, which would lead to top quartile returns on invested capital relative to our peers and a higher P/E (price earnings multiple) for

Don Washkewicz, chairman of the board and CEO, often refers to Duane Collins, who retired as chairman of the board and CEO in 2004, as one of his mentors.

Parker stock," noted Washkewicz. Heeding Collins' directive to "get out and see a lot," Washkewicz traveled more than 200 days in his first year as president and COO, visiting 200 of the company's 250 global facilities to learn about divisions in which he hadn't worked directly.[3] Ingrained with Pat's continuous improvement program, Targets, Washkewicz understood its mission of productivity, production throughput, quality, cost reduction, and customer service from his days as a general manager in the 1980s. Yet the obstacles in the new millennium would prove daunting in terms of implementing this methodology.

Possibly the result of the burst dot-com bubble and excessive spending on technology to combat the never-realized Y2K bug, the early 2000s brought the beginning of the worst industrial recession the United States and many Western countries had seen in decades.[4] Parker Hannifin was facing declining orders and falling profits.[5] In spite of the recession, Washkewicz could have simply maintained operations. Instead, he developed a plan to add value, a strategic plan of overall operational excellence, improved return on invested capital, and continued to acquire companies, including Commercial Intertech and Wynn's International, in the two largest deals in the company's history.

Left: Don Washkewicz visited Parker Hannifin facilities worldwide in search of the best corporate practices, which became the initiatives embedded in the company's Win Strategy.

Below: Parker Hannifin's Win Strategy was created and organized by Don Washkewicz. Driving operational excellence and growth, it would become the game plan for empowering employees and adding value throughout the company.

"Our focus on premier customer service, strategic acquisitions, and continuous improvement through Targets was working well, but I wanted to take Parker to the next level," said Washkewicz. "The idea was to identify pockets of excellence throughout the company and benchmark best practices throughout industry, and then rally the entire global workforce to implement proven tools for success."

While traveling through hundreds of Parker Hannifin facilities, Washkewicz carried a blank sheet of paper. He intended to fill the paper with an easily understood strategy—an instrument for change. With a vision to be the No. 1 worldwide motion and control company, he focused on the $6 billion potential for growth in the

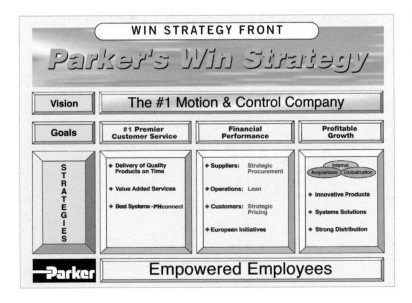

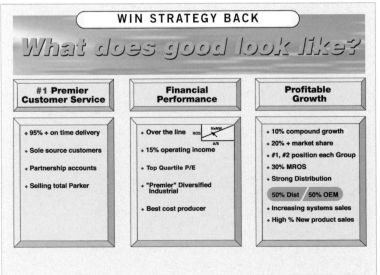

$50 billion market. Washkewicz was hopeful his employees would offer suggestions to create a Win Strategy.[6] Strongly rooted in his faith, Don also felt he received guidance on a more personal level as he set out to transform the company.

One part of the strategy was found in a division of Parker Aerospace in Ogden, Utah. This particular facility utilized lean manufacturing, a management philosophy focused on reducing seven wastes to improve overall customer value, including transportation, inventory, motion, waiting time, over-production, processing, and defective product.[7] The process was pioneered by Toyota and utilized single-piece flow, waste elimination, just-in-time production and delivery, and minimizing inventory.[8] According to lean philosophy, the elimination of waste improves quality and reduces production time and costs.

By incorporating lean initiatives, which include a constant process of analysis, "pull" production, and mistake-proofing, the Aerospace plant in Utah demonstrated impressive reduction in inventory, increased productivity and operating returns, and rising cash flow.[9]

"It was the most impressive presentation I had seen yet," Washkewicz said. "I thought, 'Wouldn't it be interesting if we could get all of Parker's manufacturing locations to execute lean?' Lean went on the paper."

"The lean enterprise initiative was a significant shift in perspective to Parker's continuous improvement journey," said Kathryn Miller, vice president, Lean Enterprise and Quality. "Once fully implemented, it would enable us to begin delivering value to our customers while remaining focused on the highest quality and lowest cost. Our lean system builds upon engaging employees to develop solutions that eliminate waste and ultimately facilitates shortened lead times in our manufacturing value streams. The next phase of development in the company's pursuit of operational excellence would include extending lean practices into Parker's non-manufacturing value streams."

Through his travels, Washkewicz also added strategic procurement to leverage the global procurement of goods and services. While Parker Hannifin was generating close to 11 percent return on sales, Washkewicz' goal

Tim Pistell joined the office of the chief executive as executive vice president of finance and administration and international chief financial officer in 2005.

was to reach 15 percent, and with the new strategy, he was certain he could close the gap.[10]

"The global procurement strategy was part of a tremendous cultural change in the way we work collectively across all divisions and groups to manage and leverage the spend of Parker," commented John Dedinsky, vice president, Global Supply Chain and Procurement. "It meant transforming a tactical procurement organization into a more strategic one. The new strategy emphasized strategic relationships between suppliers and Parker as the foundation for long-term agreements that required significant commitments from both sides."

"One division presented an impressive purchasing plan," noted Washkewicz. "When you are a decentralized company, it's hard to leverage what you spend. Decisions that direct the $3 billion-plus we were spending each year on materials and services are made by 125 divisions. We needed a strategic plan in order to leverage the entire company's purchasing power."

Parker Hannifin implemented a strategic purchasing program that established competitive, long-term contracts with a reduced number of suppliers. It collaborated more closely with its suppliers on product development to save money.[11]

For the third financial performance measure of the Win Strategy, Washkewicz examined Parker Hannifin's pricing system. Historically, the company had added a margin to manufacturing costs when establishing prices, yet after driving down manufacturing costs and then adding a margin to the newly lowered cost, Parker Hannifin was giving away its gains.[12] All the improvements from the company's lean and strategic procurement efforts would be lost with this approach.

After studying the pricing of products, Washkewicz discovered that more than half were considered "high-volume runners," which are priced competitively, with a lot of elasticity in product demand. The remaining

THE WALL STREET JOURNAL.

TUESDAY, MARCH 27, 2007

CHANGING THE FORMULA

Seeking Perfect Prices, CEO Tears Up the Rules

Parker's Washkewicz Weighs Market Power Of 800,000 Parts

By Timothy Aeppel

CLEVELAND—In early 2001, shortly after Donald Washkewicz took over as chief executive of Parker Hannifin Corp., he came to an unnerving conclusion. The big industrial-parts maker's pricing scheme was crazy.

For as long as anyone at the 89-year-old company could recall, Parker used the same simple formula to determine prices of its 800,000 parts—from heat-resistant seals for jet engines to steel valves that hoist buckets on cherry pickers. Company managers would calculate how much it cost to make and deliver each product and add a flat percentage on top, usually aiming for about 35%. ... the method

Donald Washkewicz

While touring the company's 225 facilities in 2001, Mr. Washkewicz had an epiphany: Parker had to stop thinking like a widget maker and start thinking like a retailer, determining prices by what a customer is willing to pay rather than what a product costs to make. Such "strategic" pricing schemes are used by many different industries. Airlines know they can get away charging more for a seat to Florida in January than in August. Sports teams raise ticket prices if they're playing a well-known opponent. Why shouldn't Parker do the same, Mr. Washkewicz reasoned.

Today, the company says its new pricing approach boosted operating income by $200 million since 2002. That helped Parker's net income soar to $673 million last year from $130 million in 2002. Now, the company's return on invested capital has risen from 7% in 2002 to 21% in 2006, putting it on the verge of moving into the top 25% of Mr. Washkewicz's list comparing Parker with "peer" industrial companies.

From the end of 2001 to present, Parker's shares have risen nearly 88% to about $86, compared to a 25% gain in the S&P 500.

For the past several years, many U.S. manufacturers have struggled to raise prices amid the growth of global competition and cost-cutting drives among customers. While this erosion of pricing power is often cited as a factor that has helped tame inflation, it put a strain on U.S. manufacturing, which contributes 12% to the nation's gross domestic product.

Fighting Back

Now, a growing number of manufacturers are trying to fight back by scrutinizing ... mption un...

manufacturer generally can't see its rivals' prices. Discussing pricing with competitors is illegal, while published list prices from other manufacturers mean little in industrial markets, where most deals are negotiated. And pricing changes were certain to alienate some customers.

In October 2001, Mr. Washkewicz unveiled his big plan, which involved creating a new senior position for pricing and bringing in a host of outside consultants. Many managers throughout the company's 115 divisions immediately balked. There was so much pushback the CEO eventually assembled a list of the 50 most commonly given reasons why the new pricing scheme would fail. If a manager came up with an argument not already on the list, then Mr. Washkewicz agreed to hear it out. Otherwise, he told them, get on board.

"You're messing with a company's DNA when you change how you do prices," says Richard Braun, Parker's vice president of corporate strategic pricing, the position created that October.

It didn't help that Parker, like many manufacturers, has a conservative culture that treasures continuity. Founded in 1918 as a maker of hydraulic brakes for trucks, the company had a descendant of the founder as its chairman as recently as 1999. Today, Parker is a leading producer of industrial parts used in aerospace, transportation and manufacturing. It makes components used in everything from the space shuttle to a mechanism that helped tilt a faux steamship for the movie "Titanic."

A Lifer

Like many Parker executives, Mr. Washkewicz is a lifer. He attended Cleveland State U...

---

products offered an opportunity for value pricing. Washkewicz explained:

We implemented a market-based pricing initiative across the company. This, along with the lean and purchasing programs, would become known as the Win Strategy's 'centrally led initiatives.' The Win Strategy initiated a huge culture shift for our decentralized organization. If you want to be the very best in our business, customer service is a given, and you better be able to do three things very well: Buy at the best value, manufacture at the best cost, and price to the market. That's how strategic procurement, lean, and strategic pricing work together to support operational excellence. Lastly, you must innovate and grow. Profitable growth would become the third leg of our Win Strategy.

The Wall Street Journal featured a profile of CEO Don Washkewicz in its March 27, 2007, edition, explaining how his revamping of Parker Hannifin's pricing strategy increased company profits. *(Reprinted with permission of* The Wall Street Journal, *Copyright © 2007 Dow Jones & Company, Inc. All Rights Reserved Worldwide.)*

After a year of deliberate planning, Washkewicz developed the Win Strategy and began implementation of it in 2001 with a single goal: Raise the performance of the company to a higher level.[13] Parker Hannifin had been created—and had excelled—under entrepreneurial leadership within each division, with minimal direction from corporate headquarters. Now, a sudden

cultural shift launched from the top required an equal, mandatory change for everyone. The new mantra to the leadership team was "execution–accountability–results."

"If we had made the strategy optional, it would not have been adopted by the vast majority because change is never easy. The only way we would meaningfully change the performance of the company was by executing the Win Strategy in every division, worldwide. Each division works very hard to achieve success, and they had all established different ways to make that happen over the years. It's a big deal to change the way you do business while you are struggling through a recession. Implementation of the Win Strategy was not an option, and we were prepared to spend the money needed to bring in the best resources to lead and educate our employees."

To discourage resistance to the change, Washkewicz created an audit team to visit facilities and make certain the Win Strategy was being implemented uniformly across the company. General managers were assured that the plan would create more effective purchasing, pricing, manufacturing, and ultimately growth. Additionally, Washkewicz created "champions" for lean, pricing, procurement, and innovation at the corporate level to ensure full implementation.[14]

"As you put in lean, and you get more visibility into each cell, each cell has a team improvement board. Each value stream has a value stream improvement board," explained Tom Williams, executive vice president and operating officer.[15]

The boards provided more visibility and promoted employee involvement. These self-directed work teams were ideal in that they allowed for employee participation. According to Williams, "the people who are doing the work know better than anybody else how to make it better. We want [employees'] ideas on how to plan better, how to improve."

"You have to grow the business, and grow it profitably," said Washkewicz. "That's where the right-hand

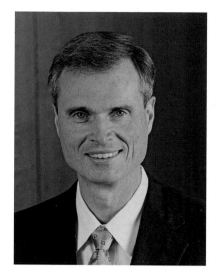

Left: Tom Williams, executive vice president and operating officer, predicts growth in the healthcare, environmental, energy, and water industries.

Below: Commercial Intertech Chairman and CEO Paul Powers (left) and Parker Chairman and CEO Duane Collins exchange company hats to show their support and enthusiasm for joining the two companies. Commercial Intertech merged with Parker on April 11, 2000, in a cash-and-stock transaction with an equity value of approximately $366 million—Parker Hannifin's largest deal at the time.

side of the Win Strategy comes into play. We provided metrics to achieve the high-level goals set forth in the strategy. We wanted to educate and assist divisions to help them be successful."

Maintaining Efficiency

There were two departments, however, that had been effectively working in a centralized manner for years. According to Raymond Doyle, manager of tax audits and special projects, and an employee since 1976, real estate taxes and personal property taxes were always handled—and would remain—with corporate responsibility. Doyle explained:

It's easier for us to do it here. For the State of Ohio, when you do a personal property tax return, it has to be a consolidated return. It has to have all your locations in Ohio put on one return and submitted to the State of Ohio. We couldn't let each location send a return in.

When I started here, we did everything for the divisions. We still do now. It's just 10 times, 20 times, bigger. More locations.[16]

The legal department would also remain centralized. "We have 18

attorneys altogether—15 in Cleveland, one at Aerospace in Irvine, two at Hemel Hempstead [in the United Kingdom], and five paralegals," said Tom Piraino, general counsel and secretary. "It's not decentralized, which is interesting about the legal department, but it makes sense to have all the attorneys right here where they can work with each other and get peer review. It helps to have everyone in one place."[17]

Determination through Turmoil

With a long-term goal of 10-percent growth per year, Parker Hannifin continued to acquire and expand. In 2000, Parker Hannifin purchased Commercial Intertech, an international manufacturer based in Youngstown, Ohio, for $366 million in cash and stock, plus the assumption of $107 million in Commercial Intertech debt.[18] The merger, which was the biggest deal in company history, allowed Parker Hannifin to market a complete range of advanced motion and control technologies to a number of industries, including truck equipment and transportation, construction, refuse and material handling, and agriculture and turf care.

"Commercial Intertech is a great fit with our growth model and long-term strategy of being the premier provider of complete motion and control systems," said Collins.

As Commercial Intertech was integrated into Parker Hannifin's Hydraulics Group, the company also acquired Gresen Hydraulics; combined, these acquisitions had facilities in Minneapolis, Sarasota, and São Paulo. It also acquired Gummi Metall Scheufele & Gienger in Germany. Landing the two acquisitions simultaneously was a major accomplishment for Parker Hannifin and catapulted the segment into the largest in the company.

Additional growth came from acquiring the assets of the Balston division of Whatman's Industrial Filtration, which manufactured high-quality purification products and gas generators for a variety of industrial applications—an asset for the Filtration Group, which was led by John Oelslager when the acquisition was completed in May 2000.[19]

As the summer began, the Seal Group, lead by Group President Nickolas Vande Steeg, completed its largest acquisition to date with the purchase of Wynn's International for approximately $497 million. The acquisition allowed Parker Hannifin to offer aerospace, marine, and mobile customers more complete assemblies, including Wynn's sealing systems for onboard air conditioning, gas, and fluid management.[20] While the purchase was an overall coup for Parker Hannifin, nearly doubling the size of the group, Vande Steeg was charged with the daunting task of making it a success.[21] Vande Steeg explained:

Wynn's had just bought a company called Goshen Rubber that wasn't making any money. Within Wynn's, some plants and divisions were making huge profits and others were losing money. [After we made the acquisition], Goshen closed 18 facilities, some of them small, consolidated field sales forces. A couple of years later they were making 15 percent. It turned out to be a great acquisition, but [it] took every ounce of energy for two years that we could muster. It was the largest number of facilities that were closed in anything that we've bought in the history of the company.[22]

Acquisitions in 2001 added more than $830 million in annual sales, in addition to representing significant systems opportunities. That January, Stainless Connections Ltd. of Australia and New Zealand was purchased to provide engineered and customized stainless steel fittings and adaptors to mobile and industrial markets. Shortly after, SBC Electronics of Milan, Italy, expanded Parker Hannifin's reach into the European markets for highly engineered motion controllers and digital servo drives used in a variety of industrial processes, including packaging, assembly, printing, and textile manufacturing. Netherlands-based Fairey Arlon, a manufacturer of hydraulic filters, rounded out the European expansion, while U.S.-based Miller Fluid Power and Wilkerson were acquired from CKD-Creatac, located in Japan.[23]

Growing through Difficulty

Yet 2001 would bring challenges that no one could have predicted. Parker Hannifin adjusted to the manufacturing recession by reducing inventory, cutting spending, consolidating facilities, and realigning production and workforce levels in the latter half of the year.[24]

On September 11, the United States was the target of a series of coordinated attacks. Four commercial passenger

AID IN A NATIONAL TRAGEDY

O N SEPTEMBER 11, 2001, FOUR planes departing from U.S. airports were hijacked by terrorists and crashed into the World Trade Center, the Pentagon, and a field in Pennsylvania, killing almost 3,000 people in a few short hours.[1] As the nation banded together, organizations such as the American Red Cross and hundreds of volunteers and city workers rushed to help with recovery efforts.[2] Given the exhausting task of hauling away the debris, Parker Hannifin products and the company's willingness to offer assistance was most welcome in the weeks following.

Debris was dumped on a conveyor belt by a front-end loader in the cleanup following September 11, and the hydraulically driven machine blew a hose. A Parker Hannifin Hose Doctor van remedied the situation in only an hour. Parker Hannifin was recognized for its efforts following the tragedy during a visit to the New York Stock Exchange.

Following the collapse of the Twin Towers, the removal of 1.8 million tons of concrete and rubble began.[3] As each load was delivered to the Fresh Kills Landfill investigation site on Staten Island, the task took a heavy toll on both the workers receiving and processing debris and the equipment that moved it throughout the site. Help for the much-strained front-end loaders and grapplers came directly from Parker Hannifin's Fluid Connectors Group. The company donated hoses, connectors, filters, and pumps through its Hose Doctor van and fully stocked trailer, which was stationed at the landfill.[4] Parker Hannifin was one of the few vendors on-site.[5]

"We wanted to do something to assist," said Brad Fischer, Parker Hannifin's mobile services manager. "What we were most qualified to do was help maintain and service the many vehicles being used to clear away debris and rubble."

The New York Police Department and the Federal Bureau of Investigation reviewed debris dumped on a conveyor belt by a front-end loader. After days of 24-hour use, the hydraulically driven machine blew

a hose. What could have delayed work for days was remedied in an hour by Parker Hannifin's Hose Doctor van.[6]

"Our mobile services van is unique in that it brings our fluid connector products right to the customer and is stocked 24/7 with things they need," said Fischer.[7]

This on-site service was also helpful for the grapplers that removed rubble from the barges delivering remains from Ground Zero. The excavator, made in Germany, experienced seal problems that caused it to shut down until a precise replacement seal was found. While workers at the landfill urgently tried locating the part from the German manufacturer, Parker Hannifin's Fluid Connector employees at the site contacted their colleagues in the Seal Group.[8]

"When the sanitation workers realized that Parker also made these seals, we were able to give them an ample supply to repair the grapplers," said Fischer. "This significantly reduced the amount of downtime."[9]

"All of us at Parker can be very proud of supporting the September 11 cleanup efforts," added Jack Myslenski, retired executive vice president of sales, marketing, and operations support.[10]

jet airliners were hijacked. Two crashed into each of the World Trade Center's towers in New York City; one into the Pentagon in Arlington County, Virginia; and another into a field in Pennsylvania. More than 3,000 Americans died within hours.[25]

The economic impact on the world would be harsh. Because the U.S. gross domestic product (GDP) was roughly 30 percent of the world GDP at the time of the attack, a recession in the United States would have ripple effects worldwide. The attacks affected the American economy through weakened consumer confidence, unprecedented cuts in the Federal funds rate, rising unemployment levels, and fears of deflation.[26]

While Parker Hannifin managed to grow 3 to 4 percent from its acquisitions earlier in the year, margins dropped following September 11, and it lost 20 percent of its volume. In addition, many manufacturing facilities were underutilized throughout the world.[27]

Washkewicz' Win Strategy became not only a tool for success, but also a means of survival.

"[Don] was really trying to get the most that he could possibly get out of that $8 billion in revenue,"

said Pamela Huggins, Parker Hannifin's vice president and treasurer, who started in 1983. "What he did was give the general managers the tools to do their jobs better, [which would allow] the divisions to perform better."[28]

Washkewicz explained:

People thought we were nuts. In the middle of a recession, we're spending millions to launch a new business strategy. We were hiring consultants and adding people at all levels of the organization to implement the new initiatives. I was either going to be right on this thing, or dead wrong, but I knew one thing for sure: We had to give it our best shot and invest in the resources necessary to get it going worldwide.

Picking Up Momentum

The recession of the early 2000s compounded with the turmoil after September 11, 2001, created a difficult environment for American industry. Parker Hannifin added value by launching PHConnect, a Web-based service system that allowed customers and distributors to conduct business across the company's divisions.[29] Previously, some groups and divisions had individual sites where customers could access their own specific products. This "divisionalized" approach needed attention, and a common technological communication system was in order. Bill Eline, chief information officer, explained:

The biggest challenge is striking the difference between a division needing to be independent and meeting … their business plan and yet having them share the lever-

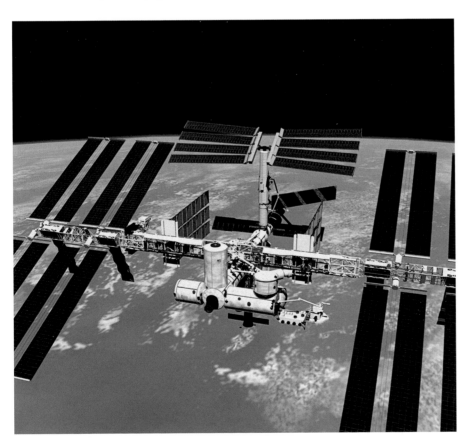

Parker's technologies are used to seal, heat, and cool the International Space Station (ISS) as it orbits 230 miles above the Earth. In a project that began in 2001, Parker Hannifin worked with NASA and its contractors for five years to design and produce more than 3,000 assemblies needed to complete the construction of the ISS.

aged technology throughout the corporation and be able to sustain the company for the long term, not just the short term.

We constantly get into, "If I do it this way, it's the cheap and cheerful way, and it gets me to my short-term quarterly or annual target." But long term, that's going to cause other problems. ... For example, in the [back end] systems of PHConnect, we had a lot of groups and divisions that had their own business-to-business portals, but, because all of them looked the same, we were able to take that to an enterprise level and provide that for the corporation, still understanding that it has to function a little differently based on a division-by-division basis. We easily could have had three software packages supporting our product development cycle, but because of the partnering effect, all had the same points of measurement for a successful R & D project. Every division that has development R & D responsibility tracks their activity on the same tool.[30]

Parker Hannifin also acquired Chelsea Products Division, a leading supplier of power takeoffs, and Eaton's Aeroquip Air Conditioning and Refrigeration business.

The support and dedication to research and development at Parker Hannifin came to fruition as technology played a vital role in the first permanent home in space—the International Space Station (ISS). In a project that began in 2001, Parker Hannifin worked with the National Aeronautics and Space Administration (NASA) and its contractors during the next five years to design and produce more than 3,000 assemblies for the ISS.[31] The company's technologies seal, heat, and cool the ISS as it orbits 230 miles above the Earth. Inside the space station, Parker Hannifin products ensure that conditions in the laboratory spaces and living quarters remain comfortable and free of contaminants.

Parker and its innovations—such as flight control actuation, thrust reverse actuation, and electro-hydraulic servo valves—were well known, its manufacturing and marketing approaches had always

been different from other groups and divisions. Although the Win Strategy focused on lowering purchasing costs in the industrial segments through strategic procurement, Steve Hayes felt this could be difficult for Aerospace. Hayes, who joined Parker Hannifin in 1972 and retired as group president of Aerospace in 2003, explained:

The challenge was that aerospace and industrial are two different animals. The technology is different. ... However, I felt [the Win Strategy] was necessary. Something had to be done to make the entire company more productive.[32]

Bob Barker, who took up the reins as president of the Aerospace Group after Hayes left and eventually became executive vice president and operations officer, was faced with the task of balancing acquisitions with organic growth.

"The aerospace community is small. Everyone knew each other, and acquisitions were simply a matter of matching a willing seller and a willing buyer," explained Barker. "The challenge is in finding a quality target [for acquisition]. I talk to the CEOs, and they talk to me at all these industry meetings that we go to."

Although the ability to grow through acquisition was a strategy applied successfully to other divisions, if an appropriate company was not available for purchase, the focus shifted to using funds for internal operations.

"If we don't have the opportunity to spend cash that we're generating on acquisitions, then let's spend it on the development of a new program," said Barker. "Let's think about [the new program] as if it were an acquisition."[33]

The Filtration Group achieved significant momentum from the 1980s acquisition of Racor Industries, which elevated Parker Hannifin to be the top supplier of diesel engine filters for pleasure boats, while another

occurring. Parker Hannifin was reorganizing its efforts internally by divesting Wynn Warranty in 2002, and United Aircraft Products in 2003. Wynn Industries, France; Zenith Pump Division; and Wynn Oil Specialty Chemicals were divested in 2004.[37]

Organic Growth

Despite three years of weakness in North American industrial and commercial aerospace markets and weak demand in Europe, Washkewicz and Collins were determined to maintain the company's leading share of the $50 billion motion and control market in 2003.[38] The company needed to focus on organic growth, as well as pushing the European operations to become more fiscally productive. That year, Washkewicz tapped Craig Maxwell, engineering manager of its newly developed Fuel Cell Systems Business Unit, for the position of corporate vice president of Technology and Innovation.[39]

"Craig's leadership and creativity would prove to be the catalyst for innovative, organic growth in the new century," said Washkewicz. "They were obviously paying a lot of attention to what was happening in California [when I served as manager of new business development for the Racor Division]. They hadn't seen that kind of explosive growth organically. They'd seen it through acquisitions, but not homegrown," said Maxwell, who started at Parker Hannifin in 1996. "I remember [Washkewicz] saying, 'You have the job. I want you to do what you did at the Racor Division, only for all of Parker Hannifin.'"[40]

After Maxwell began as corporate vice president of Technology and Innovation, taking a lead from Washkewicz, he visited Parker Hannifin facilities throughout the world. While he admitted that these decentralized business units were excellent at making individual products, he was concerned that the ability to innovate had been lost. Instead of searching for new ideas, facilities were operating under mantras of the 1990s that touted "manage what you

application became newsworthy.[34] The patented V118/V110 Filtration/Oil Cooler Module, an oil filter, fuel filter, and oil cooler all in one used on V8 diesel engines, was the first of its kind in North America.[35]

Other new developments included the Segway Human Transporter, the first self-balancing, electric-powered mobilizer controlled via a Parker Hannifin–created seal-actuation base. It allows the operator to rise up on two wheels without tipping. The company's new solenoid valves also set a higher industry standard for commercial refrigeration in retail outlets, restaurants, and distribution operations.[36]

While the groundwork for growth was under way with additional acquisitions in 2002—such as Camfil Farr's engine air filter business in Mississippi, and Acroloop Motion Control Systems in Minnesota—divestitures were also

Above: Parker Hannifin executives and board members ring the closing bell at the New York Stock Exchange on April 21, 2005, to celebrate the 40th anniversary of Parker's listing on the NYSE.

Right: The Segway Human Transporter, the first self-balancing, electric-powered mobilizer of its kind. Parker Hannifin's seal-actuation base (inset) controls the space-age vehicle.

Craig Maxwell, named corporate vice president of Technology and Innovation in 2003, would play a critical role in driving innovation throughout the company, thus promoting growth and fulfilling the third leg of the Win Strategy: profitable growth.

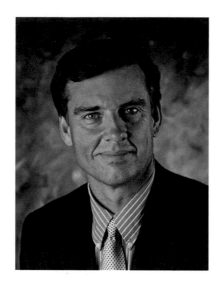

have" and "maximize efficiency."[41] Maxwell explained:

I recognized there are four things that drive an innovative culture. There's the process. You need to have some processes driving you. There's the resource—people. There's infrastructure, which would be labs and funding, money. Then finally, there's the culture piece, which is the hardest of the four to deal with, and results from an understanding of the other three, of what it takes to innovate. Here is what innovative companies do to drive innovation. They do things like portfolio management. They align strategically to markets and customers. Then they follow a very rigorous process.

We call it "stage gate." It's a funnel of ideas coming in, but you want to be very selective about the projects that you work on and understand strategically why they're significant. And, most of all, to understand how they create value in the market for the end user. You must be able to clearly articulate the unfulfilled customer need.

We had a lot of engineers working on a lot of things, but when you looked at the top line, it never moved. It's not that they're not working hard or are working on the wrong things. They're not focused on value. The value comes from the customer's eye.[42]

To find out what the customer valued, Maxwell encouraged Parker Hannifin engineers to leave the laboratories and meet with end users. The engineers visited farm co-ops that used machinery made by John Deere, a big customer of Parker Hannifin products. Through these farmers, Parker Hannifin engineers learned firsthand what was needed to service their machinery. Because the engineers were considered neutral business parties, they could also gather information about competitors, such as General Motors and Chrysler, all while serving the individual needs of each.[43]

"They're all competitors, and competitors never talk to each other. But they'll talk to me because I've got this 'immunity,'" said Maxwell. "I can pretty quickly weave this very convincing tapestry of what's really significant to the market."[44]

Sales in Europe

Europe proved challenging in a very different way. The variety of languages and marketing and sales efforts were more difficult to streamline. The Win Strategy focused on improving the bottom line, and progress has been steady.

"We're thrilled, and so, I think, is the investment community," said Tim Pistell, a Parker Hannifin employee since 1969 who was named executive vice president of finance and administration and international chief financial officer in 2005. Pistell, the first graduate of Parker's Financial Trainee Program, explained:

We identified that it would be hard to do, but we said we're not happy with the margins in Europe, and we're going to work on getting them up. ... People are now sitting up and taking notice. Part of it is critical mass. Duane [Collins] ... decreed standardization of IT hardware and software and other things ... Well, we now have an infrastructure in place that can support a lot more business than we have. The key here is to grow the business. We've done a lot of deals and added a lot of mass in Europe.

The last bit though are the Win initiatives. Then there's the European Union. People didn't know if this union and the euro would work. Well, it's there. It still has problems. It gets shaky every now and then, but it's holding together, and you really need to adapt to the "United States of Europe." ... The borders are down. So you don't need inventory in every country.[45]

Although inventory issues were addressed, organizing the sales force proved a bit more daunting. According to Washkewicz, the number of warehouses was reduced from 58 to three primary locations. Sales companies were established in three major countries—the United Kingdom, France, and Germany—giving the company a more unified presence.[46] This "One Parker" concept was

introduced with early support from Marwan Kashkoush, who explained:

The sales company model would propel operations in Europe to achieve double-digit growth under the leadership of Jack Myslenski [retired executive vice president of sales, marketing, and operations support]. Providing one contact point, strategically located in Europe's largest countries for our customers, helped to reduce delivery costs, standardize operations, improve customer satisfaction, and pull together complete systems solutions composed of products from multiple groups. This model exemplifies a unified "One Parker" presence for our customers. The sales company's strength in providing premier service lies within their knowledge of local customs and currency and the ability to communicate in their customers' native languages. Today, Parker has a unified "One Parker" presence with sales companies in 22 countries, allowing service and support to be wherever distributors and customers need it.

"Europe is now significantly more profitable than it was and is … meeting the corporate goal," said James Perkins, corporate communications manager for Europe.[47]

Another manner in which global economics affected the market was through pricing. Different markets would have different prices. For example, ordering a part from Germany and having it shipped to São Paulo, Brazil, would incur expensive freight charges.

"The strategic pricing program at Parker utilizes statistical analyses to determine the best local prices for Parker products wherever they are sold," said Dick Braun, vice president of strategic pricing. "Market prices are still more local than global, and Parker responds to local competitive conditions. This allows us to fulfill global demand economically while continuing to price to the local market."

In January 2002, to help ease the duplication of efforts by the European sales force, and as part of the Win Strategy, the sales forces were consolidated. According to Charly Saulnier, president of Europe, Middle East, Africa, the market opportunities in Europe were even greater than those in the United States.[48]

"Our strategy is to develop strong partnerships with our customers, to bring them the best solutions in order to help them achieve their goals," said Saulnier.

Anticipating Needs

The first three years of the new millennium were challenging for Parker Hannifin, with quarterly sales decelerating in 2002 to a low point of $1.5 billion and a consequential drop in operating margins.[49] Yet 2004 was the beginning of a new chapter.

Acquisitions played a significant role in 2004, with Denison Hydraulics broadening Parker Hannifin's technologies in hydraulic vane pumps, hydrostatics, and digitally controlled fan-drive systems throughout Europe, Asia, and North America. Webb Enterprises added benefits for the manufacturing of fuel conditioning systems.

"This idea of making acquisitions and having a philosophy of acquisitions is a style, a technique. This is very unusual, and it's something that is uniquely Parker," said John McGinty, an analyst for Credit Suisse First Boston.[50]

Above: Lee C. Banks began his career at Parker Hannifin in 1991 as a national sales manager for the Refrigeration and Air Conditioning Group after an advantageous meeting with Larry Hopcraft, vice president of Automotive and Refrigeration. Banks would eventually become president of the Worldwide Hydraulics Group and executive vice president and operating officer.

Right: Health care is an industry that constantly requires improved technology. Parker Hannifin engineers redeveloped the hydraulics on a line of hospital gurneys—including pumps, cylinders, hoses, and fittings—to allow health-care workers to utilize beds with greater reliability and smoother operation.

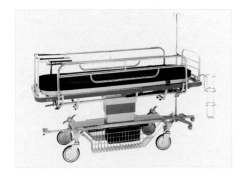

Jack Myslenski, retired executive vice president of sales, marketing, and operations support, advised associates to tell a story when speaking with customers, rather than sell parts separately. Myslenski retired in May 2008, after a 34-year career with Parker Hannifin. Marwan Kashkoush was named to succeed Jack.

Parker Hannifin's well-tuned acquisition philosophy was used again in 2004 when it acquired Sporlan Valve Company, the market leader in refrigeration and air-conditioning components, controls, and systems such as See-All moisture and liquid indicators and Catch-All filter driers. Despite some initial uneasiness after the acquisition, those at Sporlan were quickly reassured. Mike Noelke, who was vice president of marketing for Sporlan at the time of acquisition and continued with Parker Hannifin as general manager for the Sporlan Division of the Climate and Industrial Controls Group, explained:

You hear all the bad things that happen with acquisitions, about [the acquiring company] gutting the companies and moving the manufacturing. Sporlan is an industry leader and very proud of what has been accomplished, but Parker is just an impressive company, which makes the whole transition a lot easier. Being a decentralized corporation, Parker is passive–aggressive. It gives us the opportunity to make the correct decision. If they see that's not happening, they'll certainly help us.[51]

Ken Ohlemeyer, former Sporlan president and a current consultant with Parker Hannifin, remembered that Parker Hannifin had been interested in acquiring the company for years before the sale was finalized.

"Parker had a lot of product lines we weren't involved with, and when we did compete it was on a minor basis. We knew them. We respected them. They knew us," said Ohlemeyer.[52]

Parker Hannifin's leaders were also focused on the potential of growth from within to meet the demand

of its 400,000 customers around the globe, as well as presenting a cohesive image to the public.[53] Parker Hannifin had struggled historically to have its customers—and industry analysts—identify with the products it manufactured as most lie deep within a machine.

"The problem is how you show the public where the markets are and the applications. We don't have too many things that are sold by themselves, but if you're able to put together a story on an excavator that is operating across the street, I can make a story around our Fluid Connector Group, our Filtration Group, our Seal Group, and our Hydraulics Group all at one time," said Jack Myslenski, retired executive vice president, sales, marketing, and operations support, who started in 1973.[54]

"What makes great companies is their ability to pay attention to their environment and to react as necessary. Parker is working very hard at that. They're applying lean manufacturing to the supply chain, new product development, distribution, strategic pricing, and human resources," said Clifford F. Ransom, II, analyst, president of Ransom Research, Inc., an independent investment research firm. "If they continue with this, they will be exemplars. These will be truly differentiating aspects of this journey to lean that will put them on the cutting edge."[55]

Understanding the depth of the product lines as well as the aftermarket poses yet another challenge. Jim Wood, a valued consultant to Parker Hannifin, explained:

At one point, Parker had a conglomerate multiple. Good and bad. And conglomerate analysts. The decision was made to seek coverage by analysts other than conglomerate analysts, and that was the job that Pat and I worked on.

In true Parker fashion, and following the company's roots begun with Art Parker's inventions and supported by Pat Parker's enthusiastic support of innovation, the possibilities remain limitless.

There have been strides made to offset criticisms from the investment community, surrounding the fact that a

lot of Parker Hannifin's products have a cyclical nature.

"Some of our technologies and where we are the strongest are cyclical. It's hard to escape that," said Pistell. He continued:

If you're No. 1 in the world of motion and control, you have three ways to do work. There's hydraulics, there's pneumatics, and there's electromechanical, and you will choose between those for their different attributes. Hydraulics are heavier, and they're more expensive, but they are necessary for greater workloads. They are used in construction equipment, agriculture, jet airplanes ... big workloads. But when you go down that list, these are big-ticket durable goods, and there is no way of escaping the cyclicality.

According to Pistell, there are two ways to counterbalance this: diversify the product line and capture the aftermarket. The ParkerStore® venture is an example of a successful way of growing the aftermarket. Besides ringing sales for repeat customers who are familiar with Parker Hannifin, the company can effectively seek out new customers, cutting into the competition. By the end of 2002, there were more than 400 ParkerStores® worldwide. Today, there are more than 1,500 worldwide.

Global Innovation in 48 Countries

With alternative energy sources becoming increasingly important for all industries, Parker Hannifin has remained focused on research and development of new technologies. For instance, its Fuel Cells Systems Business Unit developed new compressor and motor technologies critical to the commercialization of fuel cell systems, which are typically very expensive.[56]

"There will be a movement in the future ... more and more activity in the area of energy recovery, alternative energy. I think all those things are a very fertile ground for the products we have in our portfolio," said Myslenski.[57]

Parker Hannifin began exploring technology for energy recovery systems in the late 1980s, but the weight of the 3,000-to-4,000 pound hydraulic accumulators

Parker Hannifin developed this air separation module to prevent explosion by replacing air with inert nitrogen in the fuel tanks of aircraft. The technology is currently being used in military aircraft, and, although it wasn't required in the past, commercial aircraft will need it in the future, according to a rule proposed by the Federal Aviation Administration in November 2005.

that stored the energy prevented the research from progressing.[58] In 2004, Parker Hannifin revisited and revived the old technology. New, lighter accumulators weigh 350 to 400 pounds because of advanced carbon fiber graphite epoxy composite technology, advancements in electronics and controls, and improved efficiency in hydraulic pump motors.[59]

"We have ... the most efficient pump motor on the planet today in terms of a hydraulic power system," said Joe Kovach, Hydraulics Group, vice president of innovation and technology. "We took an old technology, dusted it off, and breathed new life into it. We did it quickly by doing a lot more in terms of advanced simulation and modeling of the entire vehicle."[60]

Through virtual reality, Kovach and his team examined the performances of garbage trucks in different terrains. By building topographic data into a computer simulation model, engineers could drive the refuse vehicles virtually to optimize the system configuration. These simulations allowed for design and performance improvements that enabled the team to complete an initial prototype in less than 11 months.

Additional technology was also being completed by the Hydraulics Group's Chelsea Division. The group worked with Kovach's team and outside designers to develop a hydromechanical gearbox that incorporates hydraulic components into a newly developed mechanical system.[61]

"There are probably seven or eight divisions that we're working with in pulling this together," said John Van Buskirk, general manager of Parker Hannifin's Chelsea Division. "That's the challenge of this. ... But now we're really beginning to pull everything together into a very value-added type of system."[62]

This application to garbage trucks has shown 54 percent energy savings and 26 percent improved acceleration while maintaining standard mechanical brakes and standard anti-lock braking systems.[63] Kovach explained:

[Our system uses] typical air brakes like on a standard garbage truck. The brake shoes are still there. That's the hydraulic mechanical part, and a lot of them are air over ... typical brake system. But the way the system works is whenever you hit the brakes, except for the freeway or anything below 45 miles an hour, we can recover energy. Our system engages. We store that energy in the hydraulic accumulators. If we run out of storage or need to stop the vehicle faster, then the mechanical brakes come on as supplemented, and the tie-in is this. If we're on ice or a rain-slick surface and the vehicle starts to skid, the anti-lock braking sensor will indicate a wheel stoppage, which means it's starting to skid. At that point, our system is immediately disengaged, and the conventional anti-lock braking system takes over.[64]

As end-market users for the prototype are waste management companies, addressing concerns for how the vehicles will handle is crucial.

"Part of the original mandate for waste management is they want the driveability equal to or better than an existing chassis. Gradability, startability, and braking distance all has to be on par or better with an existing chassis," explained John Treharn, vice president of business development, hydraulics.

While still in its initial testing phase, Parker Hannifin's energy recovery system for garbage trucks and other similar-weight trucks is just the beginning in exploring alternative energy sources.

Parker Hannifin has also been studying ways to create safer fuel tanks. According to Jim Baker, corporate vice president and deputy general counsel, Parker Hannifin has been at the forefront of "overnight" technology for decades. The company is known for its work on hydraulic hybrids and energy recovery, but has also worked directly with the Federal Aviation Administration (FAA) on changing the fuel systems in aircraft.

"Years ago, Parker was working on inerting systems for fuel systems in airplanes," explained Baker. "Fish live in water because there's oxygen in the water. If you put a cup of water in a vacuum, you'll see all the air bubbling out of the water and how much air is in water. It's amazing. It's solution mixed in with the water."[65]

In a similar fashion, air is also mixed in with airline fuel and present in the fuel tank, which can spark and cause an explosion. Parker Hannifin has developed systems to remove the air from both the fuel and fuel tank. The technology is already being used on military aircraft, and although it wasn't required in the past, commercial

Left: Parker's hybrid hydraulic technology, designed to harness kinetic energy and use it to generate power, has yielded prototype results of up to 70 percent improvement in miles per gallon on delivery vehicles and refuse truck applications.

Right: Beta display in an artial chassis at a 2006 Las Vegas trade show.

Winmap   Winovation   Winvalue

aircraft will need to use it in the future, according to a rule proposed by the FAA in November 2005.

"This is a very, very hot current topic," said Baker. "But we've been working on the technology for 25 years. That [seemingly timely recognition] could happen with the hydraulic hybrids. You don't know."

"What we're doing is looking at many nontraditional areas, places with either industries that didn't exist before or industries in which we couldn't participate before, and we're going to have huge growth in the next 10 years in those areas," added Don Raker, marketing services manager, Hydraulics Group.[66]

Win Initiative

As 2005 progressed, the Win Strategy was gaining momentum under Washkewicz, in his new position as chairman of the board and CEO, and Vande Steeg as president and COO. Company-wide sales had climbed to $8.2 billion, an increase of 17 percent over fiscal year 2004. Income from continuing operations increased to $548 million, or $4.55 per diluted share, compared with $336 million, or $2.82 per diluted share, a year prior. Cash flow from operations had grown stronger as well, reaching $872 million, or 10.6 percent of sales.

Above: Parker Hannifin's business-development process involves three initiatives: Winmap, Winovation, and Winvalue. Beginning with a market action plan, Winmap identifies customer needs. Ideas then move on to Winovation, which takes the project through concept, feasibility, development, qualification, preproduction, and launch. Then, Winvalue guides the sales force to articulate value to customers by understanding their applications.

Left: Parker Hannifin's IQAN electronic control system integrated more than 200 controls on Taylor's Rubber Tire Gantry Crane for smooth, proportional control of container loading and unloading.

"The Win Strategy began to take hold, thanks to Parker's 50,000 employees. I couldn't accomplish much of anything without the efforts of the entire organization supporting the initiatives. It wasn't easy. It's change, and any time you try to execute change, there's resistance," said Washkewicz. "It's tough at first, but it becomes easier. Then change becomes the norm and once that happens, you start seeing the results you want. The Win Strategy was becoming part of Parker's DNA."

An addition to this profitable growth strategy was a disciplined process that assessed the viability of innovative product ideas called Winovation. A formal business system to drive excellence in product commercialization, Winovation promotes collaboration among the business groups and divisions. It also produces strategic new products that align with the Win Strategy.

"Winovation puts a complete process in place to monitor the activities in the R & D area," said Myslenski. "It's forced us to identify between true R & D and sustaining engineering."[67]

"We said, 'Okay, enter all the projects you're working on into the Winovation process, and start tracking them.' Over half of the projects got killed at the first gate review," said Maxwell. "People couldn't understand why they were working on them, which is what we suspected. They were destroying value because we were paying people to work on the answer to nobody's question."[68]

Roger Sherrard, president, Automation Group, agreed. "The more difficult thing is not being able to do all these things that are on the Win Strategy, but how does it fit to where you are headed because all businesses are different," he said. "You can lean out plants and increase price and get money from suppliers, but if, at the end of the day, the underlying technology is a melting snowman, you're toast."[69]

Tom Healy, now president of the Climate and Industrial Controls Group, remembered welcoming the implementation of Winovation, because, at the time, he had just been appointed group vice president of oper-

Dan Serbin, vice president, Human Resources, was instrumental in forming a bridge between engineering colleges and Parker Hannifin to encourage students to consider Parker as a future employer.

ations for the Climate Systems Division. He was excited to begin his new role, yet admits that he had found some aspects of the planning processes a bit "mind boggling." For example, at the time, there was an Aerospace plant just 7 miles away, yet the two plants never communicated about best practices or compared ways in which they were each run efficiently.

"We're going to use best practices because if there are 50 Parker divisions going about innovation 50 different ways, if you rank them, one of them is doing it the best way. And somebody is doing it the 50th-best way," said Healy. "Why would we want one of our divisions doing something the 50th-best way?"[70]

New Acquisitions

Added value would come by way of systems solutions, a key Win Strategy initiative, which were the pinnacle of Parker Hannifin's success in 2005. Its systems portfolio grew substantially that year when it was awarded the contract for the hydraulic subsystem for the new Boeing 787 Dreamliner passenger jet, as well as individual components on the airframe and GE and Rolls-Royce candidate engines for the Airbus A350XWB. This presented the potential of more than $2 billion in revenues over the life of the program.[71]

The company grew again in 2005 through the purchase of several companies, including Hanil Hydraulics in Korea, Markwel Hose Products in India, Kuiken Hytrans BV in the Netherlands, and Tianjin Tejing Hydraulic Company, Ltd., in China. In North America, Parker Hannifin added Acadia Elastomers Corporation and Advanced Products to grow its leading position in sealing technology.[72]

"When we made the decision to sell the company, clearly, Parker was the acquirer of choice," said Nancy Nicholson, president and CEO of Advanced Products. "There are some very strong synergies between Parker and Advanced, and we're confident the combination will greatly benefit both companies' employees and customers."[73]

Losing Part of the Past

Although Parker Hannifin was on an upswing in 2005, its chairman emeritus had quieted his customary energetic tone. Several years earlier, Pat Parker had been diagnosed with cancer—a condition he kept to himself. Although Pat's initial radiation treatments kept the disease at bay, it soon returned.[74]

"He didn't want anybody to know about the cancer, which made it very difficult for me because he had so many friends worldwide who would call and ask about him," said the now retired Dolores Lyon, who had been executive administrative assistant to Pat since 1970. "All I could say was, 'He's in a little bit of a slump right now, but he's going to bounce back.'"[75]

While subsequent attempts to immobilize the cancer gave Pat and his family glimmers of hope and renewed energy—and brief visits to corporate headquarters also gave Pat great joy—the disease eventually metastasized.

"The pain was so intense, and he was a guy that never, ever, ever complained. No matter what was going on, I never heard him complain," said Pat's son Streeter.[76]

On July 6, 2005, Pat Parker died peacefully, surrounded by his family in his Cleveland Heights, Ohio, home. The man who had guided Parker Hannifin's expansion from the 1960s into the 1990s, and solidified its position as the global leader in motion and control technologies was gone. He was 75.

"Pat, to everyone who ever met him, was a man of influence, integrity and warmth, with a lifelong enthusiasm for innovators and their inventions," said Washkewicz. "His drive to grow the company was rooted in his desire to serve customers better, whether through globalization or a business model that places decisions close to customers. He made it a regular habit to talk with employees on the factory floor

to get their ideas on how to improve the business. Pat touched the lives of many throughout the company and within the community."

A special memorial service was held at Severance Hall in Cleveland, Ohio, where thousands paid tribute to Pat's many contributions to his company and his community.

"Condolence letters were sent even from Parker competitors," Pistell said. "Pat was truly an ambassador for motion and control."

Bolstering the Future

Stemming from the difficulties Parker Hannifin had in hiring qualified engineers during the late 1980s and early 1990s, when there were few graduates of engineering programs, the company became more active in supporting higher education, both for possible candidates for employment and current staff members.

"There are a number of colleges that we partner with," said Dan Serbin, vice president, human resources.

A NEW BRANDING STRATEGY

IN 2007, PARKER HANNIFIN EXPERIENCED A CORPORATE unification. Throughout the company's history, it had grown through many divisions and many acquisitions. The small, Ohio-based company was now a multibillion-dollar global enterprise. It was time for a cohesive program to unify the company worldwide. According to Vice President of Communications and External Affairs Christopher Farage, the process was challenging because of Parker Hannifin's broad range of products and global reach.

How do you decide what type of company you want to be known as in the minds of all of your customers around the world? This is not an easy question to answer for a company that serves so many customers in so many ways. So, we had a lot of discussions, globally, with Parker's management team, marketing communications professionals, and, probably most important, our customers. At the end of the day, we had to be sure that our final branding conclusions were aligned with what our customers found desirable, and believable, in a partner, and yet was still distinctive from our competitors.

The new branding effort was announced in the fall of 2007. Because of the many acquisitions over the years, the company needed to incorporate the new brands under the Parker umbrella in a way that was recognizable to customers. Also, due to the expansion into new markets, it was also important to have a strong brand presence to make an immediate impression to win market share. Elements of the brand strategy encompass the logo, company description, brand promise, tagline, advertising campaign, and brand architecture.

The Brand Promise

It was a collaborative process. Customers, executives, and communications professionals were all involved in the final creation, which began with the brand promise:

Parker is the global leader in motion and control technologies, partnering with its customers to increase their productivity and profitability.

A strategic process for the integration of new brands was also developed. Acquisitions are integrated into the Parker brand in one of three ways. First, they can be immediately absorbed into the Parker brand. Second, they can be integrated into an existing sub-brand. Or, they can transition to an approved, separate sub-brand. Sub-brands use both Parker and the acquisition's existing name together. There is a process—the brand decision tree—through which these decisions will be made, mostly depending on the marketability

"We have engineering labs we've put in. We spend a couple hundred thousand dollars to put in an engineering lab, and then provide ongoing support. ... We also give scholarships."

The idea is to familiarize students with the Parker Hannifin name so upon graduation, they might be interested in applying for employment. Pistell, at one time, had been very active in campus recruiting, but he always warned new candidates: "Be careful about taking a job with Parker because you will never leave."[77]

"We hire a lot of engineering grads who then use their engineering degrees to help sell the product," said Pistell. "That's how they cut their teeth, and if they're really good and they show some aptitude to do more, then they have to be brought out of the field into operations. If they're good, they become a general manager, and if you become a division general manager, in Parker, then you're ... on the way to move up through the ranks and be group president or even chairman/CEO."

of the acquisition's name. If the name is recognizable and already has a share of the market, it may be approved for an existing as a sub-brand. If the name is not recognizable, it may be absorbed immediately into the Parker brand. The four-step integration process for all acquisitions includes:

Vice President of Communications and External Affairs Chris Farage was instrumental in leading the new branding strategy.

1. An assessment of brand equity.
2. Completion of the brand decision tree.
3. Submission of the brand-integration request form.
4. Creation and implementation of a brand-integration plan.

"Our company needs to have one name, one master brand, and one identity worldwide to define what our customers can expect from us," said Don Washkewicz, chairman, CEO, and president of Parker Hannifin. "We are a global company, and we need to be seen as one."

These transitions can take as little as six months or as long as three years.

Business, group, or division names would no longer be printed on standard marketing materials. Instead, the types of technology will be listed in a separate call-out box, with the appropriate technology tag highlighted in Parker gold. Technologies are listed as aerospace, climate control, electromechanical, filtration, fluid and gas handling, hydraulics, pneumatics, process control, and sealing and shielding.

A Brand-New Look

Along with the streamlined nomenclature, the look of Parker is more defined. The new brand requirements include the black-and-white Parker logo, a gold bar, and the tagline, "Engineering Your Success." There are also specific measurements that apply to the use and placement of the logo. This will ensure that all materials will have a cohesive look no matter what location or division from which they originate.

All materials, including stationary, business cards, and even fax memos, now adhere to the new look.

Along with incorporating the tagline, "Engineering Your Success," a new marketing advertising campaign was launched. "Together, we can ... " focuses on the relationship with the customer and highlights how the products can improve both productivity and profitability. All advertisements incorporate a consistent appearance and carry the same message.

Pistell was also familiar with training employees. After extensive involvement in both domestic and international acquisitions, he decided to share his experience. He wrote a lengthy "how to" manual on approaching and finalizing acquisitions for Parker Hannifin staff. He combined his personal knowledge of how to make deals with his understanding of the Parker Hannifin culture to create a guide tailored perfectly for his fellow staff members.

Parker Hannifin also offers tuition reimbursement and has even partnered with Lake Erie College to offer an MBA program inhouse. At World Headquarters, employees will be able to attend special classes given at Parker Hannifin, and not have to "rush off to class," according to Serbin.[78] The company also established a scholarship endowment for aerospace engineering students in 2003.

To assist employees even further, the company is instituting an internal "sales school" or virtual university to teach an effective and cohesive way to approach customers, according to Marwan Kashkoush, who had been recently promoted to executive vice president of sales, marketing, and operations support.

"We [have to] understand what the customer is looking for because they're trying to improve their bottom line and increase their top line. You figure that out and show the customer what Parker can do for them

to bring value, they're going to buy from you more than they're going to buy from someone else," said Kashkoush. "We are instituting something called the Parker Sales University to teach the Parker way of selling, which is what Winvalue is about."[79]

This dedication of Parker Hannifin employees to the Win Strategy demonstrated record results in 2006. Sales climbed to $9.4 billion—a 16.3 percent increase over 2005—with organic growth driving nearly half of the increase. Income from continuing operations increased 19.7 percent; cash flow from operations reached a record $954.6 million.[80]

Under Washkewicz, the company increased its annual dividend for the 50th consecutive year, one of the longest records of dividend increases among the Standard & Poor's 500 index. Additionally, Parker Hannifin achieved near top-quartile return on invested capital among its peers and ranked in the top 10 percent among *Barron's* magazine's 500 best-performing companies.[81]

Shifting the perception of the company to that of a global organization, rather than a North American–based operation, has been a challenge. Customers in North America have an understanding that they can access Parker Hannifin all around the world, but in other countries the perception is not so clear, according to Tony Piscitello, vice president of operations for the Fluid Connectors Group, who retired in December 2007.

"If we are in Europe where we don't have a lot of the major customers, … we're looked at as a second-tier supplier. When we say we have operations here and there, [U.S. customers] say you're an international company," he explained. "As we get a greater presence in the rest

Above: In 2007, Marwan Kashkoush was named executive vice president of sales, marketing, and operations support, as well as a member of Parker Hannifin's Office of the Chief Executive.

Left: Parker Hannifin opened its 1,000th retail store in 2007. The ParkerStore® venture was a means to reach the aftermarket and gain a greater customer share.

Right: This chart represents Parker Hannifin's customer demographic—original equipment manufacturers and maintenance, repair, and overhaul—in 2007.

Below: Parker's group presidents and officers (left to right): Bob Bond, Fluid Connectors; Michael Chung, Asia Pacific; Jeff Cullman, Hydraulics; Heinz Droxner, Seal; John Greco, Instrumentation; Tom Healy, Climate and Industrial Controls; Ricardo Machado, Latin America; Peter Popoff, Filtration; Charly Saulnier, Europe, Middle East, Africa; and Roger Sherrard, Automation.

50%
OEM Customers

50%
MRO Customers

of the world, we will start to be looked at as a global operation rather than a company with a bunch of plants all over the world."

Parker Hannifin acquired 13 motion and control businesses that year, adding nearly $1 billion in annualized revenue and thousands of employees.[82] Most notable among these acquisitions was United Kingdom–based domnick hunter. A dramatic addition to its Filtration Group—one of the company's strongest and fastest-growing businesses—domnick hunter had been on Parker Hannifin's radar for many years

because of their strong 20-plus-year working relationship.[83, 84]

"The most important, and certainly the product they had the name in and the product that we were already in and most interested in, is compressed air coalescing filters," said Oelslager. "They're No. 1 in Europe, and probably No. 1 on a global basis. We were No. 1 in the United States, and we had a very small presence in Europe. I think from that standpoint it gave us market share and position in Europe and, to a certain extent, in Asia also. It gives us, overall, more critical mass in the process filter business."

The result was Parker domnick hunter—the domnick hunter name had extensive brand recognition, which Parker Hannifin intended on utilizing—a division that became the global leader in filtration of oxygen, nitrogen, and zero air for air purification.[85] Complementing this acquisition was additional overseas expansion in Japan and the Asia–Pacific region through an alliance with Taiyo and Kuroda Pneumatics.

The importance of Parker Hannifin's 12,000 independent distributor locations grew in 2006 as the global network served both OEMs and the market for maintenance, repair, and overhaul (MRO) of working

machinery, from cement mixers to combine harvesters.[86] With customer service innovations, such as retail ParkerStores®, Hose Doctor emergency repair vans, mobile Tech Tours, and the PHConnect Web portal, the operating divisions were at or near 95 percent or above on-time delivery in 2006.[87]

Looking to the Future

As 2006 progressed, 10 additional acquisitions occurred from May through early 2007 benefiting almost all of Parker Hannifin's groups.[88] At the beginning of 2007, Vande Steeg ended his 35 years of service to Parker Hannifin, and Washkewicz reassumed the presidency. Lee Banks, Bob Barker, and Tom Williams were promoted to oversee the company's operations, each as an executive vice president and operating officer.[89]

The company was more profitable than ever, as the Win Strategy was fully utilized, and it began driving the company to achieve its full potential. The North by Northwest directive, which referred to a chart that tracked a ratio of operating margin to net assets/sales, challenged every Parker Hannifin division to control costs and assets while growing sales.[90] The name originated from a description of where progress should be noted on the chart—the upper left quadrant.

"This North by Northwest chart showed me that look, [suppose] my margins are low, but if I can turn the assets fast enough, I can more than return the cost of capital to Parker Hannifin," said Collins. "That was

Parker Hannifin's Board of Directors (left to right): Markos Tambakeras, Linda Harty, Robert Kohlhepp, Klaus-Peter Müller, Wolfgang Schmitt, Don Washkewicz, Candy Obourn, William Kassling, Giulio Mazzalupi, Joseph Scaminace, and James Wainscott.

BOARD OF DIRECTORS TIMELINE

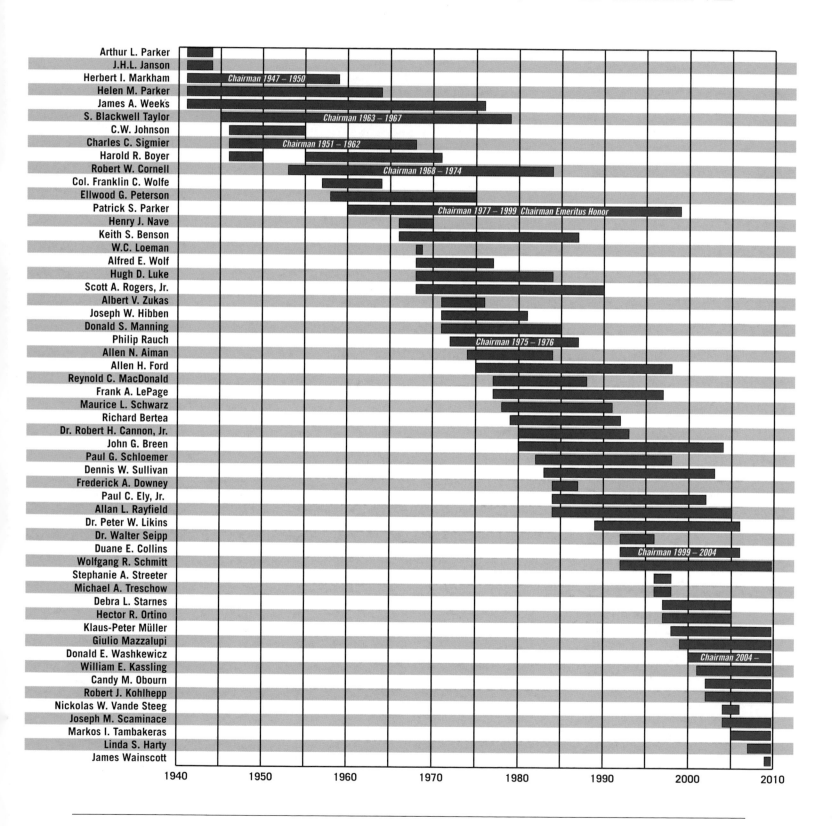

Arthur L. Parker
J.H.L. Janson
Herbert I. Markham — *Chairman 1947 – 1950*
Helen M. Parker
James A. Weeks
S. Blackwell Taylor — *Chairman 1963 – 1967*
C.W. Johnson
Charles C. Sigmier — *Chairman 1951 – 1962*
Harold R. Boyer
Robert W. Cornell — *Chairman 1968 – 1974*
Col. Franklin C. Wolfe
Ellwood G. Peterson
Patrick S. Parker — *Chairman 1977 – 1999   Chairman Emeritus Honor*
Henry J. Nave
Keith S. Benson
W.C. Loeman
Alfred E. Wolf
Hugh D. Luke
Scott A. Rogers, Jr.
Albert V. Zukas
Joseph W. Hibben
Donald S. Manning
Philip Rauch — *Chairman 1975 – 1976*
Allen N. Aiman
Allen H. Ford
Reynold C. MacDonald
Frank A. LePage
Maurice L. Schwarz
Richard Bertea
Dr. Robert H. Cannon, Jr.
John G. Breen
Paul G. Schloemer
Dennis W. Sullivan
Frederick A. Downey
Paul C. Ely, Jr.
Allan L. Rayfield
Dr. Peter W. Likins
Dr. Walter Seipp
Duane E. Collins — *Chairman 1999 – 2004*
Wolfgang R. Schmitt
Stephanie A. Streeter
Michael A. Treschow
Debra L. Starnes
Hector R. Ortino
Klaus-Peter Müller
Giulio Mazzalupi
Donald E. Washkewicz — *Chairman 2004 –*
William E. Kassling
Candy M. Obourn
Robert J. Kohlhepp
Nickolas W. Vande Steeg
Joseph M. Scaminace
Markos I. Tambakeras
Linda S. Harty
James Wainscott

1940   1950   1960   1970   1980   1990   2000   2010

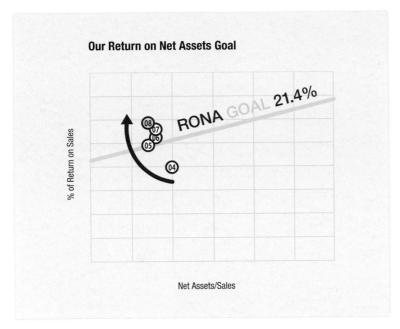

Our Return on Net Assets Goal

RONA GOAL 21.4%

% of Return on Sales

Net Assets/Sales

the slope of a line. The further left you go, the fewer assets you have and the less margin you require to get a return that exceeds the cost of capital. Now, the one thing was that it didn't really tie together with all the returns and so forth. ... We made the slope of the line a proper number that gives Parker Hannifin a return on capital that exceeds cost of capital, and that line, at that time, turned out to be 21.4 percent."[91]

It also was a great equalizer among all divisions, as those with any level of sales or assets could be compared directly.

Washkewicz explained:

We always want the divisions heading in the direction of north by northwest to achieve the return on net assets goal. Each division's goals are directly tied to personal incentives. Strategic procurement drives them in the right direction because it improves return on

 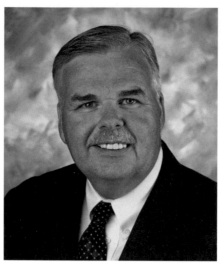 

sales. Lean moves them in this direction by reducing asset intensity and cost. And pricing takes them north by northwest by improving margins. Lastly, innovation is the driver for both margin expansion and sustained growth, moving Parker "North by Northwest."

From left to right: Dick Braun, vice president, Strategic Pricing; John Dedinsky, vice president, Global Supply Chain and Procurement; and Kathryn Miller, vice president, Lean Enterprise and Quality, played key roles that led to the success of Parker Hannifin's Win Strategy initiative.

"We've paid [dividends] for over 50 years, but we've increased them 50 years in a row," said Pistell. "And we're among the top five in the S&P 500."[92]

Fiscal years 2007 and 2008 were the best years in the history of Parker Hannifin, with net sales topping $10 billion and $12.15 billion respectively. The culmination of Win Strategy success is delivered through the company's record-breaking financial results for several years running. Specifically, higher performance levels are evident in Parker's sales, income from continuing operations, net income as percent of sales, cash flow from operations, international margins as a percent of sales, annual dividend increases, and return on invested capital.

A new branding strategy was also implemented— "Engineering Your Success"—which seeks to unify the company as a whole, worldwide, which is a welcome challenge as the company continues to reach globally.

"The brand strategy helps us present Parker in a way that makes sense to our customers," said Washkewicz.

"Instead of a collection of acquisitions, we want to look like 'one Parker,' Parker Hannifin."

From its grassroots beginnings, struggles through wars and recessions, Parker Hannifin continues to excel by promoting what essentially was never a commodity: its customers. By adhering to the spirit of innovation that Art and Pat Parker so lovingly cultivated, and always recognizing that customers and employees are its most precious assets, the company has reached unprecedented success.

As its new era of leadership moves forward, adapting to an evolving technological world, the basics still apply.

"If you listen to the customer, you'll always stay in business," said Washkewicz. "If you listen to the customer and do what is best for the customer to enhance their productivity and profitability, you will survive and grow through good times and bad."

Chairman Pat Parker created a legacy of integrity, humor, and humility, both in his business methods and in his personal life.

PATRICK S. PARKER: A TRIBUTE TO AN ENTREPRENEUR

OCTOBER 16, 1929–JULY 6, 2005

I never saw him take credit for any of it. He'd take credit for a barbecue, for a joke, anything—but never for his successful business.

—Streeter Parker,
son of Patrick S. Parker

BORN IN CLEVELAND ON OCTOBER 16, 1929, Patrick "Pat" Parker grew up in Shaker Heights, Ohio, where he claimed to have learned the traits necessary for success—all found in the sandbox of his elementary school. These "sandbox rules" included fair play, leadership among peers, and honesty.

Pat spent time with his two sisters and brother, and took several vacations with his parents Arthur and Helen Parker, which included trips to Atlantic City and sailing excursions. Pat was also introduced at an early age to Parker Appliance, the company his father founded. While Pat spent his teenage years at Shaker Heights' University School, his summers were spent with the company.

"I ran a machine in the summer of '44 next to a guy named Frankie Laine, the singer," recalled Pat. "He was a torque lathe operator at Parker making fittings during the war."

Pat was also involved with the machining and testing of the first fuel nozzles made for the first jet engines flown in the United States. Yet, his world changed dramatically on January 1, 1945, with his father's untimely death while shoveling snow. In addition to the terrible impact of Art's passing, Parker Appliance's only customer, the U.S. government, ceased all its orders with the end of World War II. Helen was faced with the possibility of bankruptcy or liquidation of her husband's company. But, as the story is told, she cashed in Art's $1 million life insurance policy and reinvested it in the company to bring in new management and revive Parker Appliance. As the rebuilding occurred, including bolstering Parker Appliance's industrial business, Pat became more involved with internal operations.

"When the war ended, I got a little lesson in continuing education when they put me in the foundry for the summer of '46," said Pat. "The only job we had was making 25,000 bronze funeral urns for the military cemeteries in Normandy, France, and after making 8,000 of those in 120 degree [heat], I decided to go to school."

Following high school and summer camps at Culver Military Academy in Indiana, Pat attended Williams

Photograph ©Mort Tucker Photography.

College in Massachusetts, majoring in English Literature. After graduating in 1951, he signed up for Navy flight training, but instead attended Harvard Business School. The admitting professor was impressed with Pat's hands-on experience from a manufacturing company. He believed Pat's presence would improve class dialog. During the summers, Pat worked at Parker Appliance as a machinist, lift truck driver, and accountant.

While at Harvard, Pat married Peggy Buckley in 1952. After he graduated, he served in the Korean War for three years as a U.S. naval supply officer. His experience with aircraft carrier fighter plane spares and repairs would come in handy in his next job, which focused on aftermarket sales. Immediately following the end of his service commitment, Pat, Peggy, and their two daughters, Nancy and Helen, moved to California. He started his career at Parker Hannifin in Parker Aircraft—a job where he would learn about the aircraft and seal business for the next 13 years.

COMMUNITY
ALLIANCES

P AT PARKER, BESIDES BEING EXTREMELY INVOLVED IN his company's expansion and innovative product lines, was an active participant in many companies, universities, and organizations.

Board Participation

- Member of the board of directors of Case Western Reserve University
- Member of the board of directors of the University School
- Member of the board of directors of the Musical Arts Association
- Member of the board of directors of the Playhouse Square Foundation
- Member of the board of directors of the Ohio Aerospace Institute
- Member of the board of directors of the Greater Cleveland Growth Association
- Trustee of the Western Reserve Historical Society
- Trustee of Woodruff Hospital
- Member of the board of directors of the College of Wooster
- Member of the board of directors of Reliance Electric Company

- Chairman of the board of trustees of Gateway Economic Development Corporation, responsible for the development of Jacob's Field and Gund Arena (now Progressive Field)
- Member of the board of directors of the Society National Bank and the Society Corporation
- Member of the board of directors of Acme-Cleveland Corporation
- Member of the board of directors of the Sherwin-Williams Company
- Member of the Advisory Board of The Salvation Army
- Trustee of the Kolff Foundation

Awards

- 1981 International Executive of the Year, Cleveland World Trade Association
- Certificate of Distinction for Executive Management by *Financial World* magazine
- 1983 Corecipient of the Achievement Award of the National Fluid Power Association
- 2004 Inductee for *Inside Business* magazine's Hall of Fame

In 1957, Parker Appliance acquired the Hannifin Corporation, a leading manufacturer of hydraulic and pneumatic power cylinders, valves, and hydraulic presses, whose products had a wide industrial application. The company's name was changed to Parker Hannifin, and the combination of company strengths allowed for great national growth, which increased business as Pat's involvement grew.

Pat was appointed to the Parker Hannifin board of directors in 1960 and he made frequent visits to the company's headquarters in Cleveland, Ohio. Soon after the birth of Pat's third daughter, Susan, and son, Streeter, Pat became president of Parker Hannifin in 1968. Later, he and his wife Peggy divorced. Pat served as CEO of the company from 1971 through 1983.

Making Connections

Pat always tried to satisfy the customer through his visionary approach. Once he had an idea, his wheels

---

Pat inherited the culture from the management before him, Ghost Taylor, Bob Cornell, and Scott Rogers. He was terrific, a very approachable person and very down to earth. I think that was the culture of Parker. The thing that made the company fun to work for was that all of us came up through the ranks.

—Duane Collins,
who started at Parker Hannifin in 1961,
and became chairman, president, and CEO

He was the type of guy you could just sit down and meet in a bar. You'd instantly like him and never know his name was on a building.

—Jack Myslenski,
a 34-year employee of Parker Hannifin, who retired as executive vice president of sales, marketing, and operations support in 2008

When I got to work for Pat, I found this is the reason we are the way we are. This is the man who has the spirit. [He] just got all these people to do their absolute best without demanding it. He knew everybody by their first name. He could go down on the factory floor, and call everybody by name.

—Dolores Lyon,
executive administrative assistant to Pat Parker
and a 36-year employee of Parker Hannifin

I've never met anybody who has such a memory like Pat. He'd walk into a place, and if he had met you once before, just once, he'd know your name. If you had any conversation, he'd remember all that. The

amazing thing is when we'd take him to a customer, the knowledge he had. It wasn't just about hydraulics and hoses. All of a sudden, the customer is just kind of amazed, but they're more amazed about how humble he was. You cannot not like Pat, and that's what the customers would see. Let me put it this way: Most of my experience with him was that when we took him to say, "Thank you" to someone, we came out with an order. I miss him, he was a friend and mentor.

—Marwan Kashkoush, executive vice president of sales, marketing, and operations support, who started at Parker Hannifin in 1977

I would consider him my mentor. We both enjoyed skiing, and we ended up with customers and distributors [on ski trips]. Pat was unpretentious. He was a brilliant engineer. The other thing was he just loved customers. He loved to find out what they wanted and needed and then to satisfy that need.

—Nickolas Vande Steeg,
president and chief operating officer,
who started at Parker Hannifin in 1971

He was a risk taker. He had this innate business sense of what was a good operation and what wasn't. He was responsible for many acquisitions personally, getting involved and deciding what companies to buy.

—Steve Hayes,
who started at Parker Hannifin in 1972 and retired as president of the Aerospace Group in 2003

Left: Pat Parker's love and understanding of sailing led him to outfit America's Cup yachts with Parker Hannifin hydraulics.

Below: Pat Parker, dressed as a pirate, alongside Jack Myslenski, tends to the barbecue at the 2004 Juvenile Diabetes Research Foundation fundraiser held at Parker Hannifin's corporate headquarters.

would spin, and Parker Hannifin would then have a new product or new division. This passion was evident to anyone who crossed Pat's path, but especially to his son, Streeter.

"If he had an idea that he needed to get going, he'd make a mental note, get on the phone, and call Dolores [Dolores Lyon, Pat's executive administrative assistant]," said Streeter. "All of a sudden, that brainstorm he had right then, he knew it was taken care of and that the notes had been made back in Cleveland. [Dolores] was jotting down this whole genesis, a whole new idea, a whole new business. The idea was safely nested back at headquarters, the proper people were being notified, and they'd already be working on it. By the time he got back, it would be halfway done."

By utilizing his entrepreneurial spirit, inquisitive mind, and hard work ethic, Pat helped launch the company overseas. After his second marriage, to Madeleine Hornickle in 1972, his family grew with a son, Maximilian in 1978, and a daughter, Astrid, in 1983.

As many Parker Hannifin acquisitions were companies located throughout the world, Pat embraced travel on both a personal and professional level. In addition to his home in Cleveland Heights, Pat and Madeleine spent summers at their home at Presqu'île de Giens in Provence in the south of France. He loved to cook local vegetables, in addition to performing galley duty on friends' yachts where he prepared grouper and lobster. Cooking aboard came naturally to Pat, who was an avid sailor and also instrumental in outfitting America's Cup yachts with Parker Hannifin hydraulics. He often wore a piece of rope for a belt in homage to his love of sailing.

Just as Pat enjoyed spending time with his family, he also valued his employees. Pat sought the advice of noted quality experts and then personally sponsored the company's first continuous employee improvement program. Thousands of employees looked at Pat as if he were a personal friend.

"He was the type of guy you could just sit down, meet in a bar, and you'd instantly like him," said Jack Myslenski, who started at Parker Hannifin in 1973 and retired as executive vice president of sales, marketing, and operations support. "When I was heading up the Juvenile Diabetes Walk in Cleveland and decided I was going to cook for everybody in the building, Pat took it upon himself to be my co-cook."

Elaine Zettelmeyer, a Parker Hannifin employee since 1973, recalled Pat's approachable and entertaining personality during one of many of her conversations with him.

"After a company golf outing, he sat with me during dinner. We all had steak and Pat said, 'You know, you're supposed to cut your steak in the middle. Everybody starts at the end, and by the time they get to the good part in the middle they're full,'" said Zettelmeyer, a clerk typist who eventually became a communications specialist. "Now I cut my steaks in the middle—the 'Parker middle.'"

This idea of always enjoying the best was one that Pat lived daily. Whether it was business or family, the man who served as chairman of Parker Hannifin from 1977 until his retirement in 1999 lived with zeal. His commitment to Parker Hannifin and its employees positioned it as the global leader in motion and control technologies.

Even after retirement, Pat wasn't found spending time on the golf course. Rather, he was busy thinking of future possibilities for Parker Hannifin, including new applications in fuel cells and marine markets. Just as he continued to embrace the company, he was also a philanthropist who supported local efforts such as the Cleveland Ballet. In a ballet performance of Elvis Presley's career, Pat was asked to don a leather outfit and ride his Harley-Davidson motorcycle on stage to "Blue Suede Shoes."

From foundry laborer to product line manager, sales manager, operations manager, war asset liquidator, and president, CEO, and chairman of the board, Pat was driven to make anything possible—and knew that every place in the world is affected by a Parker Hannifin product that is improving our standard of living.

"I can't think of anything that I did that I wouldn't do over again," said Pat. "Maybe they all didn't succeed quite the way I thought they would, but it's the old saying that if you're not making some mistakes, you're not really out there trying hard enough. We've had a lot of success, and, equally as important, is [that this] team—that's such a cohesive team at Parker—wouldn't be so cohesive if they weren't having fun doing it."

Above: On October 25, 2002, Pat Parker participated in the company's first ever bell ringing at the NYSE.

Right: This statue of Pat Parker stands outside the Parker Hannifin headquarters in Cleveland, Ohio, and captures Pat's free spirit.

Notes to Sources

Chapter One

1. 1920 United States Federal Census Record, Cleveland Ward 7, Cuyahoga, Ohio, Roll: T625_1363, 15A.
2. Parker Appliance Company, internal memo, 9 January 1947.
3. Case Western Reserve Archives, available at http://www.case.edu/its/archives/index.htm/.
4. Ibid.
5. Arthur LaRue Parker, obituaries, *Cleveland Press*, 2 January 1945.
6. "Life of Arthur LaRue Parker," Parker Appliance Company, internal memo, January 1945.
7. U.S. Patent and Trademark Office, publication no. 00935051.
8. Ibid.
9. U.S. Patent and Trademark Office, patent no. 1,268,764, publication no. 01268764.
10. Ibid.
11. "Great War & Jazz Age," The Library of Congress, available at http://www.americasstory.com/cgi-bin/page.cgi/jb/jazz/ww1_3/.
12. World War I Draft Registration Card, Draft Board, 1915.
13. "The History of Parker," PowerPoint presentation, Parker Hannifin Aerospace Group, 2006.
14. "Great War & Jazz Age."
15. U.S. Patent and Trademark Office, patent no. 1,315,683, publication no. 01315683.
16. "Glenn L. Martin Company," Wikipedia, available at http://en.wikipedia.org/wiki/Glenn_L._Martin_Company/.
17. "The History of Parker."
18. The Newcomen Society of North America, Patrick S. Parker, publication no. 1107, 1980, 12.
19. Ibid.
20. James O. Wood, personal recollection of conversations with Patrick S. Parker, 2005.
21. "Cleveland, Ohio, Along the Nickel Plate Road," Cleveland State University, available at http://web.ulib.csuohio.edu/nkp/index.htm/.
22. The Newcomen Society of North America.
23. Parker Appliance Company, internal memo, 9 January 1947.
24. U.S. Patent and Trademark Office, patent no. 1,619,755, publication no. 01619755.
25. Parker Appliance Company, internal memo, 9 January 1947.
26. Parker History Wall, Parker Hannifin corporate headquarters, Mayfield Heights, Ohio.
27. "Lockheed Corporation," Wikipedia, available at http://en.wikipedia.org/wiki/Lockheed/.

28. "Douglas Aircraft Company," Wikipedia, available at http://en.wikipedia.org/wiki/Douglas_Aircraft_Company/.

29. The Newcomen Society of North America.

30. Parker Appliance Company, internal memo, 9 January 1947.

31. Ibid.

32. "The History of Parker."

33. "A Short Summary of a Long History," Parker Hannifin Corporation, 2002.

34. "Charles Lindbergh: An American Aviator," available at http://www.charleslindbergh.com/history/index.asp/.

35. Ibid.

36. "The History of Parker."

37. "Charles Lindbergh: An American Aviator."

38. Ibid.

39. "Great War & Jazz Age."

40. James O. Wood, personal recollection of conversations with Patrick S. Parker.

41. Ibid.

42. Ibid.

43. "Life of Arthur LaRue Parker."

44. U.S. Patent and Trademark Office, patent no. 1,774,841, publication no. 01774841.

Chapter One Sidebar: The U.S. Patent Process

1. Jason O. Watson, "A History of the United States Patent Office," available at http://www.historical-markers.org/usptohistory.cgi/.

2. Ibid.

3. Constitution of the United States of America.

4. Michael Russell, "History of U.S. Patent Office," available at http://ezinearticles.com/?Patent---History-Of-U.S.-Patent-Office&id=145719/.

5. Ibid.

6. "A History of the United States Patent Office."

7. B. Zorina Khan, "An Economic History of Patent Institutions," Bowdoin College, available at http://eh.net/encyclopedia/article/khan.patents/.

8. "A History of the United States Patent Office."

9. Christopher A. Rothe, J.D., "Using Patents to Advance the Civil Engineering Profession," *Civil Engineering*, June 2006, 73.

10. Ibid.

11. Ibid.

Chapter One Sidebar: An Industry Takes Flight

1. "Glenn L. Martin Company," Wikipedia, available at http://en.wikipedia.org/wiki/Glenn_L._Martin_Company/.

2. "Airplane collection," Western Reserve Historical Society, available at http://www.wrhs.org/crawford/template.asp?id=128/.

3. "1930s National Air Races: Speed and Spectacle," The History Net, available at http://www.historynet.com/exploration/adventurers/3032876.html/.

4. "Cleveland, Ohio, Transportation," Wikipedia, available at http://en.wikipedia.org/wiki/Cleveland#Transportation/.

5. "Glenn Curtiss," Ohio History, available at http://worlddmc.ohiolink.edu.OMP/NewDetails?oid=2469110&scrapid=3449&format=y/.

6. "Glenn L. Martin Company."

7. "Airplane collection."

8. "1930s National Air Races."

9. "Cleveland's Aerospace History: the Hotbed of Aviation," NASA Glenn History, available at http://www.nasa.gov/centers/glenn/about/history/index.html/.

Chapter Two

1. U.S. Patent and Trademark Office, patent no. 1,619,755, publication no. 01619755.

2. U.S. Patent and Trademark Office, patent no. 1,894,700, publication no. 01894700.

3. "Life of Arthur LaRue Parker," Parker Appliance Company, internal memo, January 1945.

4. "The American Experience: The Great Depression," available at http://www.pbs.org/wgbh/amex/dustbowl/peopleevents/pandeAMEX05.html/.

5. Ibid.

6. Ibid.

7. "A Short Summary of a Long History," Parker Hannifin Corporation, 2002.

8. Parker Appliance Company, internal memo, 9 January 1947.

9. Parker History Wall, Parker Hannifin corporate headquarters, Mayfield Heights, Ohio.

10. U.S. Patent and Trademark Office, patent no. 2,102,214, publication no. 02102214.

11. Parker Appliance Company, internal memo, 9 January 1947.

12. *Fitting News*, Parker Appliance Company, internal newsletter, October 1934.

13. *Fitting News*, Parker Appliance Company, internal newsletter, February 1935.
14. The Newcomen Society of North America, Patrick S. Parker, publication no. 1107, 1980.
15. Ibid.
16. *Fitting News*, Parker Appliance Company, internal newsletter, 15 December 1935.
17. Ibid.
18. Parker Appliance Company, internal memo, 9 January 1947.
19. *Fitting News*, Parker Appliance Company, internal newsletter, 15 January 1936.
20. Ibid.
21. *Fitting News*, Parker Appliance Company, internal newsletter, 15 April 1937.
22. Parker Appliance Company, internal memo, 9 January 1947.
23. E. W. Ned Hollis, "The History of Parker Seal," Parker Seals, R&D Report, March 1976.
24. The Newcomen Society of North America.
25. Ibid.
26. Ibid.
27. James O. Wood, personal recollection of conversations with Patrick S. Parker, 2005.
28. "Franklin D. Roosevelt," Grolier online, available at http://www.grolier.com/wwii/wwii_roosevelt.html/.
29. The Newcomen Society of North America.
30. The Parker Appliance Company, internal memo, 9 January 1947.
31. The Newcomen Society of North America.
32. "A Short Summary of a Long History."

Chapter Two Sidebar: Assembling American Industry's Future

1. "Henry Ford Changes the World," EyeWitnessToHistory.com, available at http://www.eyewitnesstohistory.com/ford.htm/.
2. "The Henry Ford: The Life of Henry Ford," available at http://www.hfmgv.org/exhibits/hf/#theengineer/.
3. "The First Mass Production of Cars, The Assembly Line," available at http://inventors.about.com/library/weekly/aacarsassemblya.htm/.
4. "The Henry Ford: The Life of Henry Ford."
5. "Life of Arthur LaRue Parker," Parker Appliance Company, internal memo, January 1945.

Chapter Two Sidebar: Surviving "Black Tuesday"

1. Encyclopedia of Cleveland History, Aviation, available at http://ech.case.edu/ech-cgi/article.pl?id=A19/.
2. *Aviation Week & Space Technology*, 29 May 1967, 358.
3. "Glenn L. Martin Company," Wikipedia, available at http://en.wikipedia.org/wiki/Glenn_L._Martin_Company/.
4. "Life of Arthur LaRue Parker," Parker Appliance Company, internal memo, January 1945.
5. Encyclopedia of Cleveland History, Aviation.
6. "A Short Summary of a Long History," Parker Hannifin Corporation, 2002.

7. U.S. Patent and Trademark Office, patent no. 1,619,755 and patent no. 1,894,700.

Chapter Three

1. The Parker Appliance Company 1941 Annual Report.
2. "Fluid Power," An Industrial Development Contributed by The Parker Appliance Company, 1943.
3. U.S Patent and Trademark Office, patent no. 2,185,564, publication no. 02185564.
4. U.S. Patent and Trademark Office, patent no. 2,189,675, publication no. 02189675.
5. U.S. Patent and Trademark Office, patent no. 2,209,135, publication no. 02209135.
6. *The Cleveland Plain Dealer*, 23 April 1941.
7. Ibid.
8. Ibid.
9. Ibid.
10. Ibid.
11. "Remembering Pearl Harbor," *National Geographic*, available at http://plasma.nationalgeographic.com/pearlharbor/ax/frameset.html/.
12. E. W. Ned Hollis, "The History of Parker Seal," Parker Seals, R&D Report, March 1976.
13. Ibid.
14. Ibid.
15. Ibid.
16. Ibid.
17. Ibid.
18. Ibid.
19. "Fluid Power."
20. The Parker Appliance Company 1943 Annual Report.
21. "Fluid Power."

22. *Fitting News*, Parker Appliance Company, internal newsletter, January 1943.
23. Ibid.
24. Ibid., 14, 19.
25. Ibid., 15.
26. *Fitting News*, Parker Appliance Company, internal newsletter, October 1943.
27. *Fitting News*, Parker Appliance Company, internal newsletter, April 1943, 8.
28. Parker Appliance Company 1944 Annual Report.
29. Ibid.
30. The Newcomen Society Address, Patrick S. Parker, 4 October 1979.
31. "Full Throttle for WWII," *Crain's Cleveland Business*, 4 December 1995, B–65.
32. Parker Appliance Company, internal memo, 9 January 1947.
33. "Arthur L. Parker Dies in his Sleep," *Cleveland Plain Dealer*, January 1945.
34. Ibid.
35. The Newcomen Society Address.
36. Ibid.

Chapter Three Sidebar: Saving the Country through Bonds

1. "Home Front 1941–1945: Buy War Bonds," Military History, available at http://militaryhistory.about.com/od/worldwari1/a/warbonds_2.htm/.
2. Ibid.
3. Ibid.
4. "Brief History of World War Two Advertising Campaigns, War Loans and Bonds," John W. Hartman Center for Sales, Advertising, and Marketing History, available at http://scriptorium.lib.duke.edu/adaccess/warbonds.html/.
5. "Home Front 1941–1945: Buy War Bonds."
6. *Fitting News,* Parker Appliance Company, internal newsletter, January 1943, 15.
7. Ibid.

Chapter Three Sidebar: Surviving Against All Odds

1. "Adolf Hitler," Wikipedia, available at http://en.wikipedia.org/wiki/Adolf_Hitler/.
2. "The Dachau Gas Chambers," Harry W. Mazal OBE, available at http://www.holocaust-history.org/dachau-gas-chambers/.
3. Ibid.
4. Ibid.
5. Ibid.
6. *Fitting News,* Parker Appliance Company, internal newsletter, September 1943, 10.
7. Ibid.
8. Ibid.
9. Ibid.

Chapter Four

1. *Fitting News*, Parker Appliance Company, internal newsletter, February 1945, 3.
2. Thomas W. Gerdel, "Parker Hannifin: Cleveland Manufacturer's Business Boosted by Plants in 30 Countries," *The Plain Dealer*, 26 June 1999, 5–S.
3. "World War II," Wikipedia, available at http://en.wikipedia.org/wiki/World_War_II/.
4. The Newcomen Society Address, Patrick S. Parker, 4 October 1979.
5. "Picketed Parker Appliance Plant Closed by Company," *The Plain Dealer*, 1945.
6. Parker Appliance Company 1945 Annual Report.
7. "Business & The Bicentennial, Full Throttle for WWII," *Crain's Cleveland Business*, 4 December 1995, B–68.
8. Parker Appliance Company 1945 Annual Report.
9. Ibid.
10. "Picketed Parker Appliance Plant Closed by Company."
11. "14 Hurt as Police, Strikers Clash at Parker Appliance," *The Plain Dealer*, 5 September 1945.
12. Ibid.
13. Ibid.
14. Parker Appliance Company 1945 Annual Report.
15. Ibid.
16. Parker Appliance Company 1946 Annual Report.
17. Ibid.
18. Parker History Wall, Parker Hannifin corporate headquarters, Mayfield Heights, Ohio.
19. Parker Appliance Company 1946 Annual Report.
20. "Parker Hannifin: Cleveland Manufacturer's Business Boosted by Plants in 30 Countries."
21. Ibid.
22. "Parker Seals, R&D report," History of Parker Seal, Winter 1978/79.
23. Ibid.
24. Ibid.
25. Ibid.
26. Ibid.

27. Parker Appliance Company 1948 Annual Report.
28. "Seventy Years of Engineering, Parker-Hannifin: Focusing on the Total Package," *Machine Design*, 23 September 1999.
29. Ibid.
30. "Fluid Power," Parker Appliance Company, 1943.
31. Ibid.
32. "Korean War," Wikipedia, available at http://en.wikipedia.org/wiki/Korean_War#Order_of_battle/.
33. Ibid.
34. The Newcomen Society Address.
35. Ibid.
36. Parker Appliance Company 1950 Annual Report.
37. Ibid.
38. Ibid.

Chapter Four Sidebar: War and Cigarettes

1. "Smoking," The History Channel, available at http://www.history.com/encyclopedia.do?zrticleId=222558/.
2. Ibid.
3. David Burns, et al., "Cigarette Smoking Behavior in the United States," Smoking and Tobacco Control Monograph no. 8.
4. Ibid.
5. "America, History of Matchbooks," available at http://sberatel.com/zapalky/en/zobrazit.php?clanek=america/.
6. *Fitting News*, Parker Appliance Company, internal newsletter, March 1945, 12.

7. Ibid.
8. Ibid.
9. "Immunotoxicology Smoking History," available at http://www.clinimmune.com/immunotoxicologylab/smokinghistory.htm/.

Chapter Four Sidebar: A Widow's Faith

1. Jim Wood, interview by Jeffrey L. Rodengen, digital recording, 20–21 September 2006, Write Stuff Enterprises, Inc.
2. The Newcomen Society Address, Patrick S. Parker, 4 October 1979.
3. Thomas W. Gerdel, "Parker Hannifin: Cleveland Manufacturer's Business Boosted by Plants in 30 Countries," *The Plain Dealer*, 26 June 1999, 5–S.
4. U.S. Patent Office, "Coupling for Tubes," patent no. 2,458,874.
5. Ibid.
6. Ibid.
7. U.S. Patent Office, "Engine Primer," patent no. 2,450,295.
8. Ibid.
9. A. L. Parker patents, Parker Hannifin internal documents.

Chapter Five

1. Parker: A Corporate Overview, 7.
2. Ibid.
3. Ibid.
4. Parker Appliance Company 1951 Annual Report.
5. Ibid.
6. Ibid.
7. Robert Barnd, letter correspondence, 8 August 2006, Write Stuff Enterprises, Inc.

8. Ibid.
9. Ibid.
10. Ibid.
11. Robert Barnd, interview by Jeffrey L. Rodengen, digital recording, 25 September 2006, Write Stuff Enterprises, Inc.
12. Ibid.
13. Parker Appliance Company 1951 Annual Report.
14. Ibid.
15. Ibid.
16. Ibid.
17. Parker Appliance Company, internal correspondence, C. E. Cleminshaw, 14 August 1951.
18. Bill Webster, interview by Jeffrey L. Rodengen, digital recording, 13 September 2006, Write Stuff Enterprises, Inc.
19. Robert Barnd interview, 25 September 2006.
20. *Fitting News*, Parker Appliance Company, internal newsletter, August 1952.
21. Parker Appliance Company, Volunteer Fire Brigade, 10 October 1952.
22. "Korean War, Korean War Timeline 1953," http://www.korean-war.com/TimeLine/1953/timeline1953.html/.
23. Parker: A Corporate Overview, 8.
24. Parker Appliance Company 1953 Annual Report.
25. Ibid.
26. Parker Appliance Company 1955 Annual Report.
27. Parker Appliance Company 1954 Annual Report.

28. Parker Hannifin Corporation, Comparative Statistics, 1945–2005.
29. Parker Appliance Company 1956 Annual Report.
30. The Newcomen Society Address, Patrick S. Parker, 4 October 1979.
31. Robert Barnd interview, 25 September 2006.
32. Ibid.
33. The Newcomen Society Address.
34. Parker Appliance Company 1957 Annual Report.
35. "Added Facility," *Los Angeles Times*, 17 February 1957.
36. Parker Appliance Company 1958 Annual Report.
37. Dun & Bradstreet, Inc., Credit Report Special Notice, 10 September 1957.
38. Parker Appliance Company 1958 Annual Report.
39. Donald J. Mabry, "Historical Text Archive, 1953–1961: Eisenhower Years," available at http://historicaltextarchive.com/sections.php?op=viewarticle&artid=537/.
40. Parker Appliance Company 1958 Annual Report.
41. "NASA," Wikipedia, available at http://en.wikipedia.org/wiki/NASA#Space_race/.
42. Parker Hannifin Corporation 1958 Annual Report.
43. Parker Hannifin Corporation 1959 Annual Report.
44. Ibid.
45. "Parker Hannifin Sees Rise in Profit, Sales, Press Business Pages," *The Cleveland Press*, 16 September 1959.
46. Parker Hannifin Corporation 1961 Annual Report.

Chapter Five Sidebar: Parker President Plays at the Hermit Club

1. "The Lambs, America's First Professional Theatre Club," available at http://www.the-lambs.org/about.htm/.
2. "The Hermit Club, Nineteen Hundred and Four, The Beginning Year," available at http://www.thehermitclub.org/history/1904/1904-Page-2.htm/.
3. Ibid.
4. Ibid.
5. "The Lambs, America's First Professional Theatre Club."
6. Robert Barnd, interview by Jeffrey L. Rodengen, digital recording, 25 September 2006, Write Stuff Enterprises, Inc.
7. Bill Webster, interview by Jeffrey L. Rodengen, digital recording, 13 September 2006, Write Stuff Enterprises, Inc.

Chapter Five Sidebar: Parker Hannifin Explores the Final Frontier

1. "The History of Aviation and Modern Rocketry," available at http://www.thespaceplace.com/history/rocket2.html/.
2. "NASA History Division," available at http://history.nasa.gov/.
3. Paul Schloemer, interview by Jeffrey L. Rodengen, digital recording, 8 November 2006, Write Stuff Enterprises, Inc.
4. "Science and Technology, Wernher von Braun: 1912–1977," available at http://www.u-s-history.com/pages/h1720.html/.

Chapter Six

1. Parker Hannifin Corporation 1960 Annual Report.
2. "Major Changes during the 1960s: United States," Wikipedia, available at http://en.wikipedia.org/wiki/1960s#In_the_United_States/.
3. Parker Hannifin Corporation 1960 Annual Report.
4. Denny Sullivan, interview by Jeffrey L. Rodengen, digital recording, 4 October 2006, Write Stuff Enterprises, Inc.
5. Ibid.
6. Robert Barnd, interview by Jeffrey L. Rodengen, digital recording, 25 September 2006, Write Stuff Enterprises, Inc.
7. Paul Schloemer, interview by Jeffrey L. Rodengen, digital recording, 8 November 2006, Write Stuff Enterprises, Inc.
8. Ibid.
9. Ibid.
10. Denny Sullivan interview.
11. Duane Collins, interview by Jeffrey L. Rodengen, digital recording, 26 July 2006, Write Stuff Enterprises, Inc.
12. William (Bill) Armbruster, letter correspondence, 18 September 2006, Write Stuff Enterprises, Inc.
13. Parker Hannifin Corporation, Comparative Statistics, 1945–2005.
14. Ibid.

15. Ibid.
16. Parker Hannifin Corporation 1959 Annual Report.
17. Parker Hannifin Corporation 1962 Annual Report.
18. Ibid.
19. *Cleveland Press*, 1963.
20. Parker Hannifin Corporation 1963 Annual Report.
21. Ibid
22. William (Bill) Armbruster, letter correspondence.
23. "Battlefield Vietnam: Timeline," PBS, available at http://www.pbs.org/battlefieldvietnam/timeline/index.html/.
24. Parker Hannifin Corporation 1966 Annual Report.
25. Parker Hannifin Corporation 1965 Annual Report.
26. Ibid.
27. Ibid.
28. Pat McMonagle, interview by Jeffrey L. Rodengen, digital recording, 16 August 2006, Write Stuff Enterprises, Inc.
29. Ibid.
30. Denny Sullivan, interview by Jeffrey L. Rodengen, digital recording, 4 October 2006, Write Stuff Enterprises, Inc.
31. Dennis W. Sullivan, 1997 Distinguished Engineering Alumni, Purdue University, available at http://www.ecn.purdue.edu/ECN/DEA/1997/Dennis_W_Sullivan.whtml/.
32. Denny Sullivan interview.
33. Parker Hannifin Corporation 1965 Annual Report.
34. Ibid.
35. Ibid.
36. "Battlefield Vietnam: Timeline."
37. Parker Hannifin Corporation 1966 Annual Report.

38. Ibid.
39. "Growing to Meet the Challenge of Growth Era in Fluid Power," Parker Hannifin, 1965.
40. Ibid.
41. Parker Hannifin Hose Hi-Liter, Wickliffe Plant, 1967.
42. "Growing to Meet the Challenge of Growth Era in Fluid Power."
43. *Sparker Newsletter* for distributors of Parker Hannifin, Parker Hannifin, March 1967.
44. R. W. Cornell, address to the Boston Security Analysts Society, 2 March 1967.
45. *Jet Set,* Parker Hannifin internal newsletter, November 1967.
46. The Otsego Union, vol. 109, no. 38, 14 March 1968.
47. Parker Hannifin Corporation 1968 Annual Report.
48. Ibid.
49. "Major Changes during the 1960s: United States."
50. Parker Hannifin Corporation 1968 Annual Report.

Chapter Six Sidebar: Parker Hannifin Supports *Apollo 11*

1. "*Apollo 11*," Wikipedia, available at http://en.wikipedia.org/wiki/Apollo_11/.
2. John Roach, "Apollo Anniversary: Moon Landing Inspired the World," available at http://news.nationalgeographic.com/news/2004/07/0714_040714_moonlanding.html/.
3. "*Apollo 11*."
4. "The Parker Hannifin Countdown with the *Apollo 11*," Parker Hannifin, June 1969.
5. Ibid.
6. Parker Valves, Apollo Glossary, available at http://www.hq.nasa.gov/alsj/apollo.glossary.html/.
7. "*Apollo 11*."
8. "The Parker Hannifin Countdown with the *Apollo 11*."
9. Ibid.
10. Ibid.
11. Ibid.
12. Ibid.
13. Ibid.
14. Ibid.

Chapter Six Sidebar: War Efforts Prompt Innovation

1. The Newcomen Society of North America, Patrick S. Parker, publication no. 1107, 1980.
2. "Parker Hannifin: Cleveland Manufacturer's Business Boosted by Plants in 30 Countries," *The Plain Dealer*, 26 June 1996, 5–S.
3. Parker Appliance Company 1950 Annual Report.
4. Michael Zawacki, "Eyes Wide Open: Patrick S. Parker Led Parker Hannifin Corp. by Seeking and Encouraging Innovation" (2004 Business Hall of Fame), *Inside Business*, October 2004.
5. "Battlefield Vietnam: Timeline," PBS, available at http://www.pbs.org/battlefieldvietnam/timeline/index.html/.
6. Parker Hannifin Tube Fittings Division advertisement, 1969.

7. Ibid.
8. Ibid.
9. Parker Hannifin Aerospace Group, Pipeline, February 1969.
10. Parker Hannifin, Fluid Power Leadership, mid-1960s.

Chapter Six Sidebar: Divisions Unite Parker Hannifin

1. Parker Hannifin Corporation 1959 Annual Report.
2. Parker Hannifin Corporation 1962 Annual Report.
3. Parker Hannifin Corporation 1963 Annual Report.

Chapter Seven

1. Parker History Wall, Parker Hannifin corporate headquarters, Mayfield Heights, Ohio.
2. Ibid.
3. U.S. Department of Labor, Bureau of Labor Statistics, Albert E. Schwenk, "Compensation in the 1970s," available at http://www.bls.gov/opub/cwc/cm20030124ar05p1.htm/.
4. "The Struggle to Cope with Recession," *Time*, 16 February 1970.
5. Ibid.
6. The Newcomen Society Address, Patrick S. Parker, 4 October 1979.
7. John Zakaria, interview by Jeffrey L. Rodengen, digital recording, 5 October 2006, Write Stuff Enterprises, Inc.
8. Ibid.
9. The Newcomen Society Address.
10. Ibid.

11. John Zakaria interview.
12. Parker Hannifin Corporation 1970 Annual Report.
13. Ibid.
14. Ibid.
15. "Nixon's Recession," *Time*, 18 January 1971.
16. Ibid.
17. "History of the United States (1964–1980)," Wikipedia, available at http://en.wikipedia.org/wiki/History_of_the_United_States_(1964%E2%80%931980)#Nixon_and_Vietnam/.
18. Parker Hannifin Corporation 1971 Annual Report.
19. Ibid.
20. John Zakaria interview.
21. Michael Zawacki, "Eyes Wide Open: Patrick S. Parker Led Parker Hannifin Corp. by Seeking and Encouraging Innovation" (2004 Business Hall of Fame), *Inside Business*, October 2004.
22. Don Washkewicz, interview by Jeffrey L. Rodengen, digital recording, 25 July 2006, Write Stuff Enterprises, Inc.
23. Ibid.
24. Ibid.
25. Ibid.
26. Ibid.
27. Ibid.
28. Ibid.
29. Denny Sullivan, interview by Jeffrey L. Rodengen, digital recording, 4 October 2006, Write Stuff Enterprises, Inc.
30. Don Washkewicz interview.
31. Denny Sullivan interview.
32. Ibid.
33. Don Washkewicz interview.

34. "Eyes Wide Open."
35. Don Washkewicz interview.
36. Denny Sullivan interview.
37. Parker Hannifin Corporation 1973 Annual Report.
38. "The History Place, The Vietnam War," available at http://www.historyplace.com/unitedstates/vietnam/index-1969.html/.
39. Parker Hannifin Corporation 1974 Annual Report.
40. Ibid.
41. "History of the United States (1964–1980)."
42. Parker Hannifin Corporation 1973 Annual Report.
43. "History of Acquisitions & Divestitures," Parker Hannifin Corporation, 13 September 2006.
44. Bill Webster, interview by Jeffrey L. Rodengen, digital recording, 13 September 2006, Write Stuff Enterprises, Inc.
45. Parker Hannifin Corporation 1975 Annual Report.
46. Bill Webster interview.
47. Ibid.
48. Parker Hannifin Corporation 1975 Annual Report.
49. Paul Schloemer, interview by Jeffrey L. Rodengen, digital recording, 8 November 2006, Write Stuff Enterprises, Inc.
50. Ibid.
51. "History of Acquisitions & Divestitures."
52. Heinz Droxner, interview by Jeffrey L. Rodengen, digital recording, 16 August 2006, Write Stuff Enterprises, Inc.
53. Ibid.
54. Parker Hannifin Corporation 1975 Annual Report.

55. Parker Hannifin Corporation Comparative Statistics 1945–2005.

56. Joe Vicic, interview by Jeffrey L. Rodengen, digital recording, 16 August 2006, Write Stuff Enterprises, Inc.

57. Parker Hannifin Corporation 1977 Annual Report.

58. Ibid.

59. Ibid.

Chapter Seven Sidebar: Rescue from Space

1. "*Apollo 13*," Wikipedia, available at http://en.wikipedia.org/wiki/Apollo_13/.

2. Ibid.

3. "Parker Takes Motion and Control Systems to New Heights," Parker Investor Relations, Cleveland, available at http://www.corporateir.net/ireye/ir_site.zhtml?ticker=ph&script=410&layout=11&item_id=479274/.

4. "*Apollo 13.*"

5. Parker Highlights in History, Parker Played Key Role in *Apollo 13* Crisis, internal document.

6. Ibid.

7. Ibid.

8. Ibid.

9. Ibid.

10. Ibid.

11. Ibid.

12. Ibid.

13. Ibid.

14. Ibid.

15. Ibid.

16. Ibid.

17. Ibid.

18. Ibid.

19. Ibid.

20. Rick DeMeis, "Engineering News," *Design News,* 15 May 2000.

Chapter Seven Sidebar: Distributing Success

1. Jim Wood, interview by Jeffrey L. Rodengen, digital recording, 20–21 September 2006, Write Stuff Enterprises, Inc.

2. Jack Myslenski, Investor Day PowerPoint presentation, 21 November 2006.

3. Parker Appliance Company 1945 Annual Report.

4. "Reliance Electric, History," available at http://www.reliance.com/aboutre/aboutre_english.htm/.

5. Bill Webster, e-mail correspondence, 11 January 2007, Write Stuff Enterprises, Inc.

6. Ben Wattenburg, "The First Measured Century: Program: Segment 8: World War II," PBS, available at http://www.pbs.org/fmc/segments/progseg8.htm/.

7. Bill Webster, e-mail correspondence.

8. Parker Appliance Company 1951 Annual Report.

9. Ibid.

10. Bill Webster, e-mail correspondence.

11. Jack Myslenski, "Parker Distributors: At Your Service," editorial, Parker European Business Report, Autumn 2006.

12. Jim Wood interview.

13. Cary Rhoten, interview by Jeffrey L. Rodengen, digital recording, 16 November 2006, Write Stuff Enterprises, Inc.

14. Parker Hannifin Corporation Comparative Statistics, 1945–2005.

15. Randy Gross, interview by Jeffrey L. Rodengen, digital recording, 13 November 2006, Write Stuff Enterprises, Inc.

16. "Parker Distributors: At Your Service."

17. Jeff Weber, interview by Jeffrey L. Rodengen, digital recording, 17 August 2006, Write Stuff Enterprises, Inc.

Chapter Eight

1. "Jimmy Carter," Wikipedia, available at http://en.wikipedia.org/wiki/Jimmy_Carter/.

2. Ibid.

3. "Fluid Controls Tap a King-Size Market," *BusinessWeek,* 14 July 1975.

4. Ibid.

5. Ibid.

6. Ibid.

7. Parker Hannifin Corporation 1978 Annual Report.

8. Ibid.

9. Ibid.

10. Nickolas W. Vande Steeg, interview by Jeffrey L. Rodengen, digital recording, 26 July 2006, Write Stuff Enterprises, Inc.

11. Michael Zawacki, "Eyes Wide Open: Patrick S. Parker Led Parker Hannifin Corp. by Seeking and Encouraging Innovation" (2004 Business Hall of Fame), *Inside Business,* October 2004.

12. Bob Bond, interview with Jeffrey L. Rodengen,

digital recording, 25 July 2006, Write Stuff Enterprises, Inc.

13. "The Latin Beat, Going Back in History," Parker Hannifin Latin American Group, Autumn 2000.

14. Ibid.

15. Patti Sfero, interview by Jeffrey L. Rodengen, digital recording, 26 July 2006, Write Stuff Enterprises, Inc.

16. Lonnie Gallup, interview by Jeffrey L. Rodengen, digital recording, 12 October 2006, Write Stuff Enterprises, Inc.

17. The Newcomen Society of North America, Patrick S. Parker, publication no. 1107, 1980.

18. Ivan Marks, "A Tale of Strawberries, Beans, and Real Estate," Parker Aerospace, 2005.

19. Richard Bertea, University of Colorado at Boulder, Alumni and Donors, available at http://www.colorado.edu/engineering/deaa/cgi-bin/display.pl?id=163/.

20. "A Tale of Strawberries, Beans, and Real Estate."

21. Ibid.

22. Dick Bertea, interview by Jeffrey L. Rodengen, digital recording, 28 November 2006, Write Stuff Enterprises, Inc.

23. Richard Bertea, University of Colorado at Boulder, Alumni and Donors.

24. Parker Hannifin, profile, available at http://www.answers.com/topic/parker-hannifin-corporation/.

25. Bill Webster, interview by Jeffrey L. Rodengen,

digital recording, 13 September 2006, Write Stuff Enterprises, Inc.

26. Ibid.

27. Ibid.

28. Ibid.

29. Steve Hayes, interview by Jeffrey L. Rodengen, digital recording, 2 October 2006, Write Stuff Enterprises, Inc.

30. Parker History Wall, Parker Hannifin corporate headquarters, Mayfield Heights, Ohio.

31. Ibid.

32. Ibid.

33. Parker Hannifin Corporation 1979 Annual Report.

34. Ibid.

35. Ibid.

36. "Jimmy Carter."

37. Parker Hannifin, profile.

38. Ibid.

39. Parker Hannifin Corporation 1980 Annual Report.

40. Parker History Wall.

41. Parker Hannifin Corporation, Comparative Statistics, 1945–2005.

42. Parker Hannifin Corporation 1980 Annual Report.

43. Parker Hannifin, profile.

44. The Newcomen Society Address, Patrick S. Parker, 4 October 1979.

45. Parker Hannifin Corporation 1980 Annual Report.

Chapter Eight Sidebar: Realizing the American Dream

1. "1970s," Wikipedia, available at http://en.wikipedia.org/wiki/1970s#Economy_of_the_Seventies/.

2. Landmarks in the Development of U.S. Housing Policy, SUNY

Albany, Pub 528/Pos 528 U.S. Housing Policy.

3. Bob Howard, "Business Booming at Irvine Industrial Complex," *The Register*, 8 September 1975.

4. Ibid.

5. Letter from H. J. Schwellenbach, Project Administrator, The Irvine Company, to Charles Cleminshaw, Parker Hannifin Aerospace, 14 April 1976.

6. Ibid.

7. Letter from Charles E. Cleminshaw, president, Irvine Housing Opportunities, Inc., and Parker Hannifin Aerospace, to John Hollenbeck, partner, Coopers & Lybrand, 24 August 1976.

8. *Fitting News*, Parker Appliance Company, internal newsletter, January 1936.

9. Woodbridge Village Homes, The Irvine Company Multifamily Division, 24 August 1976.

10. Letter from Charles E. Cleminshaw.

11. Parker Aerospace, internal memo, September 1976.

Chapter Nine

1. Michael Zawacki, "Eyes Wide Open: Patrick S. Parker Led Parker Hannifin Corp. by Seeking and Encouraging Innovation" (2004 Business Hall of Fame), *Inside Business*, October 2004.

2. Parker Hannifin Corporation 1980 Annual Report.

3. James Wood, "The Parker Paradox Log," as told by Patrick S. Parker, 29 March 2005.

4. Encyclopedia of the Nations: Asia and Oceania: Japan,

available at http://
www.nationsencyclopedia.com/
Asia-and-Oceania/Japan-
INDUSTRY.html/.

5. Ibid.

6. Parker Hannifin Corporation
1981 Annual Report.

7. Patrick S. Parker, speech at the
Corporate Staff Cost Goal
Meeting, 20–21 September 1985.

8. Paul Schloemer, interview
by Jeffrey L. Rodengen,
digital recording,
8 November 2006, Write
Stuff Enterprises, Inc.

9. Parker Hannifin Corporation
1981 Annual Report.

10. Ibid.

11. Ibid.

12. Ibid.

13. David Rudyk, interview
by Jeffrey L. Rodengen,
digital recording,
28 September 2006, Write
Stuff Enterprises, Inc.

14. Ibid.

15. Ibid.

16. Ibid.

17. Parker Hannifin Corporation
1981 Annual Report.

18. Parker Hannifin, profile,
available at http://
www.answers.com/topic/
parker-hannifin-corporation/.

19. Encyclopedia of the Nations:
Asia and Oceania: Japan.

20. "Economy of the United
States," Wikipedia, available
at http://en.wikipedia.org/wiki/
Economy_of_the_United_States/.

21. Parker Hannifin Corporation
1979 Annual Report.

22. Bob Bond, interview
by Jeffrey L. Rodengen,
digital recording,
25 July 2006, Write
Stuff Enterprises, Inc.

23. "Ronald Reagan, The
American Presidency," Grolier
Multimedia Encyclopedia,
available at http://
ap.grolier.com/
article?assetid=0243360-
0&templatename=/article/
article.html/.

24. Parker Hannifin Corporation
1983 Annual Report.

25. Ibid.

26. "History of Acquisitions
& Divestitures," Parker
Hannifin Corporation,
13 September 2006.

27. Pete Buca, interview
with Jeffrey L. Rodengen,
digital recording,
6 October 2006, Write
Stuff Enterprises, Inc.

28. Patrick S. Parker, speech
on Parker Hannifin's
acquisition philosophy,
30 November 1983.

29. "History of Acquisitions
& Divestitures."

30. Ibid.

31. Parker Hannifin Corporation
1984 Annual Report.

32. Parker Hannifin Corporation
1985 Annual Report.

33. Parker Hannifin Corporation
1984 Annual Report.

34. Dana A. Dennis, interview
by Jeffrey L. Rodengen,
digital recording,
27 July 2006, Write
Stuff Enterprises, Inc.

35. John Oelslager, interview
by Jeffrey L. Rodengen,
digital recording,
27 July 2006, Write
Stuff Enterprises, Inc.

36. Parker Hannifin Corporation
Fiscal 1985 Annual Report.

37. Parker History Wall, Parker
Hannifin corporate

headquarters, Mayfield
Heights, Ohio.

38. Parker Hannifin Corporation
Fiscal 1986 Annual Report.

39. Parker Hannifin Corporation,
Comparative Statistics,
1945–2005.

40. "Information Age,"
Wikipedia, available at http://
en.wikipedia.org/wiki/
Information_Age/.

41. Patrick S. Parker, speech
at the Innovations
Management Conference,
12–13 May 1983.

42. Parker Hannifin Corporation
1986 Annual Report.

43. Ellen Parson, "The 1980s,"
EC&M, 1 June 2001.

44. Paul Schloemer interview.

45. Parker Hannifin Corporation
1987 Annual Report.

46. Patrick S. Parker, speech in
Brazil, 2 March 1988.

47. Patrick S. Parker, Harvard
Business School Club of
Cleveland Address,
21 January 1987.

48. Duane Collins, interview
by Jeffrey L. Rodengen,
digital recording,
26 July 2006, Write
Stuff Enterprises, Inc.

49. Ibid.

50. Ibid.

51. Ibid.

52. Parker Hannifin Corporation
1987 Annual Report.

53. Parker Hannifin Corporation
1988 Annual Report.

54. Parker Hannifin, profile.

55. Parker Hannifin Corporation
1989 Annual Report.

56. Patrick S. Parker, speech to
employees, 20 April 1989.

57. Parker Hannifin Corporation
1989 Annual Report.

58. Patrick S. Parker, "Bet on the Yankees," *Cleveland Plain Dealer*, 3 February 1989.

Chapter Nine Sidebar: Harnessing the Information Age

1. Ellen Parson, "The 1980s," *EC&M*, 1 June 2001.
2. Jim Wood, interview with Jeffrey L. Rodengen, digital recording, 20–21 September 2006, Write Stuff Enterprises, Inc.
3. Patrick S. Parker, interoffice speech, 14 September 1989.
4. Ibid.
5. Melvin Kranzberg, "The Information Age: Evolution or Revolution?" In Bruce R. Guile, *Information Technologies and Social Transformation*, The National Academy of Sciences, 1985.
6. John Zakaria, interview by Jeffrey L. Rodengen, digital recording, 5 October 2006, Write Stuff Enterprises, Inc.
7. Bill Webster, e-mail correspondence, 11 January 2007, Write Stuff Enterprises, Inc.
8. John Zakaria interview.
9. Bill Webster, interview by Jeffrey L. Rodengen, digital recording, 13 September 2006, Write Stuff Enterprises, Inc.
10. Bill Webster, e-mail correspondence, 10 January 2007, Write Stuff Enterprises, Inc.
11. Ibid.
12. Ibid.

Chapter Nine Sidebar: Parker and the World of Entertainment

1. Steve Camp, interview by Beth Kapes, 5 February 2007, Write Stuff Enterprises, Inc.
2. "Parker Stars in Latest Epic Film *Master and Commander: The Far Side of the World*," Parker news release, 13 November 2003.
3. "Parker in the Movies," Parker Hannifin PowerPoint presentation, 31 August 2005.
4. Charles J. Murray, "Raise the Titanic!" *Design News*, 19 January 1998.
5. "Sinking the Titanic," Spring 1998, Milwaukee School of Engineering, Centennial 1903–2003, available at http://www.msoe.edu/centennial/alumni/paddock.shtml/.
6. "Parker in the Movies."
7. Steve Camp interview.
8. "Parker in the Movies."
9. "News from the Fluid Connectors Group," Parker Hannifin, January 2002.
10. "Parker in the Movies."
11. "Lights, Camera … Hydraulics?" Hydraulics Unlimited, Parker Hydraulics Group, October 2006.
12. Steve Camp interview.
13. Ibid.
14. Ibid.
15. Ibid.
16. Streeter Parker, interview by Jeffrey L. Rodengen, digital recording, 13 December 2006, Write Stuff Enterprises, Inc.
17. Ibid.
18. "News from the Fluid Connectors Group."
19. Steve Camp interview.

Chapter Nine Sidebar: Investigating a Tragedy

1. Peter Hoffman, "A Bad Seal Is Blamed for the Shuttle Disaster," *Chemical Week*, 18 June 1986.
2. Report of the Presidential Commission on the Space Shuttle Challenger Accident (In compliance with Executive Order 12546 of 3 February 1986), released 6 June 1986, available at: http://history.nasa.gov/rogersrep/genindex.htm/.
3. Brian Malloy, "Firm Says Shuttle Seals Met Standards," United Press International, 12 February 1986.
4. "Company Claims Seal Cord Met Specifications." *Aviation Week & Space Technology*, 24 February 1986.
5. "Firm Says Shuttle Seals Met Standards."
6. Report of the Presidential Commission on the Space Shuttle Challenger Accident. Volume 2: Appendix L—NASA Accident Analysis Team Report. [Part 2]. STS 51-L Data & Design Analysis Task Force Accident Analysis Team Solid Rocket Motor Working Group, released 6 June 1986.
7. "At Home In Space," *On the Move*, Parker Hannifin company newsletter. January/February 2001.
8. Ibid.
9. "Stratoflex: High Performance Quick Disconnects and Hose Assemblies for Space Flight Applications," Stratoflex Products Division, Parker Hannifin Corporation, catalog

106–Space, 5M, February 2000, available at http://www.parker.com/stratoflex/.

Chapter Ten

1. "Berlin Wall," Wikipedia, available at http://en.wikipedia.org/wiki/Berlin_Wall/.
2. "1990s," Wikipedia, available at http://en.wikipedia.org/wiki/1990s/.
3. Parker Hannifin, profile, available at http://www.answers.com/topic/parker-hannifin-corporation/.
4. Ibid.
5. Parker Hannifin Corporation 1989 Annual Report.
6. Patrick S. Parker, speech, 12 October 1990.
7. Paul Schloemer, interview by Jeffrey L. Rodengen, digital recording, 8 November 2006, Write Stuff Enterprises, Inc.
8. Patrick S. Parker, speech, 12 October 1990.
9. "Higher Education in Science and Engineering," Science and Engineering Indicators, 2002, National Science Board, available at http://www.nsf.gov/statistics/seind02/c2/c2s2.htm/.
10. Lee Banks, interview by Jeffrey L. Rodengen, digital recording, 27 July 2006, Write Stuff Enterprises, Inc.
11. Parker Hannifin Corporation 1992 Annual Report.
12. Lee Banks, Parker Hannifin Biography, March 2004.
13. Lee Banks interview.
14. "Seventy Years of Engineering: Parker Hannifin: Focusing on the Total Package,"

Machine Design, 23 September 1999.
15. "Parker—40 Years in Europe," News from the Fluid Connectors Group, Summer 2000.
16. Parker: European Business Report, Parker Hannifin: News from Parker Europe, Spring 2005.
17. Ron Arthur, interview by Jeffrey L. Rodengen, digital recording, 12 October 2006, Write Stuff Enterprises, Inc.
18. Parker Hannifin, profile.
19. Parker Hannifin Corporation 1993 Annual Report.
20. Patrick S. Parker, speech to employees, 20 April 1989.
21. Ricardo Machado, interview by Jeffrey L. Rodengen, digital recording, 16 August 2006, Write Stuff Enterprises, Inc.
22. Parker Hannifin Corporation 1994 Annual Report.
23. Kjell Jansson, interview by Jeffrey L. Rodengen, digital recording, 29 September 2006, Write Stuff Enterprises, Inc.
24. Joe Vicic, interview by Jeffrey L. Rodengen, digital recording, 16 August 2006, Write Stuff Enterprises, Inc.
25. Ibid.
26. Parker Hannifin Corporation 1995 Annual Report.
27. Denny Sullivan, interview by Jeffrey L. Rodengen, digital recording, 4 October 2006, Write Stuff Enterprises, Inc.
28. Nickolas W. Vande Steeg, interview by Jeffrey L. Rodengen, digital

recording, 26 July 2006, Write Stuff Enterprises, Inc.
29. Parker Hannifin Corporation 1998 Annual Report.
30. Steve Hayes, interview by Jeffrey L. Rodengen, digital recording, 2 October 2006, Write Stuff Enterprises, Inc.
31. Ibid.
32. Parker Hannifin Corporation 1998 Annual Report.
33. Ibid.
34. Craig Maxwell, interview by Jeffrey L. Rodengen, digital recording, 25 July 2006, Write Stuff Enterprises, Inc.
35. Parker Hannifin Corporation 1997 Annual Report.
36. Rick Kanzleiter, interview by Jeffrey L. Rodengen, digital recording, 12 October 2006, Write Stuff Enterprises, Inc.
37. Syd Kershaw, interview by Jeffrey L. Rodengen, digital recording, 3 October 2006, Write Stuff Enterprises, Inc.
38. Patrick S. Parker, speech for the Support Our Managing Change Program, 22 November 1995.
39. "Seventy Years of Engineering, Parker Hannifin: Focusing on the Total Package," *Machine Design*, 23 September 1999.
40. Ibid.

Chapter Ten Sidebar: Distributors: Cornerstones of Business

1. European Business Report: News from the Fluid Connectors Group. "DAC: Wealth Springs from Exchange,"

Winter 1997/98, available at http://www.parker.waaps.com/uk/lit_page30bf.html?page+992&id+111/.

2. David Parks, interview by Jeffrey L. Rodengen, digital recording, 27 March 2007, Write Stuff Enterprises, Inc.

3. Ibid.

4. Gustavo Cudell, interview by Jeffrey L. Rodengen, digital recording, 28 November 2006, Write Stuff Enterprises, Inc.

5. Randy Gross, interview by Jeffrey L. Rodengen, digital recording, 13 November 2006, Write Stuff Enterprises, Inc.

6. Carey Rhoten, interview by Jeffrey L. Rodengen, digital recording, 16 November 2006, Write Stuff Enterprises, Inc.

7. Klaus Kohler, interview by Jeffrey L. Rodengen, digital recording, 3 April 2006, Write Stuff Enterprises, Inc.

8. Ibid.

9. Carey Rhoten interview.

10. Edward Roberts, interview by Jeffrey L. Rodengen, digital recording, 30 November 2006, Write Stuff Enterprises, Inc.

11. Mike Boyles, interview by Jeffrey L. Rodengen, digital recording, 4 June 2006, Write Stuff Enterprises, Inc.

Chapter Eleven

1. Parker Hannifin Corporation, Investor Information Book 2007.

2. Don Washkewicz, interview with Jeffrey L. Rodengen, digital recording, 25 July 2006, Write Stuff Enterprises, Inc.

3. Ibid.

4. "Early 2000s Recession," Wikipedia, available at http://en.wikipedia.org/wiki/Early_2000s_recession/.

5. "One Well-Oiled Machine," 20 September 2004, Industry Insider, *BusinessWeek* online, available at http://www.businessweek.com/print/magazine/content/04_38/b3900012_mz009.htm?chan=gl/.

6. Don Washkewicz interview.

7. "Lean Manufacturing," Wikipedia, available at http://en.wikipedia.org/wiki/Lean_manufacturing/.

8. Nelson Teed, "Lean Manufacturing: Achieving the Lean Dream," Six Sigma, available at http://www.isixsigma.com/offsite.asp?A=Fr&Url= http://www.advancedmanufacturing.com/March01/leanmanuf.htm/.

9. Don Washkewicz interview.

10. Ibid.

11. John Shryock, "Perpetual Motion: How Don Washkewicz Took Parker Hannifin to the Next Level," *Smart Business*, October 2005.

12. Don Washkewicz, interview by Jeffrey L. Rodengen, digital recording, 25 July 2006, Write Stuff Enterprises, Inc.

13. Parker Hannifin Corporation, Investor Information Book 2007.

14. "Perpetual Motion: How Don Washkewicz Took Parker Hannifin to the Next Level."

15. Tom Williams, interview by Jeffrey L. Rodengen, digital recording, 16 August 2006, Write Stuff Enterprises, Inc.

16. Raymond Doyle, interview by Jeffrey L. Rodengen, digital recording, 17 August 2006, Write Stuff Enterprises, Inc.

17. Tom Piraino, interview by Jeffrey L. Rodengen, digital recording, 25 July 2006, Write Stuff Enterprises, Inc.

18. *On the Move*, Parker Hannifin newsletter, January/February 2000.

19. "History of Acquisitions & Divestitures," Parker Hannifin Corporation, 13 September 2006.

20. "Parker to Acquire Wynn's International in $497 Million Transaction," Parker Hannifin press release, 13 June 2000.

21. Nickolas W. Vande Steeg, interview by Jeffrey L. Rodengen, digital recording, 26 July 2006, Write Stuff Enterprises, Inc.

22. Ibid.

23. Parker Hannifin Corporation Annual Report 2001.

24. Ibid.

25. "September 11, 2001 Attacks," Wikipedia, available at http://en.wikipedia.org/wiki/September_11,_2001_attacks/.

26. John M. Virgo, "Economic Impact of the Terrorist Attacks of September 11, 2001," *Atlantic Economic Journal*, vol. 29, no. 4, December 2001.

27. "Perpetual Motion: How Don Washkewicz Took Parker Hannifin to the Next Level."

28. Pam Huggins, interview by Jeffrey L. Rodengen, digital recording, 25 July 2006, Write Stuff Enterprises, Inc.

29. Parker Hannifin Corporation 2002 Annual Report.

30. Bill Eline, interview by Jeffrey L. Rodengen, digital recording, 16 August 2006, Write Stuff Enterprises, Inc.

31. "At Home In Space," *On the Move*, Parker Hannifin newsletter, January/February 2001.

32. Steve Hayes, interview by Jeffrey L. Rodengen, digital recording, 2 October 2006, Write Stuff Enterprises, Inc.

33. Bob Barker, interview by Jeffrey L. Rodengen, digital recording, 16 August 2006, Write Stuff Enterprises, Inc.

34. John Oelslager, interview by Jeffrey L. Rodengen, digital recording, 27 July 2006, Write Stuff Enterprises, Inc.

35. Parker Hannifin Corporation 2002 Annual Report.

36. Ibid.

37. Parker Hannifin Comparative Statistics, 1945–2004.

38. Parker Hannifin Corporation 2003 Annual Report.

39. Craig Maxwell, interview by Jeffrey L. Rodengen, digital recording, 25 July 2006, Write Stuff Enterprises, Inc.

40. Ibid.

41. Ibid.

42. Ibid.

43. Ibid.

44. Ibid.

45. Tim Pistell, interview by Jeffrey L. Rodengen, digital recording, 21 September 2006, Write Stuff Enterprises, Inc.

46. Don Washkewicz, interview by Jeffrey L. Rodengen, digital recording, 31 October 2006, Write Stuff Enterprises, Inc.

47. James Perkins, interview by Jeffrey L. Rodengen, digital recording, 5 January 2007, Write Stuff Enterprises, Inc.

48. Charly Saulnier, interview by Jeffrey L. Rodengen, digital recording, 6 December 2006, Write Stuff Enterprises, Inc.

49. Parker Hannifin Corporation 2004 Annual Report.

50. John McGinty, interview by Jeffrey L. Rodengen, digital recording, 10 October 2006, Write Stuff Enterprises, Inc.

51. Mike Noelke, interview by Jeffrey L. Rodengen, digital recording, 5 October 2006, Write Stuff Enterprises, Inc.

52. Ken Ohlemeyer, interview by Jeffrey L. Rodengen, digital recording, 11 October 2006, Write Stuff Enterprises, Inc.

53. Parker Hannifin Corporation 2004 Annual Report.

54. Jack Myslenski, interview by Jeffrey L. Rodengen, digital recording,

29 January 2007, Write Stuff Enterprises, Inc.

55. Cliff Ransom, interview by Jeffrey L. Rodengen, digital recording, 10 October 2006, Write Stuff Enterprises, Inc.

56. Parker Hannifin Corporation 2004 Annual Report.

57. Jack Myslenski interview.

58. Joe Kovach, interview by Jeffrey L. Rodengen, digital recording, 6 October 2006, Write Stuff Enterprises, Inc.

59. Ibid.

60. Ibid.

61. Ibid.

62. John Van Buskirk, interview by Jeffrey L. Rodengen, digital recording, 11 October 2006, Write Stuff Enterprises, Inc.

63. Joe Kovach interview.

64. Ibid.

65. Jim Baker, interview by Jeffrey L. Rodengen, digital recording, 7 December 2006, Write Stuff Enterprises, Inc.

66. Don Raker, interview by Jeffrey L. Rodengen, digital recording, 17 August 2006, Write Stuff Enterprises, Inc.

67. Jack Myslenski interview.

68. Craig Maxwell interview.

69. Roger Sherrard, interview by Jeffrey L. Rodengen, digital recording, 21 September 2006, Write Stuff Enterprises, Inc.

70. Tom Healy, interview by Jeffrey L. Rodengen, digital recording, 26 October 2006, Write Stuff Enterprises, Inc.

71. Parker Hannifin Corporation 2005 Annual Report.

72. Ibid.

73. "Parker Acquires Advanced Products," Parker Hannifin news release, 4 December 2004.

74. Streeter Parker, interview by Jeffrey L. Rodengen, digital recording, 13 December 2006, Write Stuff Enterprises, Inc.

75. Dolores Lyon, interview by Jeffrey L. Rodengen, digital recording, 27 July 2006, Write Stuff Enterprises, Inc.

76. Streeter Parker interview.

77. Tim Pistell interview.

78. Dan Serbin, interview by Jeffrey L. Rodengen, digital recording, 25 July 2006, Write Stuff Enterprises, Inc.

79. Marvin Kashkoush, interview by Jeffrey L. Rodengen, digital recording, 27 July 2006, Write Stuff Enterprises, Inc.

80. Parker Hannifin Corporation 2006 Annual Report.

81. Ibid.

82. Ibid.

83. John Oelslager interview.

84. "Parker Completes Acquisition of domnick hunter," news release, 25 November 2005.

85. John Oelslager interview.

86. Parker European Business Report, Autumn 2006.

87. Parker Hannifin Corporation 2006 Annual Report.

88. Erica Isabella, e-mail correspondence with Beth Kapes, 27 February 2007, Write Stuff Enterprises, Inc.

89. "Parker President and COO Nick Vande Steeg Retires after 35 Years of Service," Parker news release, 12 December 2006.

90. Parker Hannifin Corporation 2006 Annual Report.

91. Duane Collins, interview by Jeffrey L. Rodengen, digital recording, 26 July 2006, Write Stuff Enterprises, Inc.

92. Tim Pistell interview.

Chapter Eleven Sidebar: Aid in a National Tragedy

1. "September 11: A Memorial," available at http:// www.cnn.com/SPECIALS/ 2001/memorial/.

2. "September 11 Recovery Program, American Red Cross," available at http:// www.redcross.org/article/ 0,1072,0_312_5646,00.html /.

3. "Remains of the Day," *Time*, available at http:// www.time.com/time/ covers/1101020909/landfill/.

4. Amy Higgins, "Heavy Equipment Doctor Is In," *Machine Design*, 5 September 2002.

5. "NYC Cleanup Effort," Parker Hannifin ON TV (CD), 2001/2002.

6. Ibid.

7. Ibid.

8. Ibid.

9. Ibid.

10. Ibid.

Index

Page numbers in *italics* refer to photographs and illustrations.